SHROP⟨

A SHROPSHIRE LAD IN THE RAF

VOLUME 1

PREPARATION

FOR

FLIGHT

RON POWELL

To Mum, Dad and Brian

Table of Contents

Introduction
Chapter 1 – Growing Up in Ludlow
Chapter 2 – Early Interest in the RAF
Chapter 3 – Trying to Join
Chapter 4 – Recruit Training
Chapter 5 – Apprentice Training
Chapter 6 – The Mighty Vulcan
Chapter 7 – Officer Training
Epilogue
Author's Note
Glossary and Abbreviations

Introduction

Four red jets streak low across an airfield. Five others, including mine, rush to meet them. The closing speed is over 700 miles an hour. I hold my breath as the four grow and grow, then flash between us, our wingtips almost brushing.

Wow!

I've been a fan of the Red Arrows for 40 years, but now I'm flying with them. It's the fulfilment of a boyhood dream, no less potent for the fact that I'm no longer a youngster, but a 48-year old Royal Air Force pilot.

I'm sitting in Red 3, just to the left of the leader, his sleek red Hawk framed against the deep blue of a late summer sky. Another red Hawk sits just to my left.

They're such familiar images, I'm finding it hard to believe I'm really up here, rather than looking at their pictures in a magazine. But I am, and we're halfway through a 20-minute display practice over their base at RAF Scampton.

It's everything I imagined, a high-adrenalin, Boys' Own comic, adventure. And, as with so many things in life, the opportunity has come as a complete surprise.

In 2001, I commanded an RAF detachment at an air base in southern Italy. From there, our Harriers provided air cover for NATO peacekeeping troops in the Balkans. During my four and a half months as 'Detco', I met many gifted Harrier pilots, including a young flight lieutenant, Spike Jepson.

I came to know Spike better than most. We took part in a 10km charity run up Mount Vesuvius. It was one of the hardest physical challenges either of us had ever faced. We both completed it, but our finishing positions led to an exchange of good-natured banter.

Despite being 15 years older, I'd beaten him to the top.

Three years later, Squadron Leader Spike Jepson is leading the Red Arrows. I've travelled from another base, a late stand-in to present a prize to a party of schoolchildren visiting the team. On meeting, Spike and I resume our banter, and he offers me a flight.

So, here I am, upside down with nothing on the altimeter but the maker's name. Not quite true. I am upside down, but a mere ten seconds after our near collision at ground level, we're at six and a half thousand feet, interlacing again at the top of a loop.

What a way to earn a living.

Some people think Red Arrows pilots are prima donnas, mere poseurs in their gaudy flying suits. But I've operated alongside them several times in my career, even had a hand in teaching some of them to fly. I've seen how much effort goes into perfecting their displays. I've also seen the risks they take on a daily basis.

Over the years, they've lost several team members, one a short time before I arrived at Scampton to train as a flying instructor in the mid-1980s, killed during a practice over the airfield. And when I returned to the base a few years later, two, including the team leader, were hobbling around on crutches after a mid-air collision. One of their jets had crashed into the upstairs bathroom of a house in the local village.

Not the most consoling of thoughts as the Hawks crowd in again and we dive toward the grass for the second half of our loop.

From the ground, I, like everyone else, have always been in awe at the tightness of their formations, and at how quickly they change from Wine Glass to Swan, or whatever it happens to be. Up here, the tiny distances between the hurtling chunks of metal are even more apparent, but I can also see constant movement as each pilot works stick and throttle, striving to keep his jet in the ideal position.

The Red Arrows are always striving for the ideal. Soon after we land, I'll sit in as they review film of their performance. Their self-analysis is hyper-critical, brutal, but it's part of what makes them the best display team in the world.

Even while I've marvelled at his skill, my pilot has been subjecting himself to some ripe self-criticism. He does it again as he fails to slot in next to the leader as quickly as he thinks he should following a manoeuvre.

I'd have been over the moon, but I find it reassuring that he's working so hard. It makes him seem more human, more akin to a mere line pilot like me. Not that I could do it. The speed with which he spots minute errors in position and reacts to correct them would be beyond me.

Spike looks across from the lead Hawk, slightly ahead and to our right. His eyes crease into a smile, and he growls another command into the radio.

'Looping, Go.'

His jet pitches up, and we follow, pulling 6g. I struggle to keep my head erect and my vision clear, but the overwhelming feeling is of exhilaration.

Somehow, although my career still has several years to run, this seems like the high-point, an experience unlikely to be surpassed. I enjoy it more than almost anything else in an eventful life. The red jets flash past, or hang within arms reach. My excitement hardly diminishes throughout. I feel fully immersed in the moment.

And yet, my mind also embarks on an unexpected bout of self-analysis, a review of my past that places it in sharper context than years of contemplation on the ground.

It's been quite a journey, from son of a dustman to group captain, from rarely leaving Shropshire to travelling the world. I've seen incredible sights and met amazing people.

A cinematic narrative begins to unfold, career high and low spots interspersed with images of family that inject sprinklings of laughter and tears. And an idea takes shape.

Hanging in the straps at the top of a loop, the green fields of Lincolnshire laid out 7,000 feet below me, I make a commitment to write my life story.

It took several years and retirement for me to actually sit down and begin writing, but that encounter with the Red Arrows was the catalyst. Some of the reasons for the delay included work commitments and other writing projects, but I also became concerned at the lack of information about my parents, their origins and relationship, even about my own early life.

These are things you pick up over the years from family photographs and anecdotes. But my parents seemed to have few mementos and even fewer stories. Beyond the merest hints, they offered no sense of where they'd come from, or where they were going.

Life happened, and you dealt with it as best you could. You didn't revisit it.

I'd spotted the gaps while they were still alive, but not until it was too late. By the time I began to probe, my mother's deteriorating health, and my father's inability to recall anything beyond a few oft-repeated war stories, meant that I was destined never to receive a coherent picture. So my reconstruction of their early lives is based on scant resources and my own, potentially unreliable, recollections. But, unless you come from a family that's famous, or infamous, one whose lives are of interest to independent chroniclers, I think we're all in the same boat.

Perhaps as a subconscious reaction to this lack of clarity, documenting my own life has been something of an obsession. I've kept diaries, letters, scrap books and reports recording almost all I've ever done or experienced. And now I'm writing this book.

In my defence, as well as pandering to my vanity, this memoir is partly an attempt to leave a record for my own children, whether they want it or not.

Of course, despite the diaries and scrap books, my memories may be unreliable, or at least partial and self-serving. Sorry, but I'm not sure I can help that.

What follows is my story, my truth.

Chapter One – Growing Up in Ludlow

I never met my paternal grandmother, but, from the one faded sepia photograph I can recall, she had the stern look of a strict disciplinarian, a necessary trait no doubt, when dealing with eight children.

Even my recollections of my grandfather are pretty vague. I was still a youngster when he died, but I have a mental image of sitting on the knee of a jovial old man with a ruddy, weathered face, thinning grey hair and a thick grey moustache.

For much of his life, he worked in the stone quarries on Titterstone Clee Hill, a distinctive craggy outcrop dominating the skyline to the east of Ludlow, the small market town in south Shropshire where he lived. Six days a week, he'd set out at five in the morning to walk seven uphill miles to dig out Dhustone, a hard-wearing basalt much treasured as a road surface in the early years of the 20th Century. After his shift, he'd descend again to arrive home at about eight in the evening.

Later, he became a stoker, feeding the boilers of Ludlow's new gas plant. This may have saved hours of walking, but it still sounds like a back-breaking job to me. And finally, he became caretaker of St Laurence's Junior School in Lower Galdeford, a school I attended many years later. The job came with a tiny, whitewashed, stone cottage, just over the wall at the top end of the school playground.

My father, Ben, was born in January 1918, ten months before the end of the First World War. He was the middle of nine children, one of whom died in early childhood. I have no idea when the family started living in the cottage over the school wall, but that's where I have a vision of Dad, his three surviving brothers and four sisters, growing up. It must have been quite a squeeze.

Only one story from his childhood survives.

All four sons were in the choir of Ludlow Parish Church. The choirmaster was another strict disciplinarian – perhaps all adults were back then. On dark nights, the brothers would try to knock the old man's hat off by hanging a piece of string across the narrow path he took to choir practice. If successful, they'd take a few moments to savour him groping around, then rush to the vestry to enjoy his flustered arrival.

No wonder he was strict.

The only other snippet, that young Ben and his friends would '*run round the town for a packet of broken biscuits*' from a local grocer, brings to mind a group of grubby, Dickensian, urchins. This may or may not be entirely accurate, but I think it fair to say that he grew up as one of the respectable poor. His father's work ethic certainly rubbed off on him.

Like all his male siblings, Dad left school at 14. Even so, he, and my mother, who left at 13, could read, write and do arithmetic to a high standard. In Dad's case, this included the ability to work out, faster than any calculator, the likely rewards of betting on a racehorse.

I don't know what he did for the seven years until 1939, but when the Second World War began, he signed up immediately. He became an infantryman in The King's Shropshire Light Infantry, which he usually called the KSLI, or, in lighter moments, the King's Silly Little Idiots.

Some of his training took place in Ireland, and any mention of that island would trigger a tale of rescuing a party of fellow soldiers, their non-commissioned officers and officers, hopelessly lost in the mists on the Mountains of Mourne.

It was at about this time that he smashed an ankle playing football. The nearest medical attention was several miles away, and the journey, by truck, was made with his shattered leg resting on chains. Unsurprisingly, the injury plagued him until his death.

And yet, who knows, it may also have saved his life, because it prevented him going into combat. He became a film projectionist, entertaining the troops, mostly on land, but also on at least two long sea voyages; the first, across the Atlantic to Halifax, Nova Scotia; the second, through the Mediterranean and the Suez Canal to the Straits of Malacca, off Malaysia. I should imagine the destination was Singapore.

Following the second voyage, he retained a lifelong fascination with sharks, which they'd caught in the Red Sea by hanging hunks of meat over the side of the boat. And whenever he saw someone of south Asian descent, or a picture of India, it would prompt the observation that you could smell Bombay (Mumbai) from ten miles out to sea.

At some point, he became a senior soldier, sporting 'two upside-down stripes', an accolade of which he was immensely proud. He remained in uniform until the war ended in 1945.

It might not sound a very distinguished war record, but, as I know only too well, to win medals for gallantry, you have to be put in harm's way. I come from a generation of Cold War warriors, few of whom had the opportunity to demonstrate heroism, or the lack of it.

Dad was the same. He did his duty.

After the war, capitalising on his army experience,

he was a projectionist in Ludlow's two cinemas. Both are now gone, although they still show occasional films in the Assembly Rooms near the site of the Old Picture House on Castle Square, and my in-laws live in an apartment on the site of the other, the Clifton, in Old Street.

Later, he worked in the building trade and for the County Council, including driving a large, left-hand-drive, road sweeper, a frightening prospect when I think of his performance behind the wheel of our little family saloon car. And I know from my birth certificate that a year after his marriage in 1954, he was a paint-plant operator for GKN, an engineering firm in Wellington, north Shropshire.

Around this time, he passed the tests to join the River Police in Portsmouth, but my mother was reluctant to move, perhaps because of my imminent arrival. For whatever reason, he never took up the post, and I know that he rued the missed opportunity.

From soon after my birth until his retirement, he worked for Ludlow Town Council, sometimes as a road sweeper, but most of the time as a dustman.

Like most inverted snobs, I'm very proud of my humble background. In fact, I used to – and still do - get a perverse pleasure from telling people I'm the son of a dustman. It seemed especially good sport as I climbed the rank ladder in the RAF and mixed in grander circles. Most folk managed not to crinkle their noses, but you could tell that, for some, it was a struggle.

Comments such as, 'Well, of course, some people just like to work in the fresh air,' were quite common, as if Dad had been an intellectual who'd decided to become a dustman, or a brain surgeon who'd fallen on hard times.

No. As I've said, Dad was not unintelligent, but he was just a hard-working labourer with no pretensions to anything else. A good man, a gentle man, but very much a dustman.

Like him, my brother Brian and I were brought up as part of the respectable lower working class. He worked for everything we had, and, during our childhoods, we never saw him drunk or, like many of our peers, had to sit on the pub doorstep waiting for him to come out. He rarely shouted at us, and I don't ever remember him raising his voice to our mother. Stubborn and cantankerous he could be, but never violent.

With one caveat. On occasion, when we were young, we felt the weight of his hand on our backsides in punishment for some gross misdemeanour. Given the greater time we spent in her company, Mum probably used the same sanction more often, but Dad's hand was the nuclear option. Even so, it was a sanction invoked very infrequently.

Throughout this period, Dad was also a part-time fireman.

Attached to the wall at the foot of the stairs, was a red electric bell. When it rang, he would jump on his bike and set off for the fire station at the bottom of Galdeford, below St Laurence's School.

While we lived near the centre of town, he used to arrive in time to jump on the engine and attend fires. But years later, when we moved to the north-eastern edge of Ludlow, with over a mile to ride on his increasingly decrepit bike, I don't think he ever made it. It was not for the want of trying, though.

Just prior to his marriage, pictures show a slim, muscular man, five feet eight inches tall, with dark brylcreemed hair, a prominent hooked nose and a neat moustache that he retained for the rest of his life. Beneath the moustache is the hint of a hair lip, something that may explain my own very high and narrow palate, a feature that arouses much interest in every new dentist I see. In most of the pictures, Dad is holding a pipe, a constant companion. Even when not lit, it sat in a handy niche it had worn in his teeth.

As the years passed, he shrank a little, and the bulk round his shoulders sank to his waist. Nonetheless, approaching his death, he was recognisably the same man as in those early pictures.

Even before poor health intervened, I always sensed that Mum was reluctant to revisit her past. Whether she found it too painful to relate, or thought it too painful for us to hear, or both, I never knew. And I never pressed the issue. So this narrative is based on my own recollections and a conversation with Mum's younger step-sister, my Auntie Mary, in the summer of 2013.

Catherine Cowell was born in March 1922 in the remote village of Coreley, on the southern flank of Clee Hill. When her mother went into a difficult labour, her father, a farm labourer, rode ten miles bareback on one of the farm horses to their doctor in Cleobury Mortimer. The doctor then drove them back to Coreley in his pony and trap.

A year later, perhaps partly from the complications of that difficult birth, her mother died.

In that day and age, there was no way a farm labourer could look after a young child unaided, so Mum spent the next few years living with her grandparents in an isolated house at Cornbrook, close to Clee Hill village and the road running from Ludlow and on to Cleobury Mortimer, Kidderminster and Birmingham. Her father visited when he could.

I recall only one sepia photograph of Mum as a young child, and I've always assumed it was taken outside the Cornbrook house. It shows a five-year old girl wearing an apron of light material over a long dark dress. She has a grubby face and dark eyes, open wide, as if in surprise, perhaps at the sight of the camera.

Only when her father re-married did the young Catherine, by now perhaps six or seven years old, move back to live with him. By this time, he was working as a labourer for the local council, and the family were living in Lower Corve Street, Ludlow.

Auntie Mary said the reunion of father and daughter had some comi-tragic results. There is no inference that her new stepmother was in any way wicked, but the young Catherine had been used to living under a different regime. This had included a bottle of beer every night, brought back by her granddad after his nightly excursion to one of the pubs on Clee Hill. The lack of beer in the Corve Street house led to nightly tantrums, which included some un-ladylike language from the six or seven year old Catherine.

She also had an aversion to school, and had to be frog-marched onto the premises every morning. Even then, she often escaped, and would arrive home looking dishevelled, having hidden away in some thicket until she felt it safe to return.

The family soon included a step-brother, Stan, and a step-sister, Mary, who was ten years younger. Mary has a few photographs from this period, but the ones with which I was already familiar are a series in which Mum is a young woman, standing beneath a clothes line in the back garden of a house toward the northern end of Ludlow. She stands in a flowery dress, sometimes alone, sometimes alongside her father, stepmother, teenage Stan, and Mary, who looks to be about ten years of age.

Stan went on to serve in the Army in Palestine during the bloody period leading up to the formation of the Israeli state. Pictures before embarkation show a handsome young man, smiling winningly for the camera. The man that returned seemed rarely to smile, or even talk, and suffered greatly with his 'nerves'. It seems this may have been the result of one traumatic experience.

While in Palestine, he and a friend spent an evening with two girls. When his friend decided to stay out late, Stan went back to barracks. The next morning, he had to identify his friend's body, hanging from a tree with its throat cut.

He lived most of his remaining life with his father, and worked as an odd job man and porter at the Feather's Hotel, a black and white coaching inn that is one of the architectural gems of Ludlow.

Several years before the set of photographs with her family had been taken, Mum had left school and gone into service alongside two other maids in a large house in Bewdley, a town on the River Severn midway between Ludlow and Birmingham. The master of the house was a successful butcher.

Only when my own daughter was 13 did I get an inkling of what it must have been like for Mum to move 20 miles from home to work in a strange household, with little time off, and no means of contact beyond letters.

I often wonder if this experience, following on from the death of her mother and separation from her father could have affected her later mental health. It's hard to believe it didn't, even if the results didn't manifest themselves until many years later.

During the War, she worked in an ammunition

factory in Hereford. From her few stories of that time, I know only that there could be accidents, even explosions, one of which claimed the life of a man she knew. Mary says the work was arduous, and that Mum was very robust at this stage of her life.

Mary also says Mum used to commute from Ludlow to Hereford daily by train, but I believe she also spent time in a hostel in Hereford, an experience that led to, or reinforced, a lifelong prejudice against Catholics.

As she put it, 'They get up to all sorts during the week, confess at Mass, then do exactly the same the next week.'

In later life, if I mentioned a girl to my parents, one of their first questions would be, 'What religion is she?'

I never knew of course. I wasn't interested. But if I'd answered Catholic, or almost any religion other than Church of England, my parents would have disapproved. They would have expressed the same displeasure over nationality or colour.

To put it plainly, they were prejudiced. This may seem at odds with the picture I am painting of a good and gentle couple, but I'm sure most of their opinions were due to an almost total lack of contact with other races or religions, or discussion of the issues involved.

During my childhood, the only people of colour in Ludlow were a few men running the single Chinese restaurant. If their families lived in the town, they were well hidden, because we never saw them. A few Sikhs visited infrequently to sell household cleaning goods door to door, but they were no more than a curiosity, and their arrival would launch Dad into a story about the smell of Bombay.

Later, in the late 60s or early 70s, an Indian

restaurant opened, but again, those who ran it were rarely seen away from the premises. Returning to the town on leave in the 1980s and 90s, I remember a few black faces, but even these seem largely to have disappeared at the beginning of the 21st Century. The boom in restaurants has continued though, leading to more Asian and South Asian faces.

Dad especially was prone to casual racism. Watching Songs of Praise on the television, and spotting someone in the congregation with a large nose, he'd say, 'He's a Jew,' conveniently ignoring the fact that he had a large proboscis himself – and that the programme was coming from some Protestant parish church in the heart of England. I've inherited the same trait – the nose that is, not the prejudice.

In the post-War period, Mum rose from being a kitchen maid to become a cook at two hospitals, East Hamlet in Ludlow, then St Chad's in Birmingham. In the early 1950s, when they were courting, Dad used to get on the bus to Birmingham and visit her at St Chad's, which later became Birmingham Childrens' Hospital. For two years from 2010, our daughter worked in a 1960s edifice next door: Birmingham Dental Hospital.

In the early 1950s, pictures of Cath Cowell show a slim young woman of medium height, dressed in hospital uniform or calf-length dresses. I think she would be described as plain of countenance, with a long, angular face and shoulder length brown, wavy, hair. I have to admit to taking a stab at the hair colour, because I can't remember it being anything other than white.

In March 1954, she and Ben Powell had a traditional white wedding in St Laurence's Parish

Church, Ludlow. From the one posed photograph in the door of the church, Mum was given away by her father, and Auntie Mary was bridesmaid. Dad's family was also well represented, and his eldest brother was best man.

In 1954, Ludlow was still a relatively small market town of some 6,500 inhabitants. Sitting roughly midway between Hereford to the south and Shrewsbury to the north, it was still several decades from its first traffic roundabout, zebra crossing or supermarket; and the orange petals of new housing estates for retirees from the Midlands were yet to blossom. These would take its population to over 10,000 by the first decade of the 21st Century.

Sitting on a hill above the Rivers Teme and Corve, the town centre is dominated by an eleventh century castle and one of the largest parish churches in England. Its mediaeval grid of streets comprises wide north south thoroughfares lined with elegant Tudor and Georgian houses, and narrower, claustrophobic, lanes of smaller properties running east west.

It had been the official and de facto capital of the Welsh Marches for much of its existence, and was still the heartbeat of the surrounding farming communities. A large and vibrant livestock market a few hundred yards from the town centre at the bottom of Corve Street filled Mondays with the sights, sounds and smells of animals - and their owners.

After their marriage, my parents moved into rented accommodation in Gravel Hill, a street of large Victorian and Edwardian houses to the north of the town centre. Many of the properties were given over to flats and apartments, and Mum and Dad occupied the first floor of one of the smaller terrace houses,

Holmleigh.

I was born 13 months later, in Apr 1955. As you would expect after 58 years, I'm sure of the date, but my conversation with Auntie Mary produced a bit of a bombshell, casting doubt on at least one other area of certainty.

My birth certificate says I was born in Berrington Hospital in Atcham, 30 miles or so to the north of Ludlow. Why this should be is a mystery, as my parents had never visited the place before, and I don't think we ever visited afterwards. I seem to remember a rarely aired story about some medical complication surrounding my delivery with which the Ludlow hospitals were unable to cope.

It has always irked slightly that I couldn't say I was born and bred in Ludlow, but that is the only way Berrington has impinged on me in any way since my birth.

But Auntie Mary is adamant that I *was* born in Ludlow, and in the bed next to a girl with whom I subsequently went to school, and who died a few years ago.

Wherever I was born, and I think I have to go with my birth certificate, I was named after Dad's youngest brother, a man I never met.

Like his older brothers, Ronald joined the Army during the Second World War. He served in Singapore and became a prisoner of war when the city fell to the Japanese.

All Dad would ever say was that Ronald had a terrible time in captivity, and that, alongside many others, he was bayoneted by the Japanese guards as their POW camp was being re-taken. Whilst his body made a full recovery, the same could not be said of his mind. He spent the rest of his life in institutions. I say institutions, but it may have been just one of what were then called 'mental hospitals': Shelton, near Shrewsbury. That's where he died in 1986.

Unsurprisingly, given this background, my father harboured a deep-seated hatred of Japan and the Japanese. It never diminished with time. For some reason, my mother felt the same; perhaps it was a generational thing, or maybe she'd been brainwashed by Dad. Either way, while he was happy to express his anger and contempt for 'the Nips' - the cruel and heartless people who'd mistreated his younger brother – she was more fragile. Any mention of Japan in her presence, even on television, could upset her greatly.

Having grown up in this atmosphere, I suppose I should have had the same prejudices, but I have no memory of that being the case. Just as well, because my career put me in contact with the Japanese military on several occasions.

In 1994, I spent a year at the RAF Staff College alongside a Japanese fighter pilot, and, in 1995, I visited Tokyo as part of a military delegation. For several years after this visit, I received a Christmas card from a Japanese Vice Admiral and second row forward, with whom I'd spent a night drinking Sake and talking rugby.

Then, in 2001, as the MOD Desk Officer responsible for our military relations with Japan and several other countries in the Far East, I visited again. I also made friends with their Defence Attaché in this country.

During all these contacts, I was never other than convinced of two things: their profound anger at the dropping of the atomic bombs on Hiroshima and

Nagasaki, and the sincere remorse of those I met for the actions of their military during the Second World War.

Of course, I couldn't mention my 1995 visit to my parents at the time. It would have been too upsetting. After my mother's death, I told Dad about the contrition I'd witnessed, but he wasn't convinced, and, from his perspective, why should he have been. He too was dead when I made my second visit to Tokyo.

Anyway, Ronald was seldom mentioned among the family. As I grew up, I assumed he was dead. Then, in the mid 80s, I discovered that my father was visiting him in Shelton.

I'm sorry to say that I never attempted to do the same. I had a ready excuse in my other commitments, but the truth is that I was fearful of visiting Shelton, and of being confronted with my uncle's mental illness.

Shortly after his death, I visited my parents, by then living in my maternal grandfather's old council house. Dad said he'd inherited his brother's Shire Horses, 11 of them, and gestured to the window.

For a moment, I was dumbstruck. How, while living in Shelton, had Uncle Ronald managed to keep a string of Shire Horses? And how was Dad going to take them on? After all, the council house had barely enough lawn to exercise a rabbit.

My eyes alighted on a motley collection of small, chipped, china shire horses, some on the window sill, and some placed incongruously in the 'rockery' just outside.

Dad was immensely proud of his inheritance, and I kept my mouth shut.

We lived in the Gravel Hill flat for the first five years of my life.

Now, some people seem able to remember every detail of their early years: 'I recall the face of my heavily bearded grandfather looking into my cradle' etc. I'm afraid I'm not one of them. I have few memories of my infancy and early childhood, and only a few stories were passed on to me. Two, though, involve trips to hospital when I was no more than a toddler.

The first visit was to treat a badly gashed head, sustained when I became so engrossed with workmen digging a hole in the road outside our flat that I fell in.

The second was late at night, after I slid chin first down the stairs into the hall. There was so much blood that Dad decided to take me to the Cottage Hospital next to the Parish Church. As he pushed my pram through the dark and deserted streets, he was stopped by a suspicious policeman. I still bear the scar on my chin, and a mental picture of Dad standing sheepishly by while the policeman pulled back the covers to check that I wasn't some burglar's swag.

After this accident-prone start, I've survived to date with few other scars, and only one breakage, a finger, sustained while playing basketball.

In November 1958, three and a half years after my birth, Brian was born. About 18 months later, we moved from the small flat on Gravel Hill into a three bedroom council house on the Dodmore Estate. Soon after this, Mum began to suffer with her 'nerves', and to be admitted to Shelton hospital, sometimes for stays of several weeks.

For most of my life, I've been unsure when her bouts of depression started, or when they became apparent to all and sundry. I believed they pre-dated the move to Dodmore, perhaps even my birth. Then, in 2012, I had a brief telephone conversation with one of Mum's old workmates and friends, a lady with whom I still exchange Christmas cards, and know as Auntie Mabel.

Biting the bullet, I asked her about Mum's mental health. She recalled no problems when they'd both worked at East Hamlet Hospital in the early 1950s, or when Mum moved to St Chad's in Birmingham, after which they'd seen less of one another.

They'd drifted even farther apart when Mum returned to Ludlow to marry, and Mabel moved back to the West Midlands to do the same. But Mabel continued to visit Ludlow a couple of times a year. She couldn't say exactly when she realised there was a problem with my mother's mental health, but her gradual deterioration became apparent as the visits continued into the 1960s and 70s.

Unknown to me, Mabel visited right up to the late 1980s or early 90s, at which point Dad told her Mum didn't want to see her any more. I can't help wondering if Mum really said this, or if Dad, in a misguided attempt to protect her, began to discourage visitors. But I've jumped too far ahead.

The conversation with Mabel seemed to confirm another possibility I'd often considered: that Mum's mental illness, or at least the seed of it, was post-natal depression following my birth. The family story of a difficult delivery seemed to tally, and I know I was quite a handful.

But Auntie Mary, in our 2013 conversation, was adamant that it was moving to Dodmore that initiated Mum's slide into depression, not the birth of me or my brother.

Located on the extreme northern edge of Ludlow, the Dodmore Estate comprised a rectangle of about sixty 1940s red brick council houses, bisected by a 'middle road' of similar dwellings. In the late 50s, a number of more modern, half tiled, or half-rendered, terrace houses had been added to the northern side of the rectangle. We moved into one of these.

I've already described our family as respectable lower working class, and most of our new neighbours seemed to fit the same category. But a sizeable minority were more feckless: large families with no visible means of support, and no handkerchiefs. The estate had a reputation for loutishness second only to Sandpits Avenue, another estate on the outskirts of town.

We gained a feeling of embattled isolation. I had no experience of some of the families we now lived among, and neither had my parents. The offspring of the large, workless, households ran wild and caused trouble. One of their favourite activities was taunting and bullying anyone who seemed weak, or different, and our family seemed to fit the bill.

We had things thrown at the windows and doors, and, on more than one occasion, I went out to find graffiti ridiculing Mum's mental health chalked on the front path. I used to try and wash it out before she saw it, but they also shouted abuse, which was harder to ignore or shield her from.

If her depression had been dormant until that point, the move to Dodmore and the treatment she received there could certainly have brought it into the open.

I don't want to be a bore on the issue, but we were poor. Like most married women with children in the

1950s, Mum was a stay-at-home mother, and Dad was a labourer, then a dustman, when such jobs were at the bottom of the wages pyramid. We had few if any luxuries, and even fewer gadgets. At the time, though, it didn't matter. With very few exceptions, all those living around us were in the same boat.

Only when I went to the Grammar School, and later, when I became an officer, did disparities in parental background, income and expectation become blindingly apparent.

But, unusually for a working class kid at the time, when Mum went into hospital, I sometimes went to a nursery in a large house. I don't remember Brian being there, and I don't know where he went instead.

I didn't like the nursery. The rooms of the rambling house were dark and smelt of boiled cabbage, as did the old lady that ran it. She scared me, and I used to look forward to Dad smiling through the window when he came to pick me up on his way from work at about 5pm.

On one occasion, when he was working as a labourer on a water pipeline being laid over Whitcliffe Common, he appeared at the window a little later than usual, his lower face hidden behind a scarf. When he came inside and removed it, all his front teeth were missing, his lips and gums caked with dried blood. The damage had been caused by the handle of a cement mixer.

When we were older, we also stayed with Auntie Mary in Westhope, a village just outside Craven Arms. And later still, when Brian and I were both at school, we looked after ourselves until Dad returned from work.

Although we missed our mother, we used to quite enjoy being looked after by our father. He used to cook simple meals, such as fish and chips, or sausages accompanied by mountains of potatoes, mashed with industrial quantities of margarine until they were really smooth and creamy yellow.

We had an old black Ford Popular car and, on Sundays, Dad used to drive us to Shrewsbury to visit Mum in Shelton. I don't remember going into the hospital much, but I do remember her coming out into the garden to see us, and, on occasion, being allowed out for a drive.

The hospital was just part of our lives, sad but normal. But for Mum, it must have been awful. I know she had Electro-Convulsive Therapy, and I can only hope it helped her.

Apart from visits to Mum in Shelton, and Sunday afternoon drives into the South Shropshire countryside to pick mushrooms or fruit according to season, the only other regular journey we undertook in the Ford Pop was to see Dad's eldest brother, John, and his wife, Marge, at Broseley in north Shropshire.

Of the three of Dad's brothers that survived childhood, John was the acknowledged brains of the family. He'd passed the 'Eleven Plus' of the time, the examination that should have allowed him a grammar school education. But, in a familiar story for bright working class kids of that era, my grandparents couldn't afford to send him to Ludlow Grammar, so he never had the chance to reach his academic potential. I was the first Powell to attend the School some 40 years later.

So, like his brothers, John left school at 14. Unlike them, though, he went to work in an office. I have no idea where, or what position he held, but earning money from a clerical rather than a manual job put him a cut above the rest of the family, at least in Dad's eyes. He was always immensely proud of his eldest brother.

At the time of our visits in the early 1960s, Uncle John would have been around 50 years of age, and his health was failing. However, as was the way in families like ours, the actual illness, or its cause, was never mentioned. I think it was cancer, but that was a word that would certainly never have been used. When illness was alluded to at all, it was like a television comedy sketch.

Two male comedians sit in a kitchen, dressed in drag. They wear headscarves over hair rollers, floral dresses and thick, wrinkled, stockings. Their arms are crossed under large bosoms, their legs apart, displaying knee-length bloomers. Gurning like Bulldogs, they talk about a friend with some undisclosed illness. But, whenever they seem close to naming the ailment, they break into an exaggerated pantomime of silent mouthing and bosom heaving.

Conversations between my relatives on the subject of illness invariably took the same format, although not always with the same dress code. And there was something else. Although the name of the ailment remained obscure, there was never any doubt that the sufferer was to blame for their condition, probably due to some profound moral failing, character defect or crime. They'd obviously brought the misery upon themselves.

This philosophy read across to most other areas of life. Responsibility for any misfortune could invariably be traced back to the individual. So, anyone caught up in scandal or disaster, man-made or natural, was bound to be at fault. This allowed the Establishment to wash its hands of any untoward event, whether responsible or not.

Nowadays, we seem to have turned full circle, with individuals blaming anyone or anything but themselves for mishaps or mistakes. But I'm of the old school. I still tend to blame any hardship on the victim, at least until wiser reflection, or the facts, point to more powerful and influential culprits, often governments or large corporations.

Anyway, I gleaned no more from family conversations about Uncle John than that he'd had the majority of his insides removed in a series of operations. In my memory, he's thin and stooped, grey in dress, complexion and manner, and not very mobile.

Aunt Marge, on the other hand, was curvy and vivacious, dressed in colourful dresses, and full of laughter. From their frequent glances of disapproval, it was easy to tell that my parents didn't think much of Aunt Marge. Her frivolity was deemed wholly inappropriate, especially in the light of her husband's illness. And she wore make up.

Mum never wore make-up, and she and Dad heartily disapproved of anyone who did, adopting a stern expression and criticising any painted 'offender' when out of earshot. It seemed that make-up was the sign of a fallen woman, something that gave me great hope in the years of teenage sexual fantasy.

Given the contrast in their age, health and attitude, I always sympathised with Aunt Marge. She seemed to me to be like a canary trapped in a rookery.

I never once spent a night away from home with my parents. But we did have summer holidays throughout the 1960s: one day, and one day only, in Borth, a 'resort' on the northwest coast of Wales.

In my mind's eye, Borth is a small village running,

one building deep, along the landward side of a straight road paralleling the coast. Westward, beyond the slate roofs and thin strip of tarmac are several hundred yards of tall sand dunes topped with tufted grass. Beyond the dunes are a wide golden beach and the freezing Irish Sea.

On the chosen day every year, we used to arrive in the late morning, having taken the scenic route from Ludlow over the Welsh mountain passes. We could have arrived earlier, but, in another annual ritual, the Ford Pop had overheated. A wiser family would have been prepared for the eventuality, but it always came as a complete surprise to us. Our orange squash would have to be thrown away so that its bottle could be filled with water from a stream. This was poured, hissing, into the steaming radiator, but not before Dad had scolded himself taking the top off the damn thing.

Dad never had an accident, but he was the sort of driver who saw quite a few, and many more near misses. He never exceeded 30 miles an hour, even on the most open of roads, and there were few of those between Ludlow and Borth. We could end up leading quite a convoy through mid-Wales, Dad proudly double de-clutching to get the Ford Pop into first gear on the steeper hills, the first hints of steam wafting from under the bonnet.

Those following prayed for a stretch of straight road. When they saw one, no matter how short, they were not to be deterred by anything, not even oncoming traffic or livestock.

'Look at him. What the bloody hell does he think he's up to?' Dad would shout as a car squeezed past and dived in front of us, narrowly avoiding an oncoming lorry, or a wayward sheep.

Dad rarely swore. And even then, it was only the

odd bloody, or an even rarer bugger when the situation required more extreme language. Mild expletives by today's standards, but strong stuff for a respectable family man back then. Such outbursts were always greeted with a disapproving look from Mum.

'No patience. Why's he in such a tearing hurry?'

And if a woman was behind the wheel, no further explanation of poor driving was required.

Mum didn't drive, and never attempted to navigate. In fact, I don't remember anyone attempting to navigate. I don't think we ever owned a road map. Dad always knew the way. Or perhaps he just never admitted to being lost, and our meandering scenic route was him trying to find Borth. Anyway, we always seemed to get there eventually.

I still recognise drivers like my dad when we visit Shropshire. Having averaged 50 to 60 miles an hour up to the border of the county, your rate of progress suddenly halves, slowed by cars being driven by men and women in sensible hats, overcoats and, often, gloves. Have they not heard of in-car heating?

There are more such drivers in Shropshire than any other part of the country, probably the world. Dad would have been appalled at the number of women among them, but he'd have approved of their cautious driving.

Having arrived in Borth, Brian and I would want to head straight for the sea, but Mum and Dad would need a drink. So we'd have to sit in one of the many roadside cafés and watch them sup one, two, perhaps three cups of tea. And to make matters worse, they'd strike conversation with the waitresses and other customers, further delaying our arrival on the beach.

Hadn't the weather been awful? Weren't the roads busy? And so many lunatic drivers. Never used to be like that, did it?

When Mum spoke, it would be in the piping 'posh' voice she used when trying to create a good impression, what would have been her telephone voice, if we'd had a telephone. We clutched our buckets and spades, looked at our feet swinging beneath the café chairs, and prayed for the embarrassment to end.

On occasion, the locals would be speaking Welsh. The waitress would serve Dad and join in his small talk in English, before lapsing back into her own language with the other customers. Similarly, the customers nearest our table would join in Dad's enforced camaraderie in English, before again speaking Welsh to their neighbours.

My parents would become increasingly stony-faced, convinced they were being snubbed, and probably insulted. In retaliation, they'd try and strike loud conversation with any other English people present. If distance precluded this, there'd be a conspiracy of gesturing and gurning across the café.

All the English visitors we met in Borth, and those my parents spoke to on our return to Ludlow, saw the Welsh speaking their own language as a demonstration of ignorance, believing they were being ridiculed. Frankly, I wouldn't have blamed the locals if they'd been having a joke at our expense.

Eventually, Mum and Dad would lead us across the road and let us run off through the dunes to the sea. A few minutes later, they'd appear and set up their aluminium fold-away chairs at the top of the beach under the sand dunes. In between frequent forays to the cafés for more tea, there they'd sit for the rest of the day. There was very little concession to the fact that they were on holiday, or on a beach.

Mum would take off her coat, but not her headscarf, and Dad would take off his pullover and roll up his shirt sleeves, maybe even his trouser legs. There was no further dressing down; in fact, because of the strong breeze off the Irish Sea, Mum was likely to put her coat on five minutes after taking it off.

I'm pretty sure they didn't own swimming costumes, although Dad said he'd been taught to swim by being thrown into the River Teme below Ludford Bridge. His survival was the only evidence I ever saw that he'd learnt his lesson.

He did, however, play cricket with us, and this has left me with a strange legacy.

Dad was left handed at a time when schools tried to beat it out of you. It didn't work, and he remained determinedly cack-handed. I'm right handed, but when he taught me to hold a cricket bat, it was as a left-hander. To this day, if I pick up a cricket or softball bat, I adopt a left handed stance.

In a break with tradition one year in the late 60s, we had our summer day out in Rhyl. Unlike Borth, it was a destination that seemed to merit the name resort. It had a proper seafront with ice cream parlours and a funfair. But the place was crawling with large gangs of Skinheads and Hell's Angels, the successors of the Mods and Rockers that had flourished earlier in the decade.

Skinheads, as the name implies, had closely cropped hair, and were renowned for their love of violence. Most wore short denim jackets, although the more fashion-conscious sported long black Crombie overcoats, even in the sunshine. All wore baggy jeans, held up by colourful braces, the jean bottoms rolled up to reveal highly polished Doc Marten boots.

These 'Bovver Boots' were their favourite weapons in the fights their presence always precipitated, although they weren't above using more sophisticated weaponry, such as knives, clubs and chains. Some arrived on highly polished motor scooters, which they parked at various points along the seafront.

The Hell's Angels tended to be a few years older and rode in on large British motor bikes, which they parked in their own segregated areas. They were easily distinguished from the Skinheads by their long hair, ragged denim waistcoats, grubby jeans and motorbike boots. These could also be used as weapons, alongside more knives, clubs and chains.

Most of the Skinhead and Hell's Angel gangs came from the English northwest or Midlands. They wandered around in groups numbering anything from tens to hundreds, laughing and joking among themselves, but glowering at and taunting their rivals. In the absence of any other foe, the Skinheads at least would have been happy to fight among themselves. But on this day, they had the Hell's Angels - and the police.

I felt sorry for the latter. In an attempt to stave off the inevitable, they marched the various groups up and down the seafront, refusing to let them face up to one another. And, equally inevitably, as we marched from café to café for the obligatory cups of tea, our family was caught up in this tide of swearing malevolence.

Every few yards, in a manner which horrified Brian and me, Dad would take the pipe from his mouth and pass scathing comment on the individuals that surrounded us.

'What on Earth does he look like? Just look at that. I didn't fight in the war for the likes of him. A bit of discipline, that's what he needs. Look at him!'

Scarred faces turned to scowl at the middle-aged man and his family. I'm convinced it wasn't the police that saved us from a savage mauling that day, but the fact that we always turned into another café before the Skinheads could get at us and kick us to death.

Sure enough, when we arrived back in Ludlow that evening and switched on the television news, running battles were reported in all the resorts along the North Wales coast, including Rhyl. Frustration, beer and contemptuous comments from men like my dad had finally become too much for the gangs, and not even the police could stop them going on the rampage.

I couldn't imagine anyone rampaging in Borth.

Uncle John and Aunt Marge had a son and a daughter, and we attended the daughter's wedding. It would have been about 1962, when I was seven and Brian three. I have a photograph of us standing together in our wedding finery, slim, fair-haired and smiling. Our outfits are identical: short-sleeved white shirts, light blue shorts, matching ties, short white socks and brown sandals.

After the wedding, we'd have worn the individual elements several more times, initially 'for best', but then, until we'd grown out of them, 'for everyday'. A few years later, in a cruel twist, Brian would have inherited my ensemble, to be worn as long as it fitted him.

Having to wear the clothes of older siblings must have been one of the greatest traumas faced by the younger children of poor families; garments that were not only fairly threadbare, but also several years out of date – wrong style, wrong colour. Brian probably had few clothes bought for him until I left home to join the RAF at the age of eighteen and a half.

Dodmore could be a rough place. Brian and I were 'beaten up' on several occasions. The day I remember most vividly saw us both cornered by a large gang and thrown into nettles. Although I was only about seven, I can still recall the shame of not being able to protect my little brother.

Perhaps surprisingly, given such episodes, and my mother's ill health, I still see my childhood from five to 11 years of age as pretty idyllic.

I enjoyed school, and our house backed onto miles of fields. From a very young age, my friends and I would disappear for the day, walking to Whitbach, a wooded escarpment two miles north of Ludlow, crossing streams and roads with very little sense of danger, beyond that of getting wet socks or falling out of a tree. As long as our mothers knew where we were going, and when we were likely to return, we were given our freedom.

Only a few years later, we would ride for miles on our bicycles, visiting castles in villages such as Richards Castle and Wigmore. Again, our parents showed little concern beyond knowing where we were going and when we were likely to be home.

I was never so relaxed about my own children.

One day, at the age of about six, a friend and I ran away from home. I can't remember why, but we turned back when we reached the edge of our usual territory and realised we had no food, or means of getting any. We were home before our mothers missed us, and they were none the wiser.

I spent many hours with Andy Clark and the Parsons children, making bows and arrows, or throwing arrows, out of hazel, string and playing cards, and then firing or throwing them at makeshift targets, or just seeing how far they would go. We made twisty tracks in corn fields and ran down as fast as we could, brushing our exposed skin against jagged stalks until covered in scratches that stung like hell.

Basically, we spent all our time out of doors, playing or wandering the local area. And while some of our contemporaries were intent on creating criminal damage or fighting, I think that, in the main, my friends and I were reasonably well-behaved. Occasionally, we were chased by farmers for damaging their crops to make our tracks, or for breaking up their bales to jump into, or berated by neighbours for kicking balls into their gardens, but these instances were few and far between.

I fell in love with Susan Parsons. It was unrequited. I'm not sure she even knew.

From the age of five, my years of play were mainly in the 1960s, the decade when, according to the media, the grey post-war world was blossoming with light and colour. And yet, nearly all the games I and my friends played were stuck firmly in the Second World War.

How could something that had ended a decade before we'd been born have remained so influential?

Well, for a start, my parents, and especially my Dad, still seemed to be trapped in the period. His six years in uniform were the formative years of his life. He talked about them several times every day, and I'm sure they were in his mind much more than even that would suggest.

Although it was the decade of the Beatles and Twiggy, cinema and television were still dominated by dramas, documentaries and films about the war. My friends' parents all seemed stuck in the same time warp. The colourful style revolution overtaking the cities never touched most people such as them. I'm not sure it ever did.

So, when we played outside, we became soldiers, preferably British, which meant we'd win, but necessarily, on occasion, German, which meant we were destined to lose, no matter how superior our toy guns, our numbers or our tactics.

When the weather forced us indoors, we'd play with toy soldiers, mass-produced figures of plastic about two inches high. Sometimes we'd merely line them up as if on a parade, but often we'd have them face one another in combat, spending long hours in complex manoeuvres around and beneath the furniture, until one commander, the German, had no forces left.

My first soldiers had been bought by my parents, but as soon as I started to receive pocket money, from about the age of seven, I used to buy a toy soldier every Saturday morning. I continued this tradition into my early teens, when part of the money earned on my paper rounds went toward increasing my army of plastic paratroopers and guardsmen. If I close my eyes, I can still smell the distinctive aroma given off when I lifted them from the little brown paper bags into which the shopkeeper put them.

Does this emphasis on war offer an explanation for me pursuing a military career? Perhaps, but all my contemporaries played the same games, and few of them followed the same path. Maybe I was just more suggestible.

All four of Dad's sisters married and had children. Rose lived near one of her brothers in Stockport, Greater Manchester, and Joan made her life in the Midlands, while Pam and Nance still lived in Ludlow. As a middle-aged woman, one of Nance's daughters,

Julie, would find Dad collapsed at home on the day he died.

Wherever they lived, Dad's relatives and their families visited just once a year. The visits lasted no more than a few hours and followed a set formula.

After catching up with any family news, including extravagant mouthing about deaths and illnesses, there would be long periods of silence, interspersed with brief outbursts on the state of the world: the ludicrous rise in prices, the worsening behaviour, especially of the young, and the general deterioration of the country in almost every regard. The conversation would be accompanied by several cups of tea and pieces of cake.

Only when the cake ran out and the silences threatened to become permanent would the visitors rise to leave with invites for reciprocal visits. In the case of Pam and Nance only, these invitations would be taken up about six months later.

No visitors escaped our house without a present, Dad loading them down with geraniums and either potatoes or tomatoes.

Brian, any visiting cousins and I would have sat in attendance throughout, fidgeting. I found the whole process excruciating, especially the silences. Perhaps it's why I now fill any slight pause in a conversation with embarrassing banalities. They just seem better than the threat of the alternative – those lingering silences.

As the guests left, we'd receive a kiss on the cheek and a coin, usually a florin (ten pence), while our cousins received similar gifts from Mum and Dad. Two shillings was a lot of money in the 60s, but I doubt it made up for the hours stuck inside while the sun shined.

The only one of Dad's relatives to visit more than once a year, and my favourite among his siblings, was his older brother, Charles. We rarely visited him because he lived near Rose in Stockport, which was outside Dad's comfort zone.

I don't remember us ever driving to, or through, a city, even though Birmingham was only 30 miles away, much closer than Borth. But Dad had the good sense to stick to the countryside, which was probably just as well for all concerned.

Uncle Charles had been a Desert Rat, that is, a soldier who'd served in North Africa during the Second World War. He'd been a motorcycle despatch rider, and the nearest the family came to a war hero, having been Mentioned in Despatches. I never found out why, but often wondered whether he'd carried the despatch in which he'd been mentioned.

After the War, Charles became an aircraft technician for A V Roe at Woodford, near Manchester. The firm later became part of Hawker Siddeley, then British Aerospace. Charles helped manufacture Vulcan nuclear bombers, and fitted the starboard wing anti-icing in all the B2 variants. Two decades later, during my two and a half years as an airframe and propulsion fitter, I worked on the same aircraft and the same system at RAF Scampton.

In 1963, when I was eight, we visited Uncle Charles and Auntie Helen and I stayed on for a week, the only time I ever stayed with any of Dad's family. I know the date because they took me to a football match at Old Trafford for which I still have the programme: Manchester United versus my favourite team, Tottenham Hotspurs.

It was the first major sporting event I'd ever attended, and the choice of fixture couldn't have been better. It was one of those matches that appears on television whenever they show a programme on the golden age of either team, or of football in general. I seem to remember the final score being 3-3, with goals from George Best and my footballing hero at the time, Jimmy Greaves.

We also visited Manchester Airport, then called Ringway. I loved aircraft, but with Ludlow being about as far from a large airfield as it was possible to be in England, I'd never seen any close up. So, it was marvellous to be near row upon row of Tridents, Viscounts and Vanguards in their British European Airways liveries, watching them taxy in and out and take off and land. I stood on the roof of the terminal building for hours, and I'm sure the visit fed my growing desire to become involved in aviation in some way.

I regret not having met Charles more often. Physically, he resembled my father, but he seemed more worldly and open about the past. I'm sure he'd have had many stories to tell.

Visits by the more distant members of Dad's family often took place on the first weekend in May, or the few days either side, the period when Ludlow May Fair is in residence.

The May Fair closes the streets around the Market Square and Castle to traffic. They fill with uncharacteristic sights, sounds and smells: colourful flashing lights and gaudy awnings; raucous laughter, chugging generators, loud pop music, sirens, the shouts of stall holders; and the odours of frying fat and onions mixed with the sweet, sickly scent of candy floss and toffee apples.

For those not interested in Shakespeare, food

festivals and other forms of higher culture, the May Fair brings real excitement to Ludlow, about the only excitement since the old Town Hall discos – the Victorian Town Hall was demolished with scandalous haste in 1986.

One of my most vivid memories is of the effect the fairground workers had on the girls of the town. I'm told it's the same now.

The girls hang around the rides in excessive make-up and the most revealing fashions of the day, watching the grubby men hopping confidently between dodgem cars, or standing nonchalantly on the speeding floor of the Waltzers, giving selected gondolas an extra shove to increase the intensity of experience for the occupants. Of course, the chosen gondolas invariably contain three or four young women who bask in the attention, screaming with fear and excitement as their cars are swung this way and that.

Occasionally, it ends in tears and a pool of vomited Vimto and onions. But sometimes the fairground worker stands proudly in front of a gondola with just one girl in it, both of them revelling in the notoriety their blatant display of exclusivity bestows.

The local lads split into two camps.

Most stand sullenly on the sidelines, looking pathetic as they watch *their* girls being seduced by the interlopers. A few try to emulate the strutting confidence of the fairground studs, standing up on the rides, or moving unsteadily about them. Their acts of bravado are destined to end in ridicule as the very people they seek to outface exert their superior skill and authority, gliding swiftly over to make them sit down, or to eject them from the rides.

Whatever the outcome, the resentment of the local lads increases and the reputation and attractiveness of the fairground lads is enhanced.

One year in my mid-teens, having heard there was good money to be made, Simon Davies and I hung around on the final night and helped one of the travelling families dismantle their rides and stalls. We worked until about four in the morning, lugging heavy equipment.

With everything packed away, we were directed to a caravan, towered over by heavily laden lorries. In the darkness, we each had a note thrust into our hands, and, assuming we'd been given at least £5, maybe £10, we made our way through the vehicles to the nearest street light.

To our vast disappointment, in an era when there were £1 notes, that's exactly what we'd been given, scant payment for five hours of backbreaking work.

With the travelling workers standing around looking intimidating, we were too timid to go back and argue the case for a more appropriate reward, and we never stayed behind to dismantle the fair again.

Until the age of 11, I really enjoyed school. East Hamlet Infants', which I attended until the age of seven, was small and friendly, and I did well. From there, I went to St Laurence's Junior, another relatively small school with friendly staff.

I particularly remember Mrs Bowdler, a short jolly woman, Miss Killworth, who taught me to swim, and Mrs Bodenham, taller and more serious, but not severe. They all inspired me, especially in a love of English and drama.

Mrs Bodenham's brother had been a pilot in the RAF, and had been shot down in the Battle of Britain. She never talked about it, but we imagined him surrounded by German aircraft, fighting gallantly until one finally nailed him.

I was already familiar with the grave of one Battle of Britain pilot. I passed it regularly when taking a shortcut through a local cemetery on the way to see friends. There was something about the stark simplicity of its Commonwealth War Graves Commission headstone that always made me stop and, in my own way, pay homage.

The inscription read: *Pilot Officer H L Whitbread, Pilot, RAF, 20th September 1940, Age 26, One of the Few*. It went on with the words: *Never in the field of human conflict was so much owed by so many to so few*.

I read these words so often that I knew them by heart long before I heard them on the radio or television, or found out they were from a speech made by Winston Churchill on 20th August 1940.

I dedicated my Battle of Britain novel, Wings Over Summer, to Laurie Whitbread. Only when it was published in the summer of 2013 did I discover, or perhaps re-discover, that Laurie was the brother of my junior school teacher, Mrs Bodenham.

The publicity surrounding the publication also put me in touch with one of his nephews, who gave me more detail of his uncle's life and death – and a photo which now adorns my desk.

Laurie Whitbread was born in Ludlow and went to the Grammar School. He joined the RAF six months before the start of the Second World War and, during the Battle of Britain, was flying Spitfires with 222 Squadron at RAF Duxford in Cambridgeshire, the same base as Douglas Bader.

On 9th September, he shot down a Messerschmitt bf109, but then, on 20th September, he was hit by another 109 in a surprise attack over Rochester, in Kent. The aircraft crashed at Pond Cottage and, although Laurie was thrown clear of the wreckage, he didn't survive.

I still visit the grave every time I visit that of my parents, 50 yards away in the same cemetery. He was probably my earliest inspiration for wanting to join the RAF as a pilot, an aspiration which, from about the age of nine, supplanted the desire to be a fireman.

I did well at St Laurence's, not only thriving academically, but starring in school plays and representing the school at football. I'm afraid I can't verify a memory that a football scout from Everton came to see me and another lad play, but he missed me because I was in hospital having my tonsils out. Whether the scout's visit would have led to anything, I doubt, but it would have been interesting to have had the opportunity to impress. In the final year, I was Deputy Head Boy.

Over this period, from 1962 to 66, The Beatles were in their prime. Doctor Who and The Man From UNCLE, a spy caper, were favourite television programmes, which we acted out in the playground, when we weren't playing football, hopscotch, skipping or conkers. We also used to play kiss chase, and I had my first girlfriends. It was a happy time.

All this changed when I passed the 11-plus examination to qualify for the local grammar school.

Ludlow Grammar School for Boys could trace its history back to the 13th Century, and some of its buildings dated from the 16th. It was run much like a public school, with its own quirky language and traditions: quads for playgrounds, heads for toilets, gowned teachers and Eton Fives courts. It even had its own fee-paying students, the Boarders, who lived in large houses in the town.

The School had a fine record of academic and sporting achievement, and sent many of its students on to the Russell Group universities, including a few each year to Oxbridge. Boards in the mediaeval hall reflected its long history, as did some of the graffiti.

My parents were immensely proud that I was to be the first Powell to attend, and I don't think they would ever have considered denying me the opportunity. But the cost of the uniform must have been crippling.

Everything from the socks, blazer and cap, to the masses of sports kit and a brown leather satchel - almost as big as me - had to be purchased from the town's most exclusive, and expensive, gentlemens' outfitter: Bodenham's. I have no idea how they afforded it all, and of course, I never thanked them properly for the sacrifices they must have made.

Knowing how much my attendance meant to them - and how much they'd spent - my own excitement was tinged with nervousness. It was very much a step into the unknown, for which I was ill-prepared. And unfortunately, I went on to shun most of the opportunities the School offered, partly because I never really recovered from my first day.

The vast majority of the other children on Dodmore - all bar my friend Andy in my little enclave - went to the local secondary school. Their uniform was an understated ensemble of dark grey trousers, light grey pullover, white shirt and grey and red striped tie. My new uniform was much more flamboyant.

The cap was an especially gaudy item, covered in concentric circles of dark blue, light blue and crimson, with a stiff peak of the same colours. You couldn't wear such a thing on the Dodmore Estate.

Andy was a year older than me, was developing into a big lad and could cope with any rough stuff. I was still short for my age, and had always found it best to try and talk my way out of trouble. But the greatest orator in the world couldn't have escaped the Dodmore bullies wearing a crimson and blue school cap. So, on the way to and from school, I hid as much uniform as possible. Of course, there was no hiding the satchel, and to avoid confrontations, I was often forced to take elaborate and time-consuming detours.

Anyway, on my first morning, I rode into the playground – the lower quad - without my cap. Immediately pounced on by a prefect, I was given 50 lines, that is, I had to write out 50 times something like: I must always wear my cap when dressed in school uniform. Not an outrageous penalty, but I was devastated. It was the first time I'd ever received a punishment in school.

It didn't end there. Alongside ritual bullying by the Second Form – various tortures in 'concentration camps' - I was made to stand on a chair in the Prefects' Room while a group of Flashman-like sixth-formers threw balls of paper at my head to try and dislodge the offending cap.

My introduction reduced me to a quivering bundle of nerves. And very quickly, the starchy formality, quirky language, masters in their gowns, prefects and ritualistic bullying became too much for me. In the first few days, I was often in tears.

I wasn't the first working class lad to attend the Grammar School, and some of my junior school friends started at the same time, but, in my eyes, they all seemed to fit in. I didn't, and there were no sympathetic voices and no-one to talk to – I couldn't risk confiding in my parents and disappointing them – so I withdrew into a protective shell and became desperately unhappy.

Things became a little less stuffy in my second year, when we amalgamated with the local Girls' High School, but it was too late. My unhappiness persisted throughout my seven years at the School.

However, on that first day, apart from looking slightly shorter and less well groomed than some of the other new boys, I doubt if anyone would have noticed me in the crowd. Andrew Griffiths, on the other hand, was instantly recognisable.

To start with, he was bald. And he had a very impressive scar running down the back of his head and under his shirt collar, like a zip. As I remember it, he'd had a brain tumour removed and everyone was told not to be too rough with him. I know this saved him from some of the more extreme initiations and bullying.

Perhaps feeling we were both somehow different, we were drawn to one another. We were both keen on sport, and we became good friends.

Since my one trip to Old Trafford, I hadn't been to any major sporting events. Andrew's family on the other hand, were regulars at Worcestershire cricket ground and at Molyneux, the home of Wolverhampton Wanderers.

One Saturday in the winter of 1966/67, they took me to a Wolves v Spurs game at Molyneux, where Derek Dougan was the star striker. Unfortunately, I don't remember anything of the game, only the malevolent atmosphere surrounding the event. As we were walking away from the stadium after the match, groups of bare-chested youths with team scarves hanging from the belts of their jeans began running the other way, shouting, 'There's a fight at the ground, a fight at the ground.'

Now I was brought up to believe fighting was something you avoided if possible, but these yobs were very obviously excited at the prospect. Sure enough, that night, the TV news was full of stabbings at football matches, including one at Wolverhampton.

Andrew and I once went to stay with his grandparents in a little cottage somewhere just over the border in Wales. It rained heavily, but we still went out to play football. Taking it in turns to be goalkeeper or striker, we played for hours, scoring fantastic goals and making magnificent saves, slowly churning the goalmouth between two jerseys into a quagmire, and getting caked in mud. It was great fun.

Had we been at home, we'd have been in big trouble for getting so filthy, but his grandparents seemed not to mind, and that only added to our enjoyment.

Andrew died when we were 13.

Because these things were not spoken of in plain English, I'm not sure why, but I think it was another tumour. The funeral was very sad. He and his parents seemed so close, and they'd done everything they could to pack his life with experiences that he could enjoy and they could remember.

Thankfully, it was a long time before I went to another funeral.

Contemporaries always express surprise that I was so unhappy at the Grammar School, saying they had no inkling of my feelings. I find this hard to believe, because I developed a pattern of absence that persisted throughout my time there.

I can't remember whether I used to spend a week at school and two weeks off, or the other way round, but I must have had an attendance rate little better than 50%. The reason for the absences was always illness, usually in the form of sinus headaches.

I think I'd discovered the possibility of missing school when tonsillitis had led to absences from junior school and, eventually, a tonsillectomy. At that stage, though, the absences had been unwelcome.

But when I went to the Grammar School, I convinced my mother, maybe even myself, that sinus headaches I'd also suffered before the age of 11, had become much more frequent, and severe, so bad that I wasn't well enough for school. The ploy worked, because Mum allowed me to stay home and wrote sick notes on my return to school.

If my father knew how much time I was missing, he seems to have deferred to my mother in managing the problem. Anyway, he usually left for work before I became ill, and arrived back after I would have returned from school and changed out of uniform, had I gone. So, he may not have known.

Often, I'd be well enough to do my paper round at 6.30 or 7.00 in the morning, but too ill to go to school, and then well enough to go out again in the evening. It seems amazing that I was able to get away with such behaviour, but I was.

It wasn't that my parents were disinterested in my education. It was just that they felt as out of their depth as I did. They didn't understand the customs or the curriculum of the Grammar School, or the potential for educational advancement and the career prospects I was jeopardising. I was able to take advantage of this.

However, I was still a fairly bright lad, and I managed to cope reasonably well in most subjects up to O Level (the forerunner of GCSEs). This was partly because I didn't spend my days off school tramping the streets, but sitting at home reading and watching daytime television, which then consisted of educational *schools* programmes, rather than soap operas and quizzes.

But, having acquired five good O Levels, my underlying intelligence was not enough to see me through my A Levels. At this point, the frequent absences became a bar to success and I failed these exams miserably.

The skiving ceased the day I joined the RAF.

Another reason for my disillusionment with the Grammar School was that they played rugby rather than what I called football. We weren't even allowed to play my idea of football in the playground.

The games master would shout contemptuously, 'You're here to play football, not *soccer*.'

One of his favourite punishments for minor errors on the rugby field, such as kicking the ball out of hand when he thought it should have been passed, was to bend you over and swing his heavy metal whistle on its length of cord to clip you on the bony part of your backside. On cold days especially, it was agony.

I still loved soccer and grew to detest rugby. But I was a natural ball player and ended up playing full back for the school all the way up to the Lower VIth, when my late flowering into puberty left me lacking the physique to succeed in the senior teams; although, I think I still played for the Second XV on occasion.

My innate ball skill also allowed me to represent my house and the School in other sports such as cricket and basketball, though none of them ever made up for losing the opportunity to play soccer.

And yet, the seven years of rugby must have brainwashed me. As soon as I joined the RAF and was allowed to concentrate on soccer again, I became an avid watcher of rugby. I even chose to socialise with the rugby rather than the soccer club, and went on a memorable rugby tour to Llandudno.

And then, who'd have thought it; four years after leaving school, I started playing rugby again, for Ludlow Fourth's at weekends.

I still love watching rugby. It was one of the reasons for retiring close to Cardiff, and, when not attending Cardiff Blues games at the Arms Park, where my wife and I are season ticket holders, or internationals at the Millennium Stadium, most weekends in the autumn and early months of the year are spent watching internationals on television.

A typical day in the Powell household during my early teenage years starts with my alarm sounding. The light from a streetlamp seeps round my curtains and paints the room in a faint orange glow. Sniffing the cold, damp air, I huddle under the woolly blankets for as long as possible. But my paper round beckons and, eventually, I throw back the bedclothes and step out, wincing as my feet touch cold linoleum. I tiptoe a short distance to flick the switch by the door.

Harsh yellow light illuminates a small room with flowered wallpaper. It's furnished with a single bed, small wardrobe, clothes-covered chair and a bookcase, laden with science fiction paperbacks – John Wyndham, Arthur C. Clarke, Isaac Asimov and Robert Heinlein - bought at a second-hand book stall on the market. Several Airfix model aircraft hang on threads from the ceiling. Breathing out silver vapour, I doff my pyjamas, don cold, damp, clothes from the chair and throw back the curtains.

The window is opaque, covered on the inside in shimmering crystalline ferns. The ice is too thick to rub away, so, hoping it's dry outside, I pull a quilted blue anorak from the cluttered wardrobe, switch off the light, step onto the dark landing and descend the narrow stairs into the pungent aroma of Dad's first pipe of the day.

'Good morning.'

The deep voice booms its welcome before I've even opened the door. As I step into the front room, Dad rises unsteadily from the upright chair next to the cluttered sideboard and limps slowly into the kitchen.

'Tea?' his retreating figure inquires.

Dad is halfway through his second cup, but I can never face his industrial strength brew first thing in the morning, or later in the day come to that. I follow him towards the kitchen, knowing that my, 'No thanks,' won't prevent him preparing his next 'fix'.

Most of his contemporaries sport expensively-earned beer guts, but Dad's protruding stomach, nestling under broad shoulders and a barrel chest, is all tea. Sometimes, I'm sure I can hear him sloshing as he walks; he'll drink at least five cups before setting out for work.

I stand in the kitchen doorway and watch him fill the kettle. He grimaces as he leans over the sink, his teeth clenching tightly round the stem of his pipe, raising it to the horizontal. Even before spending the day emptying dustbins, his ankle is sore. In the evening, it will be swollen to the size and shape of a rugby ball. Overnight, it will subside, only to swell again every day for the rest of his working life, and beyond.

Having lit the gas under the kettle, he turns his

weathered, moustachioed, face towards me, takes the pipe from his mouth, and says in a broad Shropshire accent, 'You be careful out there. The roads'll be like glass.'

His concern is genuine, and apposite. I can hardly reach the pedals of my second-hand bike, and the brakes barely work. But even this is an improvement. My previous bikes were ancient contraptions with big black frames and wooden blocks on the pedals so I could reach them. This one is red, with a whiff of modernity.

Dad limps past me into the front room and sinks back into his chair with a world-weary sigh, then stares straight ahead, humming absentmindedly. He'll sit like this until Mum comes down in about 15 minutes, to the offer of, 'Tea?'

I zip my anorak, pull on my gloves and step into the cold.

At this age, I work for a newsagent half a mile away at the bottom of Corve Street, and my round takes me up into the town, down Broad and Mill Streets, past the Grammar School, or to The Linney and north onto Bromfield Road. I can't remember what I earned, but it was no more than a few shillings for six mornings a week, say twenty five pence in today's money.

When decimalization came along in 1971, I was working for Mr Kennard, the butcher. I well remember him trying to explain to Mrs Bradley that, although he'd said her piece of meat cost five pence, she had to give him a shilling, or 12 old pence.

'How can fivepence be a shilling?'

She just couldn't, or wouldn't, understand.

I no longer think of money in terms of 12 pennies to a shilling and 20 shillings to a pound, but I still think of weights in pounds and ounces, even after years dealing in decimal measurements in school and the RAF. And I still most easily visualise short distances in inches and yards, although I cope in both kilometres and miles when greater distances are involved. All very muddled.

I return from my paper round. Mum is up and Dad has gone to work, although the aroma of his pipe still fills the house. He's lit the fire in the front room, but it's still very cold, and Mum, who feels the chill, is wrapped in layers of woollen upper garments and a heavy skirt. It will be several hours before the warmth from the fire pervades the rest of the house. Even then, the frost on the inside of the upstairs windows won't thaw, perhaps for several weeks.

As usual, for breakfast, I have cornflakes sprinkled with sugar and full cream milk.

I don't remember how I decide whether I feel well enough to go to school, or how Mum and I interact to decide whether or not I go. If I do, I cycle the mile or so to the school buildings I've already seen on my paper round.

After morning lessons, I return home for dinner – I'm not sure when I started to call a midday meal lunch, but my family never had anything other than dinner. On some days, that will be it, I'll take the afternoon off, and again, I don't remember how Mum and I interact for this to happen.

If I stay home, I sit on the settee, reading or watching school television programmes, while Mum goes about her daily routine: cleaning, laundry, shopping and preparing for the evening meal.

Brian returns from St Laurence's Junior School at about 3.30, and we sit and watch programmes like Jackanory, Blue Peter or Crackerjack until Dad comes home at about 5.30. He looks tired, and is limping more noticeably than in the morning. Sometimes, as he drinks the first of many more cups of tea, one of us massages his ankle.

If I'm the masseur, I fetch a small hexagonal brown bottle from the kitchen and pour a glistening pool of camphor oil into the palm of my left hand. The initial smell is overpowering, enough to make me turn away to protect my nose from the invisible fumes. But after a short while, it seems quite pleasant. And ten minutes later, I've stopped noticing it, although someone entering the room would still find it overpowering.

Dad's left ankle is bloated, like the bulge in a snake digesting a large rodent, the white skin unnaturally stretched and shiny, still bearing the faint imprint of the tubular bandage he wears under his sock. At first, even the gentlest touch makes him wince. But soon, the stiffness and pain ease and he sighs contentedly.

The scene is one of unembarrassed intimacy. Dad always occupies the same seat in front of the fire, with Mum busy in the kitchen, cooking tea.

When the meal is ready, we eat at the table under the window in the front room. We have no dining room.

Cooked meals all come with chips, mashed or new potatoes, depending on season. The other vegetables, cabbage, cauliflower, broccoli, or runner beans, have been boiled to within an inch of their lives. They lie on the plate, limp, submissive and virtually tasteless. Unsurprisingly, I hate vegetables, and only discover they can be crisp and flavoursome several years later, when persuaded to try them again by my wife.

I don't think Mum was a bad cook. Back then, vegetables had to be cooked until the kitchen windows steamed up and all the flavour had evaporated, filling the house with a dense fog that smelt of rotting vegetation. It was the same in my friends' houses. It was the law.

We usually eat the cheapest cuts of meat, things like beef skirt or braised beef, and various kinds of offal. I much prefer things like baked beans or egg on toast. And Mum makes magnificent puddings: steamed sponge, spotted dick, pineapple upside down, all covered in delicious custard.

Brian and I are real chatterboxes, talking enthusiastically about television programmes and football.

Dad tells us how some racehorse has fared: 'Ten to one. Should have walked it. It's all a fix.'

He pretends never to put money on horses, but much later, I find out that despite his concerns at the crookedness of the sport, he's a regular at the Bookies. Brian inherits the same interest in gambling, although I never do.

After tea, if I don't go out to wander the town with my mates, I watch more television, programmes such as Tomorrow's World, Top of the Pops or The Avengers. Other times, Brian and I go out to play football or some other street game. We do this even if I haven't been to school. After all, I'm unlikely to bump into any of my schoolmates. None of them live by me.

I go to bed at about 10pm, slipping a hot water bottle under the covers and onto my pyjamas. There's still ice on the inside of the window. I undress as quickly as possible, put on the pyjamas and jump into bed. I push the bottle slowly down with my feet, unfolding my body onto the bits of bed it's warmed. When my legs are fully extended, I turn onto my stomach and read a book propped on my pillow for a while. Finally, I steel myself, dash out of bed, switch out the light, climb back in and lie within the line of warm bedclothes.

I try to get to sleep before the hot water bottle cools completely.

Dad worked hard to bring home enough money for us to have sufficient clothes and wholesome food, but, as already mentioned, there were few luxuries, such as holidays, electrical gadgets or expensive toys. Fashionable clothes counted as luxuries, and I was never 'with it', sporting the same haircut as my dad, pretty much short back and sides, until I joined the RAF.

Dad was, however, always bringing home items he'd *rescued* from the bins. The odd one or two were useful, and welcomed by one or other of us, but most were complete tat. He refused to see this and would add the rejected items to the treasures in his shed, which was always rammed full with junk.

He was a very gentle man, especially when it came to my mother. Her health remained poor. Physically, she'd always suffered with bronchitis – not helped by a life in rooms full of pipe smoke – but she was also diagnosed with pernicious anaemia, which seemed to reduce her energy levels, and to make her even more vulnerable to chest infections. And mentally, there were still lapses into depression, some of which required hospital stays.

But, at this time, when she was at home, she very much ran the household. She shopped, cooked and cleaned, and had the authority to banish Dad's clutter from the house. It was, in many ways, an archetypal family of the period. Dad was the breadwinner and Mum the home-maker.

Brian and I always seemed to get on well. As children, we played together for hours and rarely fell out. Our fights were nearly always in play.

He was much brighter than me, and a better all round sportsman. But, while playing football in the spring of his final year at junior school, he suffered a complicated break/dislocation of his elbow which left him permanently unable fully to straighten his left arm.

Following several months off school, he failed the 11-plus and went to Ludlow Secondary Modern, where he did well, gaining a good set of Certificates of Secondary Education - CSEs, most at Grade 1, which made them equivalent to O Levels. He then transferred to the Sixth Form of the Grammar School, where he also did well, gaining good A-Levels.

In retrospect, he was very forgiving during this period. Despite him doing everything better than me, I think I always gained, or sought, more attention, firstly for being at the Grammar School, then as I progressed through my early RAF training.

At times, he could easily have tarnished my image with my parents. For a start, he could have told them that I smoked, and later, that I drank much more than was sensible. To the best of my knowledge, he never did.

Brian decided not to go on to university and stayed in Ludlow, where he lived with my parents until shortly before their deaths. Whether a feeling of responsibility for their welfare affected his decision not to leave the town, I don't know, just as I don't know whether he felt trapped by their deteriorating health in later years. What I do know is that despite my absence and his loyalty, my career still seemed to garner more attention than his solidity in remaining with them.

He's never shown any resentment, an emotion to which I think he could well be entitled.

I hope I haven't given the impression that Ludlow Grammar was a bad school, because nothing could have been further from the truth. I think it was probably an excellent school, evidenced by the strong academic performance of my contemporaries. I just didn't warm to the atmosphere or teaching methods, or take advantage of the many things it had to offer.

I remember only one of the teachers with any real warmth, an English teacher, Mr Barge. It was he that fostered my interest in drama, but, alas, he didn't teach me for long, and I usually met him thereafter only through my involvement in school plays.

The teachers who made the strongest impression were the disciplinarians, such as Mr Woolley, a tiny, hawkish Maths teacher, who terrorised us all despite his slight frame. Another I won't name enjoyed corporal punishment, sometimes with a slipper, and sometimes with a long cane. He would line up half a dozen boys, make them bend over, direct them to inch forward or back and whack them all at the same time. I think we were all meant to enjoy the joke.

About the only genuinely humorous episode I remember involved one of the older generation of teachers, Johnny Jones.

He never taught me, but I remember him invigilating exams in the hall. Unlike some of the teachers who sat, ever-vigilant in front of us, Johnny would wonder up and down between the rows of desks. Every so often, he'd skip forward and perform a bowling action, then walk on. Some time after turning into the next row, he'd play a cricket shot, say an off-drive, pausing to watch the imaginary ball before resuming his slow walk. A few rows later, he'd bowl again, then, somewhere in the following row, play another shot, occasionally something aggressive like a sweep or a hook, watching the ball and smiling contentedly as if he'd scored a boundary, or tutting as if he'd been caught. It was very distracting, but endlessly fascinating and entertaining.

Perhaps nothing says more about my seven years at the School than that, beyond these few episodes, I remember very little, other than my antipathy towards it.

And yet, I think grammar schools provided a major path to social mobility for the likes of me, a dustman's son. Had I been more diligent, the world would have been my oyster. Even after the skiving that led to my failure at A Levels, I ended up with enough qualifications to pursue careers for which a secondary modern education may well have left me unqualified. And despite the impression that I was on my own during those seven years, I made some life-long friends.

The School met its demise when Ludlow's secondary schools amalgamated into a comprehensive in the 1980s, and the Mill Street site became a sixth form college.

I'd starred in school plays at St Laurence's, and continued with major parts for my age in my early days at the Grammar School. Mr Barge tended to direct these, and I'm pretty sure he put me forward for an audition that led to my major acting accomplishment.

In 1968, when I was 13 years old, I was chosen to play Edward V, the elder of the two Princes in the Tower, in the Ludlow Festival production of Richard III.

Ludlow Festival is an arts event that takes place in

the town over a two-week period every summer. Until 2012, the centrepiece was a Shakespearean play, staged twice a day in the inner courtyard of the mediaeval castle. It was a tremendously atmospheric setting, and, over the years, attracted a prestigious list of directors and actors. In the 1960s, it also offered a few locals the opportunity to appear as extras, or even, as in my case, in some of the minor roles.

I remember the whole process with great fondness.

The director was Joan Knight, to my eyes, a stereotypical luvvie – darling this and darling that - and the first woman I ever met who smoked cigars. Come to think of it, I haven't met many since.

The part of Richard III was played by the major draw, Alfred Lynch. At the time, he was most famous for a television drama, Manhunt, in which he played an RAF pilot trying to escape Second World War France. Other actors included Michael Graham Cox, Valerie Lush, Heather Stoney and Ronald Herdman, a delightful man who dubbed me Little Ron to his Big Ron.

In all, five lads from the local schools were chosen to take part. With rehearsals, we had a month off school. It was great, and I wasn't ill once.

A lad from the Secondary Modern, David Cadwallader, played my younger brother, the Duke of York. David was the archetypal cheeky chappy. You could imagine him rivalling Jack Wilde for the part of The Artful Dodger in Oliver. But like me, I think the Festival was the high point of his acting career. He still lives in Ludlow.

David and I became firm friends, but he was a terror. I noticed that he waved his right hand in a small circle when he walked on stage for our major scene together, an affectation undoubtedly brought on by nerves. I made the mistake of pointing it out.

During the next performance, he accentuated the action into a camp sashay, and pursed his lips. I collapsed in laughter, not very professional in front of a matinee audience of 1500 people. Thankfully, he never did it again, but for the rest of the run, we were always on the verge of corpsing.

Because we performed in the open air, the production was at the mercy of the British summer, and, in the years running up to 2012, they lost several performances to heavy rain. I believe it was the insurance costs associated with this that led to the eventual demise of the plays. A sad loss.

I don't think we lost a performance in 1968, but there were occasions when we were very wet. I remember one especially.

In the final scene, Richard III is killed at the Battle of Bosworth Field, and his body lies on stage until the play ends with a long victory speech by the Earl of Richmond, now Henry VII. One very wet afternoon, with Alfie Lynch already suffering from a cold, he fell to the stage with his upper body in a large puddle. It continued to rain, and Alfie was getting wetter and wetter, not least because the puddle was growing. Halfway through Richmond's speech, it all became too much. With an exasperated, nasal, 'Enough is enough,' he rose from the stage and walked off.

Again, not very professional, but it raised the biggest laugh of the production, and was something the school parties that made up the bulk of matinee audiences would never forget.

Like all good things, the experience had to come to an end, but it finished on a suitably theatrical high. At two o'clock in the morning, after a magnificent party, the whole cast performed the Okey Cokey on the town square beneath the castle battlements. Marvellous.

I'm not sure why I didn't pursue my interest in acting with more tenacity thereafter, but my physical immaturity increasingly ruled me out of the major parts in school plays, especially during my later teens, when I remained stubbornly fresh-faced and lacking in stature. My frequent absences probably didn't help. Anyway, acting was not the career I wanted.

Chapter 2 - Early Interest in the RAF

As I've already said, from the age of about nine, I was determined to become a pilot in the RAF. Perhaps Laurie Whitbread's headstone in the local cemetery had provided the spark, but there were many other influences.

RAF pilots, especially Battle of Britain pilots, were still revered as heroes, and the comics I read, such as the Lion and the Victor, were full of stories of their derring do, as were many of the small Commando comic books popular at the time. And then, there were pictures and films of the Red Arrows, whose pilots I idolised, although it was many years before I saw them perform live.

But I think it was films such as Reach For The Sky, The Dam Busters and, in 1969, Battle of Britain, that really inspired me. Battle of Britain was probably the most powerful recruiting tool the RAF had until the Tom Cruise film, Top Gun, inspired another generation of recruits from the mid-1980s onwards - even though it's about US Navy pilots.

I first wrote to the RAF when I was 10 years old. In reply, I received a large envelope containing a number of brochures and posters, a sympathetic letter explaining that I was a little too young for them, and information about a youth organization I could join when I was older. The very fact that they'd taken the time to reply so fulsomely to someone unlikely to affect their recruiting figures for several years strongly reinforced my desire to join, a powerful lesson for recruiters in any field.

The movement mentioned in the letter was the Air Training Corps (ATC), an organization partly financed by the RAF to foster air mindedness in the nation's youth.

In early 1969, as soon as I reached the magic age of 13 years nine months, I joined Ludlow's ATC unit, a detached flight of 156, Kidderminster, Squadron. There were about 20 regular attendees, all boys at that time, with ages ranging from nearly 14 to 18½. Before I left to join the RAF in 1973, the numbers had swelled sufficiently for the flight to become a squadron in its own right, No 333 Ludlow Squadron.

The flight was run by a small group of civilian volunteers and commanded by a local racehorse trainer, Jack Peacock, who was a pilot officer in the RAF Volunteer Reserve. His right hand man, the person who did more than any other to ensure that we youngsters got the most out of everything the organization had to offer, was Derek Crowther, a warrant officer in the Volunteer Reserve.

We cadets wore a blue uniform similar to that worn by RAF airmen, and we met once a week for two hours on a Friday evening. The hierarchy of ranks also mirrored the RAF, with corporals, sergeants and flight sergeants, my eventual rank. A few years after I left, Brian became the highest ranking cadet on the Squadron, the Cadet Warrant Officer.

Alongside the rank structure was another hierarchy, based on progress through a syllabus of military and aviation subjects, such as drill, meteorology and aerodynamics. Successful completion of practical tests and exams allowed you to rise from 1st Class, to Leading and then Senior Cadet, each stage with its own distinctive badge; and finally, to Staff Cadet, at which point you wore a yellow lanyard – a thin rope of interwoven cord - at the shoulder.

I remember lots of drill, marching up and down the

small car park outside the squadron building, but also lessons in various aviation topics and opportunities for other activities, such as shooting, building radios and welding. I enjoyed it all, even the drill, but the biggest draw for me was the opportunity to fly.

On the 1st of June 1969, almost undoubtedly accompanied by Derek Crowther, I and a small group of other cadets from Ludlow travelled to RAF Shawbury, just north of Shrewsbury, to fly on Number 7 Air Experience Flight. I was 14 years and just under two months old.

Air Experience Flights were – and still are - based at more than a dozen airfields around the British Isles. Each had a permanent staff of one RAF pilot, aided by a small number of serving and retired RAF pilots who gave up their free time to give youngsters like me 20 minutes in the air. At the time, they operated De Havilland Chipmunks, a monoplane development of the Tiger Moth.

My penultimate job as a group captain was a study into the future viability and basing of Air Experience Flights, and my final post included command of them, something I certainly hadn't envisaged on my first visit to one, 35 years earlier.

On that occasion, I was given a helmet, shown how to use the microphone in its oxygen mask, and fitted with a parachute, a bulky item that dangled beneath my bottom and made it difficult to walk. It would double as a seat cushion when I sat in the aircraft.

Next, we were briefed on what to do if there was an emergency so dire that we had to take to our parachutes. I'd have to open the canopy, stand up, jump from the aircraft and pull the parachute D-ring. I listened intently, but couldn't help thinking it unlikely

I'd be able to complete all the necessary actions in a real emergency. But the parachute and helmet made me feel the part, even if I didn't look it.

My confidence took a further knock when I was given a little blue and white bag, for when I was airsick, pretty much a certainty on my first flight the old hands told me. Missing this bag and throwing up into your oxygen mask or over the cockpit - and the occupant of the front seat - was the worst crime you could commit. The punishment was to spend the rest of the day cleaning up the mess, and, presumably, apologising to the pilot.

As I waited for my flight, I practised unclipping the mask and finding my sick bag.

By the time I eventually waddled onto the flight line, I'd worked myself into quite a lather, but I was also very excited. My allocated Chipmunk taxied in, turned and stopped in front of me, leaving its engine running. A cadet clambered out of the seat behind the pilot and waddled down the wing and onto the tarmac. He was white in the face and clutching a bloated blue and white bag.

I swallowed hard and waddled to the wing root. My legs were so short, and the parachute so cumbersome that I had to be lifted onto the wing - and into the cockpit.

An inauspicious start.

I sat down. With the instrument panel and the pilot's head obscuring the view to the front, and the cockpit sills rising above my shoulders to either side, I found it quite claustrophobic. It was also smelly, the aroma of exhaust fumes, fuel and engine oil, mixing with the rubber of the oxygen mask and the faint whiff of sweat and…and vomit.

I later discovered that Chipmunks always smelt of

all these things, and that each military aircraft type has its own, distinctive, smell. Even now, if I put my head into the cockpit of an aircraft I've worked on or flown, the aroma transports me straight back to the period of our last acquaintance, and more forcefully than watching film or looking at photographs.

At that first exposure to the smell of the Chipmunk, I was unimpressed and put my hand on my sick bag, just in case. I remained apprehensive all the time we were taxying for take off, the pilot weaving from side to side so he could see down the side of the high engine cowling. But, once we were airborne, it became a magical experience.

I was, and still am, fascinated by the appearance of the ground from the air. In the days of Google Earth and aerial and satellite imagery, perhaps today's youngsters are less impressed, but I was captivated.

I was also given control of the aircraft for brief periods, and was delighted to find that we didn't fall from the sky. Then the pilot performed some basic aerobatics, turning the aircraft upside down, looping and rolling. The feelings of added weight as he pulled up into manoeuvres, and of weightlessness as we floated over the top, were magical. And I wasn't ill.

The 20 minutes passed all too quickly, but I returned to fly again in the November of the same year, and up to four times a year thereafter. I was hooked, which is why the RAF does it of course. They'd ensured that I'd always want to be an RAF pilot, but also, if I couldn't become a pilot, that I'd always want to be around aircraft, preferably RAF aircraft.

I was also able to spend a week every year at an RAF base with hundreds of like-minded youngsters. I attended five of these Summer Camps: RAF Manby in

Lincolnshire in 1969, then RAF Lindholme in South Yorkshire, RAF Locking in Somerset, RAF Catterick in North Yorkshire and, finally, in 1973, RAF Aberporth in Ceredigion, West Wales.

As a sign of my age and the shrinking size of the RAF, most have been closed for many years.

The Summer Camps were not my first weeks away from home. Springing from my involvement in the church choir, I'd spent a week in each of the previous two summers with a group of youngsters from Hereford Diocese – the first on the Gower Peninsula in South Wales, and the second near Swanage in Dorset. I enjoyed these, but they didn't inspire me like the visits to RAF bases.

For a start, the Summer Camps offered the opportunity for extra flying, usually in Chipmunks, but I also flew in a Varsity, a bulbous light transport aircraft used to train navigators, and a Devon, another twin piston-engined transport aircraft. And there was shooting, day and night navigation exercises and war games, and visits to various sections on the bases, even, on occasion, the opportunity to spend the day with a tradesman working on aircraft.

Then, in 1972, I was chosen to go to Germany for a week. Having thought I'd never have the opportunity to travel overseas, I had a marvellous week at RAF Bruggen, near the Dutch border, a base that operated Phantom air defence fighters at the height of the Cold War.

During the week, we visited attractions in the local area, including some in Holland. I particularly remember a flying saucer-shaped building in Eindhoven, containing a futuristic electronic exhibition run by Phillips; an open air military museum at Overloon; and Cologne, with its magnificent cathedral.

But the highlight was a day spent alongside RAF tradesmen working on the Phantoms in the hangars at Bruggen.

The next year, I was considered for an exchange visit to Canada. I lost out at the final interview to a lad with whom, five months later, I joined the RAF.

But the ATC offered something I enjoyed more than any of these things, even powered flying: gliding.

I've already said that I found the back cockpit of a Chipmunk claustrophobic. But there were two types of glider, the Sedbergh, for those of normal stature, and the Mk III, ideal for short arses like me.

Neither looked anything like the sleek white gliders we see today. Battleship grey with chunky wooden frames covered in doped fabric, they were one step removed from the troop-carrying gliders towed into the air over Arnhem and Normandy.

The cockpit of the Mk III was low-sided and open to the elements, the cadet sitting in front of the instructor, thrust into the airflow forward of the high wing. So, there was no chance of claustrophobia, although, compared to the Sedbergh, it flew like a brick.

I didn't care. On the occasions, a couple of times a year, when I visited 633 Volunteer Gliding School at RAF Cosford, near Wolverhampton, I loved it.

The take-off, especially, was breathtaking. You sat in the glider at the launch point, your backside a few inches above the grass. At the other end of the airfield was a winch, basically a powerful engine turning a drum wound with cable. A Land Rover unwound the cable from the drum and pulled it across the airfield to the glider, where it was attached to a strong point under the nose. The slack was taken in, and, at a predetermined hand signal, the winch roared and wound in the cable - with you and the glider on the end.

The acceleration was more stomach churning than any fair ground ride, and, before you knew it, or could even register the airspeed, you were airborne, climbing steeply, with the wind whistling past you. As the glider approached the overhead of the winch at about 600 or 700 feet, it would start to be pulled down rather than forward, so you released the cable by pulling a toggle in the cockpit.

Again, I found the sight of the ground stunning, and this time it could be viewed in serene silence, or near silence, just the merest whooshing noise as you sliced through the air.

If you had time, you could search for thermals – rising air - and spiral upwards, staying airborne for long periods. But most air experience trips were short circuits of the airfield, descending all the time to line up for a final approach to land, the ground rushing up at an alarming rate. At the last moment, the pilot would raise the nose and you'd float along, bottom a few inches above the ground again, before touching down and bouncing to a halt on a small wheel and tail skid, one wing gently settling onto the grass.

When you were 16, you could apply for a course during which you'd be taught to glide and, if you were good enough, to fly solo. This meant spending several weekends at Cosford, a problem for me. It was about 35 miles from Ludlow, Dad had stopped driving and there were no obvious public transport links. But one of the great friends I made in the ATC, Nick Goldthorp, applied for the same course. When we both gained places in the summer of 1971, his father drove us to and from Cosford.

Over five weekends, we learned to control those

amazing take-offs, to climb at the correct angle, keeping the wings level, and to fly a circuit of the airfield and land. I don't know about Nick, but my instructors showed endless patience with my cack-handed attempts to kill them on take off and landing. But, on 15 August 1971, at just under 16½ years of age, I piloted three flights with no-one else in the glider.

I wish I could say I remember my solo flights in detail, but I don't. What I do remember is the feeling of exhilaration and pride. Several months before I was old enough to drive, someone had let me fly an aircraft on my own. Nick was also successful, and we were allowed to wear a small set of silver wings on our uniforms.

I'd never been so proud of anything in my life.

When not in school or with the ATC, I and my friends, Nick, Andy, Simon, Ian Price and John Steele, who later became a champion motor-cyclist, would wander Ludlow in search of adventure. Usually, we were disappointed, even when searching for ghosts around the castle and the Cromwellian trenches on Whitcliffe.

But, occasionally, there was some excitement, like when Ian froze climbing a cliff along the Bread Walk above the River Teme, and we had to coax him down. Or when parties of girls stayed at the Youth Hostel near Ludford Bridge and we followed them, waiting – usually in vain - for some opportunity to engage them in conversation.

And then there was the time when Andy saved my life.

Aged about 16 and 15 respectively, he and I were on the River Teme in a friend's ancient canoe, HMS Amethyst, when we capsized. Laughing, I stood up in about three feet of swiftly flowing water, facing upstream. I'd managed to hold onto the canoe amidships, but it started to fill with water and force me backwards. After a couple of steps, I realised I needed to get out of its way, but my backside came up against a submerged tree. The rapidly filling canoe rode over my upper body, bending me back over the tree and threatening to push my head under water.

It's amazing how quickly joy can turn to terror. Luckily, Andy grabbed one end of the kayak and levered it off me, at which point it set off downstream and sank. I don't think it's too melodramatic to say that he saved me from drowning.

I can't remember how we did it, but we retrieved the canoe and no-one was any the wiser.

It wasn't the first time Andy had 'saved my life'. On one of our expeditions to Whitbach from Dodmore when we were both much younger, I fell into a stream. It was only a few inches deep, but, for some reason, rather than standing up and stepping out, I tried to swim. Even if I'd mastered the skill, the water wasn't deep enough, and Andy lifted me out, coughing and spluttering.

This is the first time I've told the story for over 50 years.

As teenagers, we used to get up to some mischief no doubt, although I can't remember any particular misdemeanours, not even much under-age drinking. I looked too young to get a drink in a pub until I was 18, and even then, in all but my usual haunts, I had to prove my age. Even when we went into pubs, we were often so broke we'd be forced to share a pint of bitter shandy between three or four of us, something I don't think they'd tolerate now.

In those days – the early 1970s – the only

alternative sources of alcohol were off-licences, but their booze was no cheaper than that in the pubs; in fact, I have a notion it was more expensive. This probably saved us from some of the excesses of modern youth.

Perhaps I lived in my own bubble, but I had no involvement with drugs. I never even saw any.

We all had part time jobs. In my case, until the age of 15, I was a paper boy as well as a Saturday boy for one or other of three local ironmongers. After that, I became a butcher's boy for a couple of years and, in my later teens, I worked Saturdays and a couple of evenings a week on the forecourt of a local garage, at a time when someone like me came out to serve you with petrol or diesel.

The work at Mr Kennard's butchers' shop could be particularly unpleasant. In a side room, he boiled off-cuts - heads, trotters and offal - in a small kitchen boiler, to make cooked meats, such as brawn, pressed beef, haslet and tongue. Afterwards, I had to clean out the boiler. The smell was awful and the feel of the jelly and fat oozing through my fingers used to make me gag.

Perhaps it was character-building, but it didn't feel like it at the time.

I spent my meagre wages on model soldiers and aircraft, and second hand books and records from local street markets. I still have the John Wyndham, Isaac Asimov, Robert Heinlein and Arthur C. Clarke paperbacks I bought then.

The long playing records were rarely by the original artists, tending to be of the Top of the Pops variety; and my singles tended to have large holes in the centre because they'd been sold on by DJs. Our record player – in a wooden cabinet with a radio – had a plastic ring you dropped over the spindle before playing these singles. I also spent money on cigarettes.

I started smoking at the age of seven.

A school friend lived in a large house on one of the posher roads in Ludlow. During the summer holidays, I went there to play. His mum smoked, and unlike most of the mums in Dodmore, she also went to work. While she was out, we used to smoke some of her cigarettes.

I'm sure the practise only lasted a few weeks, and I have no recollection of smoking again until I was 13. But when I began again at that age, I carried on for over two decades.

I can only think I cadged most of the cigarettes during those early years, but I must have bought some. My parents never knew, or never let on that they did, although it's hard to believe they couldn't smell the stale smoke in my hair and clothes. Since stopping myself, I can smell a smoker at 50 yards. Perhaps the smell was masked by my poor personal hygiene, or by the all-pervading stench of Dad's pipe.

Over the years, I gave up fairly regularly, but always returned to the habit soon after, usually by starting to cadge the odd cigarette from very understanding and generous friends and workmates. I finally stopped smoking cigarettes in my early 20s, only to start smoking small cigars in the evenings.

I joked that I only smoked when I drank – about 40 a day. There was some truth behind the quip, because I was also a terrible boozer. On an unexceptional night out, I could easily drink eight pints of beer and smoke a similar number of Panama cigars. And, unlike Bill Clinton, I used to inhale.

I finally gave up when I was 39, but that's another

story.

On Friday and/or Saturday nights when we were older teenagers, we used to go to discos in Ludlow Town Hall or the local village halls. From the age of 17, most of us were drivers, but I remember only Nick having regular use of a car, so either he drove or we cadged lifts. The discos were always entertaining, in a morbid sort of way.

While we were perpetually strapped for cash, the local louts always seemed to have enough money to get drunk. At some point in the evening, they'd start a fight. These could be quite vicious affairs, but were easily avoided by stepping outside or moving into a different room until the trouble was over.

The girls danced in groups. It sounds too much of a cliché, but they really did dance round their handbags, the groups, varying in size from two to ten, dotted around the dance floor. Interposed in the gaps would be a few lads dancing with their girlfriends. They'd be the only males on the dance floor. The rest of us, the vast majority, would be standing around the walls, beer in hand, watching.

I lie slightly. There were a few lads, usually regarded as weirdoes, who danced on their own. They'd probably be trying to emulate the trance-like movements of the Woodstock hippies, or maybe head-banging to Status Quo.

But men did not dance with other men. It was the law.

Even if you really liked the music, and I usually did, you weren't allowed to dance unless you could prise one of the girls from her group. The only way to do this was to walk onto the dance floor under the full gaze of everyone in the room and attempt to gain the young lady's attention in some way – a cough, a touch on the shoulder – and ask them if they'd like to dance.

And of course, if – or in my case, when – they said no, you had to walk back to your mates, facing, at best, sympathetic, smiling shrugs, at worst, jeering taunts.

It was hell. Which was why, if we had the money, we generally just drank beer.

The ideal, and something we all put much effort into as the night wore on, was to establish eye contact with one of the girls. This could take considerable time, but if she deigned to meet your gaze for long enough, you tried to strike a tacit telepathic agreement that she'd dance with you if you plucked up the courage to walk onto the floor.

But there were all sorts of nuances to complicate matters.

Of course, you could just totally misread the situation, walk onto the dance floor and be rebuffed. This was an increasing problem as the night wore on and an excess of beer made you delusional.

Then there was the issue of your intended partner's friends. If she was dancing in a big group, it wasn't a problem. When she turned to dance with you, her remaining friends could carry on. But if she was dancing with only one friend, she wasn't going to turn to you and leave the girl to walk off the floor on her own, with all the shame and ridicule that seemed to invoke. So, you had to induce one of your friends to take on hers.

And there would be another complication. The other girl was usually much plainer, if not downright ugly. A terrible thing to say, and beauty is in the eye of the beholder and all that, but it was often true. Perhaps pretty girls like to accentuate their good looks by dancing with someone of plainer disposition, but the girl you wanted always seemed to have a less attractive friend. You needed help from someone who, either had lower standards, or was more desperate.

Another terrible thing to say, but there it is.

And if your friend and hers didn't hit it off for at least a couple of dances, you were likely to end up at square one anyway.

Discos were a minefield, almost always destined to end in frustration and ridicule, from your own mates if no-one else.

When, in 1985, I became a flying instructor on my first University Air Squadron, I was surprised to find that the rules had changed. When the students, male or female, heard a record they liked, they just went out onto the floor and danced.

That could mean, not only mixed groups, or groups of girls, but also groups of boys dancing with boys, sometimes even just two boys dancing together. And they didn't get taunted and beaten up, as they surely would have done at Diddlebury Village Hall in 1972.

You could actually spend the whole night dancing. Well, they could. I still couldn't. My conditioning was too strong. It took me several years to be able to dance uninhibitedly without an exclusive female partner, and I could never dance solely with another man. But the female students used to take pity on me every now and then, so I didn't have to stand on the side with my beer all night.

There were still nuances and complications. Young men and women still yearned for an exclusive partner, and the old eye contact thing seemed just as important. But at least male students could avoid the walk of shame. They could just go out with a mate and dance next to a couple of girls. Hopefully, at some point, both sets would turn through ninety degrees and pair off. If not, they'd just carry on dancing with their mate. Either way, they'd get to dance.

It all seemed very sensible. I've no idea what the modern etiquette is.

During my 32 years in the RAF, I served in 27 locations for periods of between 6 weeks and three years, and in many other places for shorter periods, ranging from a few days to a few weeks. During all that time, I met many people, most of whom I'd have classed as acquaintances, but others who, at the time, I would also have counted as friends.

But even where I'd claim friendship, the relationships have rarely lasted beyond the periods we served together. On occasion, we'd meet again, and, when we did, it was usually possible to slip back into an easy camaraderie, even if we hadn't seen one another for several years. But, on parting, we'd become strangers again.

Only a dozen friendships have stood the test of time slightly better, but only inasmuch as we've remained Christmas card buddies. Two of these I correspond with an extra couple of times a year, but only one, my best friend from apprentice training at RAF Halton, do I see regularly, and that because he and his wife have moved in 500 yards from us in south Wales.

And, as I write this in 2013, I remain in Christmas card contact with only four friends from my teenage years in Ludlow. One of these, who served a full career in the Metropolitan Police, I never see; another, Nick, one of the friends from the Air Training Corps for whom I was best man, still lives in Ludlow, but I see him only infrequently; and two, Simon and Ann, I correspond with regularly and see at least once a year on reciprocal visits. Ann is a friend purely from schooldays, while Simon is another of the strong friends from school and the ATC, and another for whom I was best man.

I'd lost contact with Andy, the friend from Dodmore days who saved my life and for whom I was also best man; that is, until the publication of Wings Over Summer, when an article in a local paper directed him to my website. He and his wife, Ann, had moved to north Shropshire, and I'd moved so often that they'd failed to keep up. We have now met on a couple of occasions, and I'm sure we'll do so again.

I've failed to regain contact with Ian, though. We virtually grew up together and spent years alongside one another in the ATC, before he joined the RAF a few years ahead of me. Several years later, we served on the same base for a while and met fairly frequently. But, after he moved on, we met only another couple of times, before losing touch.

I still feel guilty at not having put more effort into keeping in contact with some of these teenage friends, especially when I think of the times Nick and, to a lesser extent, Andy, picked me up from far-flung railway stations on Friday nights. I've never repaid them as they deserve.

I always describe myself as a bit of a street urchin over this period, and I think there's at least some truth in this; although, when not wandering the streets, I used to play a lot of sport: football, tennis and, in a local church hall, table tennis.

I attended church regularly until the age of about 16, and was in the choir of St John's on Gravel Hill for at least seven years. I was, I was told, a very good treble, and sang regular solos, usually in St John's at Christmas, Easter and the like, but once in the Parish

Church of St Laurence for a visit by the Archbishop of Canterbury, Lord Ramsay.

I remained a treble much longer than was cool, and did very little singing outside church from the age of about 13.

Church for me was a ritual. I don't think I ever had any religious faith. And as I've aged, I've lost patience with all religions. The wilful or ignorant misinterpretation of their texts exacerbates many regional and global problems, including misogyny, racial intolerance, terrorism and over-population. If anything, I'm a humanist, believing that individuals must take responsibility for their own actions, good or bad, not pretend they are dancing to the tune of some supreme being.

But the ATC was the major focus of my teenage years. I became a staff cadet and flight sergeant, a glider pilot, a marksman and represented West Midlands Wing at various sporting events. My enjoyment of all its activities was in sharp contrast to my loathing of school.

Deep down, I must have realised that only school could help me gain the two A Levels required for commissioning as a pilot. So I have no real excuse for my stupidity in concentrating on the ATC, beyond a naïve belief that it could somehow secure me the career I wanted.

Chapter 3 - Trying to Join

Just after my 17th birthday in April 1972, I started my quest to be a pilot in the RAF in earnest, with the first of several visits to the RAF Officers and Aircrew Selection Centre at Biggin Hill. I was attending for a Test in Advance, a means of finding out whether there was any medical or aptitude reason to prevent me applying to become aircrew when I was old enough.

I travelled by train from Ludlow to London, via Newport, and was amazed by my first sight of the capital. The outskirts seemed to stretch all the way from Reading to Paddington, the buildings becoming much taller than any I'd seen before. I took the Underground to Victoria, then another train to Bromley South, and a bus to Biggin Hill. It was my first independent journey of such complexity and distance, and I can still remember both the excitement of travelling on the Tube, and the pride at arriving safely at my destination.

At Biggin Hill, I joined a group of about 30 lads of similar age, all there for the Test in Advance: one and a half days, comprising a medical, aircrew aptitude tests and an interview. Despite their youth, most of the others seemed much more self-assured and confident.

The medical took several hours and seemed to include everything short of surgery, including an ECG. I passed, but several others failed, some with problems of which they'd been totally unaware, such as poor eyesight or hearing loss. These medical failures caught an early bus back to Bromley South, and our numbers dwindled.

Many years later, when given access to my medical documents, I found that I should probably have joined them. It seems there was some justification behind my childhood ailments. My nasal passages were noted as constricted and bent, meaning I could suffer sinus and respiratory problems if I became aircrew. Several years later, during my flying training, this turned out to be the case, and I had an operation to widen my nasal passages.

Next came the aptitude tests. These lasted more than four hours, and comprised IQ-style tests of verbal, non-verbal and mathematical reasoning; and machine tests of dexterity, mental capacity and hand-eye coordination. I remember two of the machine tests particularly vividly.

For the first, I sat in one of several mock wooden cockpits lining both walls of a long room. To my front was a large, old-fashioned, grey TV screen. It had a thin vertical and horizontal line that crossed through a spot of light in the centre. When the test started, the spot began to wander off. Using a control column and rudder bars, I had to return it to and keep it in the centre of the screen. It may sound fairly easy, but the sense of the controls was reversed, so to move the dot up, you pushed the control column forward, and to move it left, you pushed the right rudder pedal. Dastardly.

For the second test, I sat before a rotating metal cylinder covered in paper. Holes in the paper formed a wobbly path that wound from left to right of the cylinder as it rotated. All I had to do was turn a little wheel to steer a pointer over as many holes as possible. Every time the pointer ran over a hole, it made an electrical connection and I heard a click. Again, it doesn't sound too difficult, but there was a time lag between the turn of the wheel and the response of the pointer. Another dastardly contraption, and those around me seemed to be making many more clicks.

Perhaps they were, because I only passed the aptitude tests for navigator, not pilot, although I was told that aptitude could improve with age, so I might stand a chance of gaining the pilot score on a later visit. Several of the others failed to show aptitude for any aircrew category, and were forced to catch an early bus home.

Of the 30 of us that had started the previous day, only about half remained to complete the final test, the interview.

A tall squadron leader pilot ushered me to a small office, where I sat opposite him and a wing commander, seated behind an enormous desk. Ancient and moustachioed, they were gods to me. After all, my ATC squadron was commanded by someone several ranks below them. They tried to put me at ease, but I felt so small and overawed by the rank differential that it could never be anything other than an ordeal.

For 15 minutes, one asked about my life, while the other took notes, then they swapped and the second asked about my aspirations for the future. Unexpectedly, he also quizzed me on military and current affairs. I answered as best I could, feeling that my achievements, knowledge and potential sounded a bit thin. When the 30 minutes were up, I was only too glad to escape their company.

I travelled home with no idea how I'd done. A few weeks later, I received a letter. Despite my self-description as a street urchin, they must have spotted some potential in me, because the letter encouraged me to apply for the full selection procedure the next year.

Thirty years later, when, as a group captain, I commanded the Officers and Aircrew Selection Centre, I discovered that I must have done better than I thought. If they'd been less impressed, they'd have suggested a return in two years, or even politely discouraged me from ever applying again.

I took up their offer and made my second visit to Biggin Hill in June 1973, this time hoping to complete the full selection process. I joined a group of about 30 men, aged from 18 to 30, all applying to join as aircrew. Again, most seemed more polished and confident than me, but I felt a little less overawed.

The first day and a half followed the same format as my previous visit. And, as before, the number of candidates reduced after each stage. I passed the medical again, but this time, I also passed the aptitude tests for pilot. Having read up on some current and military affairs, I felt better prepared for the interview, and did well enough to go forward to the second part of the selection procedure.

Only about half of us remained.

For the afternoon of the second day and morning of the third, I became a member of one of three syndicates. The five or six of us in each were kitted out in identical grey overalls, over which we wore blue bibs bearing a white syndicate letter and a number. I became C6, known as Charlie Six.

Throughout Part 2, we were assessed by a wing commander and squadron leader, often joined by a group captain, other senior military officers and groups of varying sizes in civilian clothes. Once again, I didn't find out why all these people were looking at us until I ran the place 30 years later.

The Officers and Aircrew Selection Centre receives visits from many senior RAF, Army and Royal Navy officers, as well as school and university careers staff and the senior managers of large companies. The RAF observers could be bound for posts requiring knowledge of the selection process, while the officers from the other Services and the civilians would be interested in how the RAF selects its future leaders.

As the Group Captain, I often escorted these visitors, but I would also be keeping an eye on my assessment staff. After all, I based my selection decisions on their recommendations, so I needed to be sure they were doing their jobs properly.

In 1973, this depth of knowledge was a long way off. All I and my fellow candidates knew was that we were performing under the glare of many pairs of eyes.

For the first exercise of Part 2, the six of us sat in a semi-circle opposite our assessors. They threw in topics – are motorways dangerous? should we be going to the moon? that sort of thing – and left us to discuss them among ourselves. There were three or four topics in all, and the assessors wrote on clipboards throughout, presumably noting whether we made any contribution, and if so, whether it was relevant and/or persuasive.

Next, there were a couple of planning exercises, one as a syndicate and one as an individual. We were told they were based on simple time/speed/distance calculations. Of course, they were only simple if you could do the maths.

For the group exercise, we had 20 minutes to discuss how to find a couple of injured climbers and lead them to safety. After we'd agreed a team plan and worked out the detail, the assessors questioned us. Which route did you use to take the climbers to hospital? How long would it take? Why didn't you choose this other route?

Once more, we presumed they were looking for a positive contribution, whilst also assessing whether we fitted into the team, or rubbed everyone up the wrong way. I thought I hadn't done too badly so far, but I found the individual planning exercise much trickier.

For this, I had 15 minutes to work out how to get a football team whose bus had broken down to a match 20 miles away. Before my planning time ran out, I had all bar the goalkeeper in place for the kick off. He was going to be ten minutes late.

'You'll be 10-0 down by the time he arrives,' the assessors joked, before prompting me to a better solution. Again, I didn't think I'd done too badly.

We spent the final morning in a large hangar undergoing practical exercises to assess our leadership potential. The hangar was split into small bays by high screens. Each bay contained some form of real or imaginary obstacle; a wooden wall; or a gap representing a pool of shark-infested custard, a bottomless pit, a minefield or raging rapids. The bays also contained the means to cross the obstacle: planks and ropes, as well as impediments to progress, bulky items, such as large blocks of wood or oil barrels.

Each exercise had its nuances, but the general rules were similar. The syndicate had 15 minutes to get its six members and their equipment across the obstacle, which usually meant climbing the wall, or bridging or swinging across the chasm, river or minefield.

To familiarise us with the rules and equipment, the first exercise had no nominated leader, although we were still assessed, presumably to see whether we got stuck in, and whether a natural leader emerged.

After this taster, each member of the syndicate had 15 minutes of glory, or not, attempting to lead the team through a different exercise. I wasn't sure exactly what the assessors were looking for, but one of my syndicate seemed too blushingly quiet to lead effectively, and another too loud and autocratic, while yet another seemed unable to devise a plan.

When my turn came, I had to get the team and equipment across a swiftly flowing river. I came up with and briefed a plan, which I modified as we went along, but we ran out of time two thirds of the way across the 15 metre gap. Even so, I didn't think I'd made too bad a fist of it. I'd certainly enjoyed myself.

I found out later that some of the exercises were nigh on impossible, and whereas finishing an exercise would do you no harm, more importance would be attached to how you controlled and led your team.

The final part of the process was an interview to confirm your chosen branch or branches – pilot, navigator, air engineer etc - and to ask whether you felt you'd been treated fairly. I had no complaints and made it clear that I was still desperately keen to be a pilot.

I knew I'd done better than the previous year, but I was also pretty sure I hadn't done well enough. And, on 29th June 1973, I received a letter from OASC, confirming that I hadn't been selected to flying duties, or a commission in the ground branches of the Royal Air Force. They explained the competitive nature of the process and held out the hope of a more favourable result if I returned in a year.

Once again, it was nearly 30 years before I gained a deeper insight into just how competitive it was.

There is no pass mark guaranteeing selection as an RAF officer. Instead, the Group Captain selects the best of the thousands that attend the Centre to fill branch targets that are sometimes measured in single figures. As a result, candidates who perform exceptionally well still might not be selected because others have preformed better. Brutally simple, but not always easy for candidates or their parents to understand.

During my two years as the Group Captain, I spent much time fielding complaints from disgruntled parents who just couldn't understand how little Johnny or Jemima could have failed something, perhaps for the first time in their lives.

I certainly wouldn't pretend I was an exceptional near miss, but the fact that OASC were prepared to see me again after only a year meant they still thought I had potential.

Even if I had been chosen, I'd have been dropped like a hot potato when my A-Level results were revealed. I failed to pass a single subject.

Of course, I'd known this was the likely outcome, so, as soon as I'd returned home from Biggin Hill, I'd applied to join the RAF as an engineering apprentice. The minimum educational requirement was 5 O-Levels, which I already had. In July 1973, I visited the RAF Careers Information Office in Shrewsbury for more tests and an interview.

As an aside, a couple of years later - when a filing cabinet was left open at RAF Halton - I and most of my flight sneaked a look at the reports written by the officers who'd interviewed us at the various careers offices. Most of my report was quite positive, but one phrase really hurt.

It stated, 'Powell is obviously from a poor working class background, as witnessed by his shabby suit.'

I may not have the exact wording, but the original was just as blunt.

Although the deduction from my appearance may have been correct, mention of it seems irrelevant to my selection as an airman. But what really gave me pause for thought was that I'd worn the same suit to school every day for years, and for my two attempts to become an RAF officer. What my better-heeled school friends and the assessors at Biggin Hill had made of my shabby appearance, I dread to think.

Anyway, despite this, at about the time I heard my disastrous A-Level results, I received a letter saying I'd been entered into the competition for an RAF apprenticeship. But I wouldn't find out whether I'd been successful until the middle of September, and I had to decide what to do in the meantime. The only certainty if I failed to be an apprentice was a determination to re-visit Biggin Hill the next year for another crack at pilot selection. So, in the absence of any other plan, I went back to school to re-take my A-Levels.

I still don't remember seeing A-Levels as a route to university. There were no family precedents or pressures to set me off down that route, and I wanted to escape formal education as soon as possible. They were a means to only one end: joining the RAF as a pilot.

On Friday 14th September 1973, Dad received a letter from the RAF informing him that, subject to a final medical, I'd been selected for an RAF apprenticeship in the trade of Aircraft Technician (Airframes/ Propulsion).

I was sensible enough to realise that this offer was better than holding on for another, potentially unsuccessful, visit to Biggin Hill, and I left school the next Monday.

For the six weeks before I joined the RAF, I had a taste of what life might have been like had I decided to remain at home. Like many school leavers who stayed in and around Ludlow, I went to work at a local chicken-processing factory.

I'm not sure I got to choose where in the plant I worked, but somehow I avoided the less pleasant tasks carried out by most of my peers. Some went to unload the live birds, catch them and place them upside down, flapping, onto the hooks that conveyed them to their deaths. Others cleaned, plucked and disembowelled the bloodied carcasses prior to freezing, and still more wrapped and boxed them ready for the large refrigerated warehouse to one side of the factory.

In comparison, my job was relatively clean and certainly free of gore. I joined about a dozen men of various ages on the loading bays adjacent to the warehouse.

Fork lift trucks would emerge through heavy plastic screen doors and drop pallets piled high with cardboard boxes of frozen chickens. We would then throw – yes throw – the boxes into the backs of huge, refrigerated lorries, or smaller delivery vans.

I only ever saw a chicken, that is, a cellophane-wrapped ball of frozen white flesh, when one of the boxes burst open. Its contents would shoot out, sliding every-which-way along the floor of the loading bay or lorry. In a madcap game, we'd chase the sliding carcasses. Once caught, if there were no external signs of damage, they were re-sealed in the box and thrown into the back of a vehicle emblazoned with a cheerily winking cartoon chicken.

Did frozen chickens bruise? I wasn't sure, but, as I pictured the birds I'd loaded thawing with large purple and yellow welts on their flesh, I vowed never to buy a frozen chicken, or, knowingly, to eat one. In the home, I've kept to that pledge, but who knows what we eat in restaurants and takeaways?

It was hard physical work, and probably helped me toughen up before I started recruit training. But boy it was boring. I'm not sure I could have stuck it for more than six weeks.

And yet, I worked alongside people who'd done the job for years, and who really enjoyed it. They extolled its virtues. It was relatively clean and carefree, and it paid a decent wage. It also offered greater variety than anywhere else in the factory, if only in the size of the boxes. At the time, I failed to share their upbeat assessment, and the long hours of loading lorry after lorry, van after van, all rolled into one.

In hindsight though, now the factory has long closed, its plant and jobs probably shipped overseas, I suppose there was a certain attraction to the work it offered, and to the comradeship to be found on the loading bay.

I sometimes wonder what the men I toiled alongside went on to do. I can't picture any of them working in IT.

The age bracket for joining the RAF as an apprentice was between 16 and 18½ years. On the day I was due to sign up, I was going to be 18 and seven months. The careers staff had said this wouldn't be a problem, so, with a few weeks to go, it was a shock to receive a letter stating that I was too old to join without an age dispensation.

There were a few tense days before the clearance came through, but it did. Only later did I find out that it was pretty much a formality, and that some of my fellow apprentices were even older.

Chapter 4 - Recruit Training

I joined the RAF at Shrewsbury Careers Information Office on Monday 5th November 1973. In a process called attestation, I filled in forms, swore allegiance to the Queen, Her heirs and successors, agreed to obey the orders of those put in charge of me and filled in more forms. I also received an advance of pay of £2 – the 1970s equivalent of the Queen's shilling – a rail warrant and 92 pence in travelling expenses.

I signed for an engagement of nine years regular service as an airframe and propulsion technician, followed by three years' reserve service. Before starting my technician training, I had to undergo six weeks 'square bashing' at the RAF School of Recruit Training, RAF Swinderby, a few miles south of Lincoln.

Three days after attestation, wearing my trusty suit and carrying a battered family suitcase, I left the house to walk to Ludlow railway station for the 9.15 train to Shrewsbury. I avoided tearful platform farewells by saying goodbye to Dad and Brian when they went to work and school respectively, and by persuading Mum not to accompany me to the station.

Wound up in my excitement, I gave little thought to how she'd be feeling after years pandering to my every need. I just walked away. Of course, she may have been relieved to be shot of me, but I don't think so, and I wish I could turn the clock back to that moment, if only to say, 'Thanks for everything,' before setting out.

At Ludlow station, I exchanged a rail warrant for a ticket to Newark and boarded the first of several trains. As I watched Ludlow Parish Church and the castle disappear behind me, the excitement began to give way to apprehension.

Just what was I letting myself in for?

Ian, the close friend who'd joined the RAF a few years before, had been the purveyor of horror stories, not least because he'd failed his engineering apprenticeship, before becoming a driver. Simon had left for Leicester University and there was no feedback on his experiences yet. Nick and Andy were staying in Ludlow as apprentices at a local factory making agricultural machinery; I wondered if I should have followed their lead.

At each successive station, noisy groups of teenagers jumped aboard carrying single items of luggage. Although dressed in anything from smart suits to torn jeans, they sat in huddles, chatting away. I soon realised we were bound for the same destination, but I was too shy to break into any of the groups, and I moved from train to train on my own.

Only later did I find out that they knew one another because they'd been attested en-masse at their various careers offices the day after me. I have no idea why I was attested early but, in later years, it allowed me to tell them to 'get some in', banter proclaiming that I'd served longer, if only by one day.

At 2pm, my final train pulled into Newark Castle Station. Nearly all its passengers stepped out onto the platform.

Before we had time to feel lost, we were rounded up by half a dozen NCOs dressed in long greatcoats, shiny shoes and hats with peaks bent so far down over their eyes that they had to tilt their heads back at improbable angles to see where they were going. Tucked under their arms were varnished wooden pace sticks.

From my ATC days, I recognised them as drill

instructors.

At this stage, with passers-by watching proceedings, they were politeness itself, gently cajoling us onto a couple of Service coaches.

After a journey of a few miles, the coaches turned through the main gates of RAF Swinderby and stopped in front of a large building. Out of sight and sound of the public, the mild-mannered NCOs changed their spots. My diary says they became, *just like in the films,* that is, the Second World War films on which I'd been reared.

Shouting in gravelly, sometimes unintelligible, but always threatening voices, they bullied us off the coaches and into a large hall where we joined another group of teenagers who looked as confused and shell-shocked as the rest of us. In total, we numbered 156.

With no explanation, we were lined up and subjected to a procedure not unlike selecting a playground football team, only in reverse. Rather than picking the taller and more athletic looking, the sergeants and corporals walked among us and pulled out the shorter, the be-spectacled, and others whose reasons for selection were less obvious.

Eventually, roughly a third of our number had been shepherded to the far side of the hall. They remained segregated as the remainder of us were split into two groups. Only later that evening did we find out that, in five weeks, two-thirds of us would join hundreds of other apprentices to line the streets of London for Her Majesty The Queen and a visiting dignitary.

As to the other third, it seemed that the Queen was not allowed to see short, bespectacled men with zits. This was why all those who were five feet six inches tall or shorter, wore glasses or had skin complaints, such as acne, had been pulled aside. They became

Number 9 Flight, known to the rest of us as The Leper Colony.

For those of us deemed tall, eagle-eyed and handsome, it was all a big joke. Not surprisingly, members of The Leper Colony found it less amusing, and it did seem a cruel way to start their new careers, especially as they were allowed to take part in the ten route linings we mounted over the following three years at Halton.

A friend who'd been in the Leper Colony confirmed this account, adding only that, although he completed the full ten route linings at Halton, for the first few he wasn't allowed to wear his glasses, so everything was a blur. For later route linings, he was allowed to wear his specs, with no explanation for the change of policy.

The Leper colony having been selected, we were marched to our barrack blocks and allocated to 14-man rooms. We found a bed, dropped our kit on it, formed up outside again, and were marched away for a haircut - whether we needed one or not.

For me, having worn short hair all my life, a military haircut was no big deal. But many had hair down to their collars, and a few sported locks hanging down to their waists. For them, the visit to the Station barber was a major life crisis.

Part of the problem was the style of cut. We weren't shorn like US Marines or skinheads. At least that would have made us look menacing. No, our hair was left long enough to be worn in a short fringe, or waved in a style that our fathers or grandfathers would have worn. More like the lead in a syrupy Doris Day romance than a teenage rebel.

And just to enhance the experience, the barber cut one side of the victim's head first, giving them a grisly before and after image in the mirror. Those awaiting their turn could only look on in horror, while the newly shorn walked around in a daze, gazing sadly into every mirror and pane of glass they passed. Some did this for weeks.

After this ritual, we were issued with a few items of uniform and fed our first meal in the Airmens' Mess, a dining hall with tens of Formica-topped tables, each seating up to 20. As we passed along a metal servery, food from large rectangular metal dishes was dolloped onto our plates by a line of cooks armed with serving spoons or ladles. The meal of red meat, mashed potatoes, vegetables and gravy, was followed by a wholesome pudding and custard.

It was designed to give us the 4,000 or so calories a day we'd need to cope with our training.

Unflatteringly, my diary says, *stodge*. Well, it wasn't Mum's home cooking, but I did get used to it, and grow to enjoy it. Although modern RAF messes would emphasise the greater choice on offer, including vegetarian and minority religious options, similar fare would still be on the menu today, especially at training establishments.

After our meal, we were given an hour or so to settle into our rooms. Some spent most of this time marvelling at their new appearance.

That evening, we met our flight NCOs, Sergeant Blackman, a grey-haired, grandfatherly, figure in his late 40s or early 50s, and Corporal 'Piggy' Tonner, a short, stocky and pugnacious, ex-RAF boxer in his 30s. They gave us a series of talks on what to expect during our six weeks at Swinderby, and told us in no uncertain terms what was expected of us.

We were to receive lessons in drill - marching and

saluting; general service knowledge - the history and roles of the RAF; ground defence training - nuclear, biological and chemical warfare, shooting, first aid and fire-fighting; physical training – fitness sessions and organized games; and more drill.

We'd be expected to conform and try hard at everything, and to keep ourselves, our uniforms and our rooms in immaculate condition. To that end, Sergeant Blackman and Corporal Tonner gave immediate demonstrations of essential skills, such as polishing, ironing and bed-making. Demonstrations over, we were allowed to disperse and settle into our rooms.

My hair had darkened to a light brown, but I was still fresh-faced and no more than five feet seven inches tall, so, although I was one of the oldest, I looked – and felt – like one of the youngest.

Over the next year or so, I grew to five feet ten inches and bulked up a bit. But, on 8th November 1973, I was a bit unnerved by some of the stubbly, streetwise, characters I met. They hailed from as far apart as Devon, North Wales, Eastern Scotland and East Anglia, with the majority being from the industrial north and the Midlands.

Several years later, the Scottish lad, Pete Rosie, went on to fly Nimrod maritime reconnaissance aircraft. He became the Nimrod display pilot and I helped train him to become a flying instructor.

Regional banter began almost immediately, and nicknames such as Taff and Jock were quick to appear, although they became difficult to sustain when the numbers of Welsh and Scottish folk in other rooms became apparent. I became firm friends with someone from a more recognisable minority, a red-haired Lancashire lad, Richard Hough, inevitably known as

Ginge.

There were no black faces in our entry, and our room had the only person of non-white appearance, the result of a marriage between an RAF Serviceman and a Singaporean.

Almost a third of the entry was Scottish, and northern and Midland accents made up most of the remainder. There were two from Northern Ireland, one from the Republic of Ireland, and several from the London area. Only the Devonian and I seemed to have rural accents, something that was a feature of the rest of my Service career, during which I met relatively few country folk.

Most of us found some of the Scots accents particularly hard to fathom, and it was months before many of us were able to understand a lad from the Outer Hebrides. If we were to see him now, it wouldn't be long before someone said, 'Yen, tway, shree,' in imitation of his piping voice counting to three.

On the other hand, everyone took the mick out of my Shropshire burr, including the ladies on the NAAFI wagon. If I ordered a Mars Bar, they delighted in repeating, 'a Marrrs barrr my dearrr.'

I'm not sure how much my accent changed over the years. On the few occasions I've heard myself, I've thought I still sound like a complete yokel. Many of the people I've worked with over the years have probably thought the same.

On that first day, my state of mind veered constantly between confidence and insecurity.

Having been in the ATC, the geography and atmosphere of an RAF station were familiar, and I knew a bit about drill and polishing shoes. I was even used to being shouted at by NCOs similar to the

Swinderby drill instructors. But their ferocity and vindictiveness was way beyond anything I'd encountered before, and parts of the training syllabus sounded truly daunting. I already wondered whether I was going to stay the course.

Reassuringly, many of my new roommates expressed the same doubts.

My first letter home, written that night, said I was missing everyone, and bemoaned the amount of civilian clothing I'd taken. It seemed I was going to have very little opportunity to wear it.

Three days later, my diary states baldly, *Our corporal is a bastard.* The same epithet is later applied to Sergeant Blackman, but it was the corporals they set on us first.

They taught us all the basic manoeuvres involved in foot drill: standing to attention – heels together, toes angled out at 45 degrees, arms straight down the sides, fists clenched, thumbs to the front running down the seams of the trousers; standing at ease – heels shoulder-width apart, open hands overlapped, right over left, behind the lower back; standing easy – an infinitesimally more relaxed form of standing at ease; turning, left, right and about – through 180 degrees; and saluting - only commissioned officers, not NCOs or Warrant Officers – moving the right arm swiftly out to the side and up, and bending it to place the open hand, palm forward, with the fingertips over the right eyebrow for three seconds, before whipping the arm shortest way down to the side again.

Then, finally, marching itself, swinging your arms to shoulder height in an exaggerated walk, naturally moving the right arm with the left leg and vice versa, but with the arms straight, fists clenched, thumbs on top. Complications were added, such as turning left, right and about while marching, and saluting officers approaching from any conceivable direction.

As anticipated, I found marching relatively easy, and most of those with no previous experience came to grips with it fairly quickly, but some just couldn't do it.

Alongside the surprising number who couldn't tell left from right, and kept turning in the wrong direction or setting off with the wrong foot, were those who, when putting their right foot forward, swung their right arm. This is called tick-tocking, and, believe me, it's quite hard to do, unless, of course, you're one of the poor souls for whom it comes naturally. They suffered a torrid time having the habit beaten out of them.

If you watch the Royal Albert Hall Festival of Remembrance on television, I guarantee that you'll see at least one person tick-tocking, usually a nurse or a member of the reserve forces who hasn't had the habit thoroughly eradicated by hours of dedicated drill practice.

And, as we had our bad habits eradicated, practising for hours on end, Piggy Tonner shouted at us, constantly criticising, never satisfied with our efforts, no matter how much we, or perhaps he, felt we'd improved.

The NCOs all spoke in a style familiar from films, but used words we'd never heard before, like *jildy* for hurry up, or *dhobi* for laundry, learnt during their previous service in the Middle or Far East.

Many of their phrases could have come straight from the pen of a comedy script writer: *if you don't swing that arm, I'm going to rip it off and hit you over the head with the soggy end*; or, *if you don't sharpen up, I'm going to stick my boot so far up your arse, you'll be spitting out polish for a week*; and many others. There were tens of them, all threatening some form of outrageous physical torture if our performance didn't improve.

Recalled later, in the warmth of our rooms, these gems were very funny, but they seemed far less amusing on the parade square, where, in November and December, it was always freezing, and often wet. All we wanted was for the incessant marching to end. And of course, because 7 and 8 Flights were to parade in front of the Queen, we were kept at it for longer than the Leper Colony. They didn't seem so sad now.

We eventually found out more about what our route lining would entail.

Visiting leaders fly into London Heathrow all the time, but a few every year are given the honour of an official State Visit. When they are, the first thing they and their entourage usually do is catch a train to Victoria Station, where they're met by the Queen, other members of the Royal Family, Ministers and senior Service officers. Then, they're driven, often in horse-drawn carriages, up Victoria Street to Parliament Square, down Whitehall to Trafalgar Square, under Admiralty Arch and along the Mall to Buckingham Palace.

Both sides of the route are lined by Servicemen and women from various Royal Navy, Army and Royal Air Force units, standing ten yards apart in the gutter, heels against the kerb.

In the 1970s, many of the Royal Navy and Army units were rotated through these duties, but the RAF was always represented by its apprentices, while the Foot Guards always formed a large part of the Army contingent.

With the apprentices from Halton, Cosford and

Locking, we were to line the section of the route from Parliament Square to Trafalgar Square. There, in front of pavements thronged with thousands of sightseers, we would stand, facing one another across the street, waiting for the Royal party to pass. We'd each be armed with a Self-Loading Rifle, bayonet fixed but no bullets.

Royal protection was the responsibility of the police constables on and around the route. But we often wondered what we'd do if someone lunged at the royal party as it passed. I for one hoped I'd try and stop the assailant, although the truth was that we were there mainly as adornments, and to prevent our rifles falling into the hands of terrorists, at the time, the IRA.

For our first route lining, on 11th December 1973, the visiting dignitary was President Mobutu of Zaire, now the Democratic Republic of Congo.

We had a month and a few days to progress from raw recruits to parading before the Queen.

Many of the more demanding, even brutal aspects of military training are based on a system called 'dislocation of expectation'. It can be applied to almost anything, from basic drill and kit cleaning, to advanced leadership training or SAS selection.

Take the example of an exercise involving map reading to a camp site. You and your team push yourselves hard against the clock to arrive in time for a hot meal and rest. But, when you arrive, your instructors tell you the enemy have discovered your location and you have to break camp and travel another five miles. Oh, and by the way, you have to carry the complete campsite with you.

Most, if not all of your expectations have been well and truly dislocated.

Whatever the changes in military training since I retired, I'm sure dislocation of expectation still features prominently, because it can be used to build so many qualities, from individual resilience in the face of hardship and disappointment, to group cohesion against the enemy, in the case of training, your instructors.

And nowhere was the system practised more effectively than in the barrack blocks at Swinderby.

Bull is short for bullshit, and encompasses all things in the military to do with cleaning of personal kit or accommodation. A more polite term would be spit and polish. Anyway, The Recruits' Handbook sent to us before our arrival at Swinderby stated, *It can be fairly said that all unnecessary bull has been eliminated from the present training course.*

If ever an expectation was set up to be dislocated, this was it.

The barrack blocks were two storeys high, and shaped much like the H Blocks of prisons such as The Maze. On each floor, the short crossbar of the H contained offices, store-rooms and ablutions – baths, showers, washrooms and toilets, while each long bar contained four large, communal, rooms, two up, two down.

I was in a ground floor room with 13 others, and my bed-space contained a bed, a slim wardrobe and a small, metre-high locker with a drawer and a few open shelves. Kit, including civilian clothes, had to be laid out in the locker and wardrobe in a prescribed manner.

We were responsible for cleaning our rooms, plus the corridor outside, half the ablutions on our floor and halfway up the stairs. This was meant to entail a quick once-over daily, first thing in the morning, to keep the place reasonable, and a thorough clean one evening a week: a bull night, which would be followed by an inspection the following morning.

At Swinderby, however, we stood next to our beds while our rooms were inspected nearly every morning.

Linoleum floors had to be polished to a bright sheen, as did any brasses and the tiles and porcelain surfaces in the bathroom. And there was to be no dust anywhere. If there was, it was sure to be found by the probing fingers of Corporal Tonner or Sergeant Blackman, or, God forbid, the Flight Commander. If he spotted something the NCOs had failed to find, we were all in for an especially rough time.

For the first few weeks, the block was never clean enough, and we had bull night after bull night, even taking to tying dusters over our shoes to glide over the floors in the run up to inspections. The smell of floor polish became all pervasive. But to no avail. Our first free weekend was cancelled.

I was homesick and thoroughly cheesed off, but the loss of the weekend was too much for some. They decided to call it a day and leave the RAF at this early stage.

We were surprised to find that beds had a decorative as well as a practical use. We were allowed to sleep in them at night, but in the morning, they had to be stripped and made up again in a very precise and unusual fashion.

One grey blanket was laid over the mattress and tucked in with hospital corners. The other blankets and the sheets were folded until each was one yard wide and two feet deep. They were then laid on top of one another at the head of the bed in the order, grey blanket, white sheet, white blanket, white sheet, grey blanket. Wound about with a colourful bedcover, the resulting rectangle of bedding was meant to be a yard wide, two feet deep and six inches tall, with perfectly square corners.

This was a bedpack, and it was topped off with two smoothed white pillows.

To prevent sagging and ensure the requisite angularity, old hands said we should place thin rectangles of wood between each layer of our bedpacks. Luckily, we weren't tempted, because when a bedpack displeased the inspecting NCO, it would be thrown across the room. The poor chap standing opposite tended to be enveloped in sheets and blankets. Any wooden inserts would have pole-axed him.

Then there was your uniform.

The two skills required to prepare uniforms for inspection were ironing and polishing. Both had been demonstrated by Corporal Tonner on the first night. He made it look so easy, especially the ironing. But for teenage boys, the very sight of an ironing board brought on another major life crisis. Not only did we have to iron four shirts, leaving no creases, but also two pairs of trousers, these until the creases front and back were straight and sharp, not multiple and rounded.

In addition, we had to polish two pairs of shoes, one pair of boots, the peaks of our caps and our brass belt buckles. And not just polish in the normal sense of a quick buff to maintain colour, but caress to a deep shine in which you could see, not only your face, but the distant hills. They had to be fit to be seen by the Queen.

The fact that she was never going to see our second pair of shoes or our boots made no difference. Everything had to be immaculate.

For footwear, the method of gaining a shine to which I maintained a career-long loyalty is to take a small wad of cotton wool, wet it in tap water – not spit – squeeze most of the water out of the wad on the palm of your hand, lightly coat it with black polish and rub gently over the surface of the shoe or boot in small circles until the polish has been absorbed. Repeat, for hour upon hour, until there is a deep, unblemished shine.

The chief dangers are any form of grease, which can lead to smearing, and grit, even microscopic particles, which can leave small circular scratches. Drill NCOs can see smears and scratches invisible to the rest of the human race.

We also discovered a totally new danger to society. Dust on the small horizontal shelf where the rubber soles of shoes and boots meet the leather uppers: the welts.

Sergeant Blackman considered dust in the welts to be a sure sign of a shoddy approach to cleaning, RAF training and life in general.

My diary mentions frequent bull nights followed by four hour polishing sessions. We'd go to bed at 11.30 and get up at 5.30 to continue cleaning and preparing kit. We had breakfast only if we felt we could spare the time, because, by 7.30, bedpacks and kit laid out, we had to stand to attention at the foot of our beds to be inspected. If not success, we at least expected recognition of the effort we'd put in.

This expectation was nearly always thoroughly dislocated.

Theoretically, there were different levels of inspection: routine and formal, either by the NCOs or the Flight Commander. But, in practice, it didn't seem to matter which type of inspection it was, or who did it. We cleaned as thoroughly as possible for all of them, and rarely managed to please anyone.

There were differences though. The inspections by the Flight Commander were quieter affairs, with little ranting, at least until the officer had left. When the NCOs were inspecting, hostile feedback was delivered immediately, and at full volume.

Sometimes an inspection took place while we were at work, and it was several hours before we knew how we'd done. An early sign of failure to impress was the sight of shoes and boots littering the grass outside the barrack block as we marched towards it.

Confirmation came on entering our rooms. Bedding from dismembered bedpacks littered the floor, as did more of our shoes and boots, those that hadn't been thrown in the rubbish bins. Some toecaps had been smashed on the metal bed ends, causing the polish to crack off, meaning many hours' work for the unfortunate owner to regain a shine from scratch.

A friend corroborated this memory, adding only that the shoes thrown out of his window suffered major damage. He lived on the first floor.

My diary and letters indicate that this treatment was unrelenting in the early weeks. It was soul-destroying. But you had to pick yourself up and, hoping for better results next time, do it all over again. And once again, a few of our number, including one of our roommates, decided enough was enough, and withdrew from training.

The rest of us bonded into an ever tighter group, one of the main reasons, of course, that the pain was being inflicted on us in the first place.

Unless you've been in the Services, or at least their lower echelons, the deference shown to officers must seem very strange. I don't intend to launch into an essay, but there comes a point when, to be truly successful, officers have to earn respect over and above this deference.

Recruit training is not one of these points.

We rarely saw the officer who commanded our flight, and we had no idea whether he merited respect for reasons other than his rank. But the mere fact that he held a commission was enough for him to receive our unquestioning deference. We learnt to look through the man to the commission, and defer to that.

For the rest of my career, I could call a brick wall sir or ma'am if it held a commission.

In the military, this is necessary, if only to give new commanders time to earn respect. And even if they fail to gain this, deference should allow them to perform their leadership function to a minimum standard.

In the early days, though, I was prepared to give our flight commander more than the usual benefit of any doubt. To my eyes at least, the bright white pilot wings on his chest gave him a god-like quality.

Only later did I develop some misgivings, doubts that profoundly affected my own approach to being an officer later in my career.

At Swinderby, we were cajoled and bullied into having immaculate kit and upright bearing, and our NCOs maintained similar standards. But some of our flight commanders cut slightly shabby figures, with, by our new benchmark, untidy hair, uniforms and shoes.

I saw the same from other officers at various stages in my 32 years of service, and always felt they were letting the side down. As a result, when I became an officer myself, I tried, not always successfully perhaps, to maintain a smart appearance. It was especially difficult when wearing a green bag – an RAF flying suit - but I must have been one of the last aircrew officers to bull the toecaps of his uniform shoes and flying boots.

I know I didn't make a conscious resolution to do this in those early weeks at Swinderby, but I'm sure it was where the idea originated. It was certainly how I used to rationalise it as a senior officer, when, on Sunday evenings, I didn't always feel like polishing my toecaps for the week ahead.

Although I was one of the older members of my entry, I'd only just started shaving, and some of the younger amongst us had never shaved.

On the first morning, we discovered that bum fluff was no more acceptable than stubble. In the future, everyone was to shave every morning.

It would take some of us days to sprout anything visible, but, somehow, if you omitted to shave, Piggy Tonner could tell. He could also tell if you'd shaved with an electric razor, and this too was unacceptable. You had to wet shave.

Skin care specialists would blanch at the results. I rarely cut myself, but some of the others, especially those with the dreaded acne, were always ripping their faces to pieces.

One of my friends relates a story of being stopped by a warrant officer and asked if he'd shaved. When he answered, 'Yes,' the warrant officer growled, 'Did you use a mirror?' On receipt of another timid, 'Yes,' the warrant officer spat, 'Well try using a razor next time,' and marched away.

One incident seems to me to indicate our ongoing transition from civilians into Servicemen. It's not a story to be particularly proud of, but it does make the point.

During my first 18 years in Ludlow, unless I'd played a particularly messy game of rugby or football, I bathed only once a week, and I'm pretty sure I only changed my underwear with the same regularity, or lack of it. As far as I know, all my mates had the same hygiene routine, and I don't remember noticing the smell of those around me. I guess we were all in the same boat; none of us had showers, and my parents only heated enough water for baths once a week, in our case, on a Sunday.

I can't believe my middle class friends and acquaintances at the Grammar School didn't notice my poor hygiene, or that they didn't pass comment. But they never did so to my face; perhaps even they followed a similar routine in the late 1960s and early 70s.

At Swinderby, the expectation was that everyone would take a daily bath or shower, and change their underwear, if not daily, more often than they had at home. Most of us settled into the routine fairly quickly, realising the sense of it when 14 athletic young men were sharing a room.

But every so often, someone had to be encouraged to pick up their soap and towel and head for the ablutions. And some unfortunates just seemed to have body odour problems no matter how often they showered. I shared a room at Halton with one such. He could only avoid verbal lashings by constant bathing and the regular use of a masking agent. Many of us took to using Brut or Right Guard deodorant sprays.

After a few weeks at Swinderby, a lad from another room in our block had earned a reputation for poor personal hygiene through sheer laziness and lack of consideration for others. To be blunt, he stank. He even seemed to think it funny. In addition, he often failed to put enough effort into either bulling his personal kit, or cleaning the communal areas. He was forever getting the whole room into trouble.

After failing one particular inspection because of him, his roommates had had enough. We were all invited to witness their solution to the problem.

On entering their room, the miscreant was sat in front of a table, behind which sat a fellow roommate wearing a dark blanket and a mop head in a very good imitation of a legal gown and wig. The 'judge' gave a very theatrical address, accusing his roommate of the obvious crimes of poor hygiene and letting down his mates, but adding, 'Making love to a wax facsimile of Mrs Mills.'

Mrs Mills was a rather large pianist, a constant feature of television variety shows at the time, and popular with our parents' generation. We all collapsed in laughter at the clever turn of phrase. It has stuck with me ever since.

I remember nothing else of the kangaroo court beyond the sentence and its execution. The lad was taken to the ablutions, stripped, placed in a cold bath and washed with scouring powder and stiff bristled scrubbing brushes. Not very edifying, but he never let his room down again at Swinderby, or, as far as I know, during our three years at Halton.

I don't remember the lad who played the judge at all after this episode; perhaps he left to pursue a career in the law.

The point is that we were learning to police ourselves, making sure individuals didn't let down either themselves or their unit.

Many hours were spent in the gym and on the sports fields, both improving our general fitness and playing games. The Physical Training Instructors always pushed us to exhaustion, whether we be running or doing circuits of various exercises, such as press-ups, sit-ups and star jumps. Some found this aspect of the course especially hard, but I enjoyed it, not only at Swinderby, but throughout my RAF career.

During Ground Defence Training, we learned military skills, including how to dismantle, reassemble, clean and fire the Self-Loading Rifle. We also learnt the rudiments of first aid and fire-fighting. But, at the height of the Cold War, a major part of the syllabus was given over to nuclear, biological and chemical warfare training, NBC. This emphasis continued on later courses, and I undertook NBC refresher training and testing at least once a year for the rest of my career.

At Swinderby, they aimed to teach us the theory of nuclear explosions and their aftermath, and how to recognise the signs and symptoms of the various chemical agents that could be used against us: choking and blood agents, and nerve gas. There was little mention of specific biological agents, only a realisation that an enemy could unleash some form of germ warfare.

The aim was to help us survive to launch the aircraft that would take the fight to the enemy.

As our first line of defence, we were issued with protective clothing: camouflaged, all-enveloping NBC suits, special gloves and overboots, and, most importantly, respirators. We learned the buddy-buddy system, the fundamental way servicemen look after one another in all situations. In this instance, it meant checking that our buddy was wearing all his complicated equipment correctly.

The culmination of the training was a test of us and

our equipment in the CS chamber, a concrete bunker in which CS gas was released. If we'd fitted our kit correctly and learnt our drills, we should be able to minimise our exposure to the gas, although we already knew there was no way we'd be able to avoid it altogether; we'd been told we had to experience its effects, just to hammer home how important it was to look after our equipment, and especially our respirators.

Immediately you come into contact with it, CS gas makes your eyes water and sting, whilst also making it difficult to breathe and causing you to cough violently. The effects are very unpleasant and only alleviated by fresh air and time, as modern day criminals sprayed by the police will know only too well.

The CS chamber was one of the major tests of character on the Swinderby course. Whether intentional or not, there was a big build up to the event, with graphic stories about just how unpleasant the exposure to the gas would be.

On the day, looking like a group of visiting spacemen in our NBC suits and respirators, we filed into the chamber in groups of ten, with two similarly attired instructors. One knelt down and set off – lit – a CS gas pellet, which filled the room with what looked like smoke, while the other guarded the door. I for one was very nervous.

There were three stages at which you could come into contact with the gas. If you were lucky, you avoided the first two.

Firstly, if your respirator didn't fit properly, or had a faulty canister, you felt the effects of the gas immediately the pellet was lit. Those unlucky enough to experience this had to stay put as the panic and pain escalated, holding up their hands until spotted by the instructors, patted on the back and let out. After some time to recover, and some remedial work on their respirators, they'd have to re-enter the chamber with another group.

The second chance came when we had to change the canister screwed into the respirator to the side of our chins. The threads were quite large, but unscrewing an old canister and fitting a new one wasn't easy, even when practising in the peace and quiet of the barrack block. That morning in the chamber, adrenaline, tension and the presence of CS gas made everything that much harder. But, I held my breath, changed the canister first time and blew out to clear any residual fumes, all with the merest whiff of CS.

Inevitably though, some of the others were all fingers and thumbs. They failed to fit the new canister before they ran out of breath and had to inhale. Even then, coughing and spluttering, they had to hold up their hands until one instructor patted them on the back and the other let them out of the door. Once again, they would be given time to recover before being allowed to re-take the canister test with another group.

Finally, came the moment the rest of us had been dreading. No matter how successful we'd been so far, there was no escape now. One by one, we had to take off our respirators and shout our number, rank and name until the instructor was satisfied, patted us on the back and let us charge out of the door.

The person before me stuttered over his speech, tried unsuccessfully to pick up where he'd left off as the fumes took hold, and was finally let out before he collapsed.

I took a deep breath, lifted off my respirator and shouted, 'C8019348 Apprentice Technician Powell, corporal.'

With my eyes streaming and my throat burning, I waited for what seemed an age before I felt a pat on the back and stumbled out of the door. Once in the fresh air, I ran into wind trying to blow the gas from my eyes and clear my lungs. I can't remember exactly how long it took to recover. A matter of minutes I think. I'd breathed in much less of the gas than some of the others, but it was enough to last a lifetime.

This was meant to be the only time we'd be forced to feel the effects of CS gas, but we had to do the same drills in a CS chamber as part of our refresher training every year, so there was always the chance you could be re-acquainted with the horrible stuff. In fact, in later years it became more likely, because they came up with additional actions to perform in the chamber, such as eating and drinking, decontaminating your respirator, and taking medication.

At some point in the 80s or 90s, CS gas was replaced with something more benign. Thereafter, if your respirator was a poor fit or you made a mistake with your drills, you received only a strong whiff of pear drops. It still made the point, but nowhere near as powerfully as CS.

I can't say I mourned its passing, though.

At Swinderby, as well as the CS chamber and other practical tests in shooting and first aid, we completed written exams in Ground Defence and General Service Training. I did well in these, probably because, in contrast to my school studies, I found the subjects interesting, relevant and enjoyable.

In early December, our drill and kit cleaning became increasingly focused on the route lining. We had a final dress rehearsal on the 7th, and left for RAF Halton at lunchtime on the 8th, travelling by train and bus to arrive in the late evening.

Stepping off the bus into the dark canyon between two of Halton's three-storey barrack blocks, with drill NCOs barking the things drill NCOs love barking, it all seemed reminiscent of scenes from the TV series, Colditz, being screened at about the same time.

My diary calls it, *a bit of a dump.*

We stood out from the other apprentices like a bunch of very prominent sore thumbs. While they were bedecked in colourful badges, hat bands and rank chevrons, we bore nothing to mark us out as part of the same breed – more of which later. And they were all streetwise, having been in the RAF for a minimum of several months.

We, on the other hand, exuded an odour of innocence. They sensed it, the way carnivores sense a tasty meal. We were fair game.

Just to make matters worse, although smart, the other apprentices lacked the glossy sheen to which our NCOs were accustomed. They'd never seen a trainee with a uniform more than 6 weeks old, and interpreted the slightly careworn appearance of the Halton, Locking and Cosford contingents as slovenliness.

Worse still, during a break in rehearsals, Corporal Tonner and one of his fellow instructors, Corporal 'Jildy' Smith, marched two of our number up and down in front of the massed ranks of the other apprentices, telling them to note the superior turnout and drill produced at Swinderby.

That night, we were raided.

There was very little room-raiding at Swinderby. By the time even the senior flights had finished bulling, sleep was more important than high jinks, and nobody wanted their room or kit trashed before the morning inspections. Where there was the odd sally, I remember fairly friendly affairs, with pillows, lots of laughter and no blood.

The tradition at Halton was somewhat different.

At the first shout of *raid*, those quick enough to jump up and confront their attackers with pillows were subjected to a wholly unexpected level of violence that led to cut lips and black eyes. And those that failed to get up quickly enough found themselves upside down, trapped between their bed and the wall, or a radiator. To cuts were added sprains and head injuries, some serious enough to require visits to the medical centre.

Worse still, the medics involved our NCOs. Unused to such things, they escalated everything to the point where those responsible for the mayhem were identified and charged with assault. Some of our entry had to appear as prosecution witnesses, which made us even more unpopular.

There were no further raids before the route lining, but we knew there'd be trouble when we returned to Halton to begin our technical training in the New Year.

After two more days of rehearsals, 11th December 1973 dawned bright and sunny. At 8am, several hundred apprentices left Halton for London in a fleet of 13 coaches. Our progress was eased by Police motorcycle outriders who continually raced ahead to block side roads and roundabouts, then overtook and raced ahead again to do more of the same. Being escorted in this way was quite an experience but, increasingly, our attention shifted to the view from the windows.

I'd been through London twice on the way to Biggin Hill. On both occasions, I'd taken the tube across town, seeing few of the major tourist sites.

Many of the others, probably the majority, had never visited the capital, so our excitement mounted as we passed one famous landmark after another.

Eventually, having given us a sight of Buckingham Palace, the buses parked along Horse Guards Road. We disembarked and formed up on Horse Guards Parade, the space to the rear of Admiralty House, Whitehall and Downing Street used for Trooping The Colour - and the Olympic beach volleyball in 2012.

At noon, led by the Band of the Royal Air Force, we marched through the arch on the eastern side and into Whitehall. I didn't have far to go, because I was positioned a few hundred yards up the road with my back to the Ministry of Defence Main Building, not far from the Cenotaph.

Although I was standing in the gutter, my pride knew no bounds.

The size of the crowds grew steadily, until, at 12.50, we were brought to attention and presented arms in Royal Salute, rifles held vertically in front of our bodies, bayonets fixed.

The first to pass, in a blaze of colour and jangling accoutrements, were two troops of Household Cavalry. They took up the full width of the road, and we'd been told the troopers might try to kick the rifles out of our hands or knock off our hats, so we should tilt our bayonets to make the horses shy away. I followed the advice, but quickly gained the impression that if I was hit by a cavalryman, it would be through incompetence rather than malice. Some seemed barely in control of their horses, and, with the Queen not far behind, they swore like, well... like troopers.

The cavalry were closely followed by an open, horse-drawn coach bearing the Queen and President Mobutu. They passed no more than a few feet from me. I had an unobstructed view that money couldn't buy, and I was being paid for it. Knowing how much people would give for such access, I've always felt privileged to take part in royal occasions, although, at this point, I never dreamt how often I'd come close to members of the Royal Family, or that I'd have two audiences in Buckingham Palace.

Successive coaches contained various Congolese dignitaries, accompanied by the Duke of Edinburgh and Prince Charles, the Duke of Kent and Earl Mountbatten, and the Duchesses of Kent and Gloucester. The coaches were followed by cars carrying government ministers and senior military officers, with a further squadron of Household Cavalry clattering past in the rear.

The procession left behind it a pungent aroma of horses, and a road littered with their dung.

It was all over in a few seconds. The crowds dispersed remarkably quickly and we marched back onto Horse Guards Parade, trying to avoid the piles of horse manure. I was also trying to ignore irrational pangs of guilt at not leaning down to scoop some up for Dad's roses. Before we'd really had chance to take stock, we were back on the coaches and heading for Halton.

Over the next three years and ten more route linings, I discovered there was something very special about being a part of royal ceremonial. The rehearsal process was invariably repetitive and tedious, but the events themselves always engendered a feeling of immense pride, none more so than when, some 17 years later, I stood on Horse Guards again to call in the flypast for The Queen Mother's 90th Birthday Parade.

After our first royal occasion, we snatched a quick meal at Halton and set off for Swinderby, where we arrived at nine in the evening.

We'd been told the Queen was apt to pass comment if something particularly good or bad caught her eye. Well, we didn't receive royal feedback after this route lining, but the General Officer Commanding London District passed a message, saying, '*Alongside the Household Division, the RAF Apprentices are the professionals of the streets of London*'.

After weeks of being kicked from pillar to post, it was great to hear such praise.

On reaching Swinderby, we went to the NAAFI (the airmen's' club, pronounced naffey) to watch ourselves on the television news, after which, flushed with pride, my diary says we *sang the senior flight into the ground.*

Singing seemed to play a prominent part in the early years of my RAF career. Not formal singing in a choir, but spontaneous singing, in joy, or in competition with rival groups, usually with drink taken.

Whether it was a hangover from the First and Second World War, or just something young men did (and perhaps still do), we sang, in the NAAFI, the rugby club and whenever we got on a bus. It was to be expected at some point during any night out, be it with fellow flight or squadron members, or a sports team.

On occasion, the songs could be raucous and rude, the ruder the better, but sometimes, they could be more patriotic or popular, with a real attempt to sing tunefully, even in harmony, for songs like Bread of Heaven or Sloop John B.

The members of Halton Rugby Club, especially, were great singers. The Club included many Welshmen, and I learnt at least to mouth many of the popular Welsh language songs, and to sing patriotic

English songs, such as Jerusalem and Land of Hope and Glory with great gusto and pride when the opportunity arose.

Singing could also be taunting and confrontational, but I remember it as a substitute for fighting, not a precursor to it, like football chants, and it rarely had the ugliness of such tribal goading.

I don't remember any singing during my three years on the C-130 Hercules, where we travelled in constantly changing crews of five, passing like ships in the night and rarely coming together as a squadron. But we often ran across fighter squadrons on detachment as a complete unit, singing enthusiastically.

Later, serving as a flying instructor on University Air Squadrons, we often sang, again with a mix of the raucous and rude, and the more tuneful. Even as a wing commander in the late 1990s, I'd join in, attempting to lead the singing toward the more tuneful end of the Squadron repertoire.

I hope karaoke hasn't totally displaced these spontaneous outbursts.

On our return from London, the NCOs tried to ratchet up the pressure for what should have been the high point of the six-week Swinderby course, our Passing Out Parade. But, even they seemed to realise that all bar the Leper Colony had already passed their major test by marching before the Queen. So, in the run-up to the Parade, my diary notes more tedium than fear, more sport than drill.

One thing we found out later was that when officers completed a course, they *graduated,* whereas we merely *passed out*. And in the printed programmes for such occasions, officers were accompanied by their *ladies*, while airmen were joined by their *wives*. We imagined the downward progression to a category of apprentices and their *scrubbers*.

Some of the institutional distinctions between airmen and officers, such as segregated toilets and separate doors to enter buildings, would seem absurd today, but I think they owed more to the class system of the early and mid-Twentieth Century than any purely military strictures. Nonetheless, at the time, they reminded me that, as the son of a dustman and an apprentice, I was at the bottom of both the civilian and the military hierarchies.

There were still differences in the treatment of airmen and officers when I retired in 2005, but many of the more ludicrous disparities had disappeared, from the RAF at least.

Over the years, I found that most RAF training courses ended with enjoyable social functions. The message was, if you could survive the pain (intellectual and/or physical), the last few days would be good fun. This gave you a target to aim for during the darker days of training, and the events themselves helped foster esprit de corps. Where the end of a course coincided with the run up to Christmas, as it did at Swinderby, this was always a bonus.

Our final few days got off to a cracking start with a dance on the Saturday before the Passing Out Parade. It was attended by the female trainees from a nearby base.

Although the Women's Royal Air Force had been formed in 1949, the WRAF acronym was still pronounced Waff, plural Waffs, after the acronym of their predecessors, the Women's Auxiliary Air Force. And, until 1979, WRAFs still did their recruit training at a separate unit: RAF Spitalgate, not far from Swinderby.

During the course of the evening, I spent some time with one of the WRAFs. Nothing more than a few dances and a farewell peck on the cheek, with no expectation of ever meeting again. But it earned me more street cred than I'd ever had before, or, if truth be told, have ever had since. She was one of Spitalgate's corporal drill instructors.

I can only say that she was far from the female equivalent of our own Corporal Piggy Tonner. She was young, slim and pretty, and I had no idea of her true identity until later in the evening. Her flight members had told all my mates, but they hadn't told me. Anyway, we had a good time and she left my reputation sky high.

On the Monday, we had our flight party, *a good night,* my diary states. And, on the Tuesday, we had the Airmens' Christmas Dinner, the meal being served by our NCOs and officers, a Service tradition. It was a jolly occasion with party hats and crackers and lots of banter, and was followed by a cabaret.

After all the fun leading up to it, the Passing Out Parade itself was a bit of an anti-climax. Not because anything went wrong, but because wet weather led to it being held in a hangar rather than on the parade ground. While our instructors had no qualms about marching us up and down in the pouring rain, even they realised it was unfair to make the visiting families suffer while we did it.

Outside on the square, I'm sure the Parade would have been a colourful and enjoyable occasion. Inside a drab hangar, with the music of the band and the shouted orders echoing around the walls, it all seemed disappointingly low key, especially after the route lining in London.

My negativity may also stem from the fact that my family didn't attend. Dad no longer drove, and even if they could have afforded the train fare and overnight accommodation, the journey was too long and complicated for them to undertake.

So, on Wednesday 19th December 1973, having successfully passed out of RAF Recruit Training, I travelled home alone, on leave until the New Year, when I was to report to RAF Halton.

I have many of the letters my family sent during the Swinderby course, and over the following three years at Halton. These indicate that all remained well at home.

My mother was now in her father's old house, away from the corrosive atmosphere of Dodmore, and a small bathroom annexe was added in 1974, making it much more like a dwelling from the 1970s than the 1930s. Brian became Head Boy of Ludlow Secondary Modern School, before doing well in his CSEs and moving up to the Grammar School to take his A Levels.

Chapter 5 - Apprentice Training

When the RAF was formed in 1918, its first leader, Lord Trenchard, realised it would need large numbers of skilled tradesmen, not only to keep its fleet of 22,000 aircraft serviced, but also to stay abreast of fast-moving developments in military aviation.

The highest quality recruits, about 1,000 a year, would be offered apprenticeships. They would have to be well educated and intelligent, because to save costs, they'd have to complete their training in three, rather than five years, as was then the norm in Civvy Street. In January 1920, while RAF Halton was being prepared, the first of four groups of 'boys' began training at RAF Cranwell in Lincolnshire.

The 5th Entry arrived at RAF Halton in January 1922, undergoing a name change from Boy Mechanics to Aircraft Apprentices. They were also known as Trenchard Brats, a nickname RAF apprentices retained until the final entry, the 155th, graduated from Halton in June 1993.

I've always been proud to be a Brat.

Unlike other entrants to the RAF, apprentices had always done their six weeks square bashing at their apprentice schools. They'd also worn distinctive regalia, such as coloured hatbands, and, most notably, on the sleeves of their tunics, a one-inch diameter brass ring encasing a four-bladed propeller; it was known as the Apprentice Wheel. And to help the adult staff maintain discipline, some members of the senior entries were made Apprentice NCOs, with rank chevrons on the sleeves of their uniforms.

Following a review in the early 1970s, my entry, the 123rd, was entering under new rules. We wore no apprentice insignia, none of us would become Apprentice NCOs, and, like all other airmen joining the RAF, we did our square bashing at Swinderby. Finally, we were known as Apprentice Technicians rather than Technician Apprentices, to ensure we were thought of as adults, rather than boys. As fine a piece of management consultant bullshit as I ever heard.

The lack of any distinguishing regalia was what had marked us out from our fellow apprentices on our visit to Halton for the route lining before Christmas.

When, two years after our arrival, the last Apprentice NCOs graduated, it was realised that getting rid of the system had been a mistake. But to re-introduce it immediately would smell too much of a climb-down, so a few individuals were chosen to be Senior Apprentices, with coloured lanyards at the shoulder instead of rank chevrons. I wore a red lanyard for my final year at Halton.

A few years after we left, the wheel turned full circle. The apprentice badge, other apprentice regalia and NCO ranks were all re-introduced.

Much damage is done by politicians, senior civil servants and senior officers keen to make a name for themselves as great innovators, wedded to change, the new corporate religion. They initiate reviews and studies, carried out, either by ambitious officers or, even worse, external consultants, who steal your watch and tell you the time, but are thought by those in authority to give a study more weight and credibility.

In reality, consultants rarely understand what they are meddling with. They assume everything they're told by those doing the job to be obstructive, and come up with totally impractical recommendations that senior staff accept because they offer savings, and because they too fail to understand, or are not interested in, the long term ramifications.

When the recommendations are implemented, they don't work and lead to extra costs. No-one can tell the truth because it would put egg on the faces of the great men. The shop floor has to lump it, at great financial and physical cost.

A few years later, the politician, civil servant and senior officer will all be working for the consultant, or the contractor given the work, or both.

End of brief rant.

During my visit for the route lining before Christmas, I'd called Halton a dump. When I returned on the 2nd January 1974, facing the prospect of nearly three years there, it made no better impression. And a few days later, I was likening it to Colditz again. My downbeat assessment could not have been due to the location.

RAF Halton sits in a wooded area of the rolling Chiltern Hills, straddling the B4009 between Wendover and Aston Clinton. Part of a country estate, it was offered to Kitchener by his friend, Alfred Rothschild, at the outbreak of the First World War, and was used by the Royal Flying Corps throughout the conflict. Afterwards, a long-running dispute over who should restore it to its former condition was only settled when Alfred Rothschild died. The estate was given to the RAF in lieu of death duties in 1919.

The gift included Halton House, a Cotswold Stone mansion with fairy tale turrets, sitting beneath a wooded hillside above the Vale of Aylesbury. Built as a weekend retreat, with its own railway spur from Wendover, an outdoor ice rink and an indoor plunge pool, it has been used as the Officers' Mess ever since, although minus the railway spur, ice rink and pool. It's still a magnificent sight, and much sought after by companies filming period dramas.

Unsurprisingly, the military architecture built over the rest of the estate is less luxurious, and much less aesthetically pleasing.

To the west of the Wendover/Aston Clinton road lies a vast area of old, single storey, factory space and classrooms, known as Workshops; a large, red brick building of laboratories and classrooms, known as Schools; and, about half a mile to the northwest, a grass airfield, dating from 1913, with more modern hangars and airfield facilities, unsurprisingly known as The Airfield.

To the other side of the B4009 is the bulk of the domestic accommodation, sitting on the flanks of two small hills, bisected by a gully. In 1974, to the south of the gully, around a large parade square, were housed the Station permanent staff, and airmen trainees undertaking various training courses. Half a mile further south was a large RAF hospital, since closed.

To the north of the gully, up a steeper hill, was another parade square, surrounded by the accommodation blocks that housed the apprentices. Often in the past there had been thousands under training, formed into several Wings, but, when I arrived, it was hundreds.

The 123s moved into the Groves area to the north of the parade square, occupying two of its six barrack blocks. Constructed of dark red brick and packed closely together, these three storey buildings seemed to shut out the light, especially on dark winter days. It's from this aspect that my prison camp analogy sprang.

And the barrack blocks themselves were a bit grim.

Pushing through a double door in the centre and walking forward a few yards, you'd find yourself in a corridor running to left and right. Over your shoulders, a few yards apart, two wide sets of stone stairs with black metal railings and wooden balustrades snaked their way up to the first and second floors. Footfalls and voices echoed around these stairwells, giving the buildings the feel of municipal car parks.

To your front, double swing doors led to the ground floor ablutions. Mirrored on the two floors above, the ablutions were large echoing spaces, with highly polished red stone floors and white tile walls. They contained bathrooms, showers, toilets, washbasins and enough brass pipework and porcelain to keep an army of cleaners permanently occupied.

There are many stories of apprentice pranks; my own entry perpetrated a few, but somehow, we seemed to lack the ambition of some of our predecessors. Myth has it that one Friday night during a particularly hot summer, an enterprising flight sealed around the doors to their ground floor ablutions, turned on the cold taps and filled the space to the window sills, five feet above the floor. Over the weekend, they used the resulting swimming pool to keep cool.

The story fails to say how the pool was discovered on the Monday morning, but I like to think the flight NCOs tugged on the doors and were washed away, like characters in a cartoon flood.

Turning along the corridor to your left, you'd pass a couple of offices before entering a long room with a large television at the far end. In 1974, this TV room was furnished with 50 or 60 metal framed, armless, lounge chairs. I can't remember the exact colours of the soft furnishings, but the seat covers would have been something like dayglo orange, the carpet olive green, and the curtains some other striking colour, such as bright yellow. The colours in any other barrack block would have been similar, but arranged in a different order, perhaps dayglo orange carpet, olive green curtains and yellow chair covers.

The furnishings at Swinderby had been the same, and we began to realise that they were standard throughout the RAF. I later found out they adorned all Army and Navy buildings, and even, when I married several years later, the Married Quarters provided for families.

Geraldine was always horrified at the clash of colours when we 'Marched In' to a new Quarter, which we did 13 times in 25 years. But the only solution would have been to buy new carpets and curtains for every move, prohibitively expensive in the case of carpets, and increasingly ruinous for curtains, when the sizes of the windows in each house were invariably different, and we might only be in residence for six months. Sometimes, though, the décor was so frightful you had to shell out.

Thankfully, in the 1990s and early 2000s, the MOD's choice of colours became a little less frightening.

Along the barrack block corridor to the right hand side of the stairwell on the ground floor, and either side of the landings on the other two floors, were offices, small storerooms, single bedrooms for apprentices from the senior entry who supervised us out of normal working hours, and our own long, communal, rooms. The floors of these were of highly polished brown linoleum, and the walls were painted light blue or yellow to shoulder height, then white up to the high ceilings, which were also white.

The bright colours and numerous tall windows made the rooms light during the day, while two lines of strip lights kept them equally bright at night. We were relieved to find that the curtains in our room – on the middle floor of Kestrel Block - were olive green, so at least we didn't have to wake up to dayglo orange windows.

Each side wall was lined with 10 metal-framed single beds, heads against the wall. Each bedspace had one large, double wardrobe and one small locker, arranged so as to provide at least the semblance of a partition; although, you were totally exposed to the gaze of your roommates across the central aisle, known as the centredeck.

With 20 in a room, we couldn't open our wardrobe doors without hitting our beds. The situation was only resolved when several of the entry decided the RAF wasn't for them, and we all gained extra space, at least enough to open our wardrobe doors fully. Even so, most of us lived in 14 to 18-man rooms for three years. And we paid for the privilege.

There's a common misconception among civilians that Servicemen and women get their accommodation and meals free. This is not true. During my 32 years in the RAF, I paid rent for all the barrack blocks, officers' messes and married quarters in which I lived, and for all the meals I took in the various messes.

Perhaps the misconception arises because the money is deducted from salary, so it's never seen, but it's certainly deducted. And most of the accommodation I lived in, both before and after marriage, would have been considered sub-standard in comparison with similar civilian properties, even some prisons. The barrack blocks at Halton certainly seemed spartan, to say the least.

The only privacy was in the cubicles of the toilets, baths and showers, but even these had walls ending short of the high ceilings. To be indelicate, in the early days, several of my entry were discovered relieving their sexual frustration. At this point, they picked up a nickname that followed them for the rest of their time at Halton. It was very important not to be caught.

Our three flights at Swinderby became two at Halton. I became a member of 7 Flight, and moved into the room in Kestrel Block with 19 others, few of whom I knew from Swinderby.

Although he was now in another flight and another block, Ginge remained a friend, and one of my early letters refers to him making a nuisance of himself as I was writing it. Otherwise, I made new friendships, something you developed the knack of doing very quickly.

The hope that we'd left the worst excesses of drill and bullshit behind at Swinderby was rudely dashed. My letters make it plain that we'd entered a harsh regime.

Discipline during working hours was provided by our flight staff: a flight lieutenant – a rakish young officer reputed to have a water bed in the Officers' Mess - a sergeant and a corporal.

The NCOs were keen to rid us of the bad habits they thought we'd picked up at Swinderby, so there were many hours of drill, and many bull nights and inspections. Often, the staff were unhappy with the standards we reached, which led to extra drill, more bull nights, and cancelled weekends. For those picked out as being particularly lax, there were individual punishments, such as scrubbing pots in the cookhouse in the evenings.

Serial offenders could be placed on a formal charge – a Form 252 - and receive summary justice, similar to a court appearance, in front of the Flight Commander.

The procedure was called an Orderly Room and could lead to fines and/or jankers – out of hours work and kit inspections, and the loss of privileges, such as weekends and leave.

The opening salvo of these Orderly Rooms was, 'March in the accused'.

We always referred to it as, 'March in the guilty bastard,' which wasn't far from the truth. Those put on charges were always found guilty. People just accepted that they wouldn't have been charged if they hadn't done something wrong.

Discipline was also dished out by the apprentices of the senior entries: the 231s - the last entry of Craft Apprentices, who were nearing the end of their two years of training - and the Technician Apprentices of the 120th,121st and 122nd entries. The 120s especially instilled fear in us. They'd been at Halton for nearly three years and knew every wrinkle of the system.

They were headed by two Apprentice Sergeants who never ceased to make me smile when they formed us up on parade every morning. One was short, not much more than five feet tall, while the other was a giant, a barrel-chested rugby player standing well over six feet. They presented an amazing contrast as they strutted up and down in front of us. And yet, in disciplinary terms, I don't remember being more afraid of one than the other. They both seemed to warrant our respect.

Both were commissioned straight out of Halton. The shorter became an engineering officer, while the taller eventually became a helicopter pilot. I met him several times over the years, the last occasion 27 years after we'd first met, when he was a squadron leader and I a wing commander commanding a Harrier detachment in Italy during the NATO involvement in

Kosovo in the early Noughties.

At short notice one Saturday afternoon, we were told to expect a Puma helicopter diverting in from, I think, Pristina. The weather was atrocious, and we opened the hangar doors and stood in the dry looking out at the sheets of rain sweeping across Gioia Del Colle airfield.

Such was the visibility that we heard the helicopter long before we saw it, but eventually it appeared out of the mist and rain and settled in front of the hangar. As the troops rushed out to wheel it into the dry, two careworn figures clambered down and walked towards me. One was the tall, ex-120 entry, apprentice, the other an equally tall young flying officer I'd also met before. They'd had a nightmare journey through the mountains of Former Yugoslavia and across the Adriatic, admitting that they'd feared for their lives on several occasions.

I knew it must have been bad to reduce such robust characters to such a state of nervous exhaustion. They'd been due to refuel and fly on, but it seemed more prudent for them to get a good night's sleep before doing so, and that's what they did.

Back at Halton, we were about as popular with the senior apprentice entries as a fart in a spacesuit.

One reason was the punishments some of them had received following the room raids during our brief visit for the route lining before Christmas. Another, more permanent source of friction, was the new pay structure.

The senior apprentices, many in supervisory positions over us, were receiving about £15 a fortnight. We, having only just arrived, were receiving £32.

Now, had this been an invisible grievance, I'm sure

it would largely have been forgotten, if not forgiven. But, at that time, we received our wages in cash at low key ceremonies called Pay Parades. In Kestrel Block, these took place once a fortnight in the TV room.

In front of the television, seated at a small desk, would be the Flight Commander, flanked by the corporal and sergeant. When the corporal read out a name, the individual would spring to attention, repeat his name and the last three digits of his Service Number, march forward, watch his money being counted out by the officer, initial a sheet, pick up the money, salute, turn about and return to his place.

This would be repeated up to 80 times, maybe more, as the sergeant admonished anyone whose drill was unacceptable and made them do it again.

The first to receive their cash were the handful of senior apprentices who lived in the block. They then had to watch about 70 of their juniors receive twice as much. By the time I, two thirds of the way down the list, shouted, 'Powell 348,' and marched forward to receive my cash, they were thoroughly hacked off.

In this way, the festering wound of our disparity in pay was opened every two weeks to have salt rubbed in it. As a result, in the early days at least, there were frequent raids by the senior entries, during which rooms were trashed and people who resisted too energetically were beaten up. It could be a brutal place.

I managed to avoid most of the physical confrontations. It just wasn't my way, and anyway, others were less reticent. The tougher members of my entry gave as good as they got. More than that.

We were the largest entry for several years. Despite the small number who'd left for a variety of reasons, there were still more than 130 of us, while the 122s numbered no more than about 20. And once the 231s and 120s passed out, we outnumbered the 121s and 122s combined. So, as the months passed and our esprit de corps grew, we were raided by others only rarely. We still used to raid one another's rooms, mainly with pillows though, rather than fists.

At social events such as the weekly discos, there could be quite a few fights. I also kept well clear of these, although I was once sitting next to a roommate who was hit over the head with a Newcastle Brown bottle by someone from a senior entry. Blood, gush, spurt, and a visit to the Medical Centre for stitches.

I appeared as a witness at the miscreant's charge hearing. If my memory serves me right, he received a £25 fine and seven days' jankers, leniency that surprised many of us, especially as one of our entry caught leaving the WRAF Block, a crime that seemed to us to be far less heinous, had just received a £50 fine and 14 days' jankers.

The guilty party in the assault case also received more brutal summary justice. He was beaten up by the hard men from our entry. It was just the way it was.

Until I went to Halton, I thought religious sectarianism was an Irish phenomenon. But I soon discovered it was also rife in Scotland and some English cities, such as Liverpool and Coventry. And with the large number of Scots in our entry, it found its way to Halton, with frequent taunting, and some fights between the Protestant and Catholic Scots, usually on the anniversary of some ancient battle that meant little to the rest of us.

I don't remember the three apprentices from Ireland getting involved. Of the two from Northern Ireland, one was Catholic, the other Protestant, and as far as I know, there was never any trouble between them.

They faced risks the rest of us didn't have to worry about, though. If some in their home towns discovered they were in the RAF, their lives, and those of their families, would be in jeopardy.

The one concession they had was to grow their hair beyond regulation length before they went on leave. It was hoped that this would prevent them being marked out as Servicemen. In at least one case, it didn't. But, perhaps surprisingly, it was the Protestant lad who was 'outed', and who had to stop going home.

I don't know whether the lad from the Irish Republic faced similar problems. He went on to become a Jaguar pilot. Last time I saw him, in the late 1990s, he was a wing commander.

Although the clue was in the title, Number 1 *School* of Technical Training, many of us were surprised to find out just how like a school RAF Halton was, a boarding school with very harsh living conditions and discipline. One thing that added to the impression, and something I'd forgotten until I read my letters, was 'lights out'.

Just like many a school dormitory, the room lights were switched off at a set time, presumably by the senior apprentice. I don't remember what time he did it, but however early or late, it sounds a bit Dickensian. I don't remember coming across the practise after Halton.

If lights out didn't cause me great anguish, another issue did. We had bull nights and inspections on Friday nights, and drill on Saturdays, or at least Saturday mornings. This left no time to get to Ludlow and back in what remained of the weekend.

I seriously considered quitting because of it.

But the country was in the middle of Ted Heath's conflict with the miners, and the resulting power shortages meant a three day working week for some industries, frequent power cuts and no trains on Sundays. So, I couldn't get home and back over a weekend anyway.

While several others decided to call it a day there and then, I resolved to stay and see how things developed – and to save for a car.

So far, I seem to have painted an unremittingly negative picture of Halton, and my reaction to it. Overly so. Perhaps it's because, initially, the infrequent examples of violence and intolerance made the strongest impression on me, a simple country lad.

But the shock of the accommodation and harsh discipline eventually began to wear off; I made new friendships, a couple that have stood the test of the subsequent 40 years; and I began to feel more at home and to enjoy myself.

Then, a few weeks into 1974, it was decided we would work only one Saturday morning a month, for route lining practices, plus the odd weekend needed to prepare for specific royal events. In practise, we rarely worked weekends at all.

There were still times over the next three years when I was thoroughly fed up, and small numbers continued to withdraw from training, but I don't think I ever seriously considered throwing my hand in after those first few weeks. For me, the positives outweighed the negatives.

One of the positives turned out to be our professional studies, which were initially divided into two complementary areas: academic and trade training.

On weekday mornings during our first 18 months, we had lessons in Schools (Kermode Hall). These academic studies were to lead us toward an Ordinary National Certificate in Engineering. The subjects covered were Maths, Mechanics, Aerodynamics, Electrics, Engineering Drawing, Materials and Structures, Applied Mechanics, Applied Heat and General Studies.

At first sight, given my poor performance at school, I found the prospect of all this study extremely daunting, and the weight of text books we received in the first few days did nothing to allay my fears. But, as time went on, I became genuinely interested in the subjects. They seemed so relevant to our trade training. I even gained a reputation as a bit of an inky swot, something that would have astounded the teachers at Ludlow Grammar School.

The highlights of the Schools curriculum for me were the practical sessions in the aerodynamic and engine laboratories, working with aerofoils in the wind tunnels, or running engines to measure the efficiency of various configurations and fuels. The laboratories even had assistants in white coats similar to those I'd seen in various war films, like The Dam Busters. It was great stuff.

I also enjoyed General Studies. I think the aim was to improve our communication skills through writing about and discussing topics such as domestic and international politics and military issues. The teacher, Flight Lieutenant Thomas, was very idiosyncratic, a Colonel Blimp figure, but he taught me how to develop arguments and commit them to paper, a skill that would become increasingly important as my career developed.

Once a week, we also had Padre's Hour.

Over the years, I've found the mix of religion and war increasingly distasteful, to the point where I now shun the purely religious elements of remembrance events, as well as visits to church services, unless they're linked to weddings or the burial of old friends.

But although taken by priests in uniform, Padre's Hours never peddled an overtly religious message. Rather, they allowed an exploration of moral issues relating to society and war. This was done in a relaxed atmosphere, free of the pressures of rank and conformity that could be found in a normal military classroom or lecture hall. I invariably found them both interesting and thought-provoking.

In 2011, an ex-head of the Army, General Sir Richard Dannatt, bemoaned the lack of such training in the Armed Services. I can only think that Padre's Hours have been cut to provide financial savings. I certainly attended them after Halton, during officer training, and it's sad if current Servicemen and women don't have the same opportunity.

Alongside academic study, there were hours of physical training in the various gymnasia at Halton. There was also an adventurous training week in North Wales, the subject of a Station magazine cutting in my scrap book. The week, in July, involved miles of hill walking between camp sites to experience activities such as canoeing, climbing and mountain rescue training.

It was a warm summer and there were several cases of heat exhaustion as we struggled over the hilly terrain around Aran Fawddy. I could barely lift my load of 60lbs, and if I slipped, which I did on a few occasions, I was stuck on my back like a turtle until someone gave me a hand up.

A few years later, among the many things I admired about the British troops who yomped across the

Falklands, was that they were carrying twice the weight I'd barely managed at a similar age.

The magazine cutting has a picture of me at the front of a stretcher carrying a simulated casualty down a Welsh hillside, another back-breaking experience. The poor chap had just been lowered down a sheer cliff, another incident caught on camera. He looks terrified.

We had the opportunity to try rock climbing and abseiling, which I really enjoyed, and then spent a day canoeing on Lake Bala, which I also enjoyed, once the obligatory capsize drills were out of the way.

My chief memory of the canoeing is that we were instructed by Warrant Officer Don Cobley, an Olympic canoeist. The prize for the best canoeist of the day was a go in his racing canoe. It was as thin as a thin thing, tapering from a narrow cockpit to sit on the water on a knife edge.

The prize wasn't as good as it sounds, because the winner, and every other mere mortal that had a go, wobbled on the knife edge and rolled into the water before they could make a single stroke. Just to prove it could be done, Don Cobley finally hopped in and paddled majestically away.

In the late spring of 1975, nearly 50 of our entry, about one third, failed the major ONC exams. The system was rocked by such a high failure rate and an inquiry was held into the reasons behind it, and to decide what to do with those that had failed. They couldn't graduate without an ONC.

I don't know whether the inquiry found any fault with the teaching, but the offending apprentices were dealt with in a variety of ways. Some were allowed to take immediate re-sits and rejoin the entry, some were sent to the other side of the Station to train as single trade fitters or mechanics, and a small number were discharged from the Service.

A group of 18, including one of my Christmas card buddies, David Griffiths – who admits he failed because he spent too much time in the bar – became a sub-entry, the 123/As.

Forever known as the Stroke As, and immensely proud of their moniker, they were the only sub-entry ever formed at Halton. After six weeks' revision, they re-sat their exams and carried on their trade training to pass out six weeks behind the rest of us.

Being a Stroke A seemed not to do David too much harm in the long term. He went on to become an engineering officer and retired as a wing commander.

With the completion of our ONCs, we began spending all day on trade training in the workshops or on the airfield, learning in earnest to be aircraft engineering technicians, airframe/propulsion (AEngTech A/Ps).

The curriculum was wide-ranging, involving both classroom and practical study. I still have a hardback A4 notebook, its blue cover bearing in black typeface: RAF Form 619A, Royal Air Force Notebook For Use In Schools And Colleges (Cadets and Apprentices). I used it to make notes during lessons on subjects that are too numerous to list, but included, Basic Engineering, Theory and Practical; Documentation and Organization; Gas Turbines; Piston Engines; Propellers; Rigging, Hydraulics and Wheels; Aircraft Systems; Aircraft Controls; and Cabin Environment.

To take just Cabin Environment, it comprised studies in Structures and Aerodynamics; Flying Faults and Performance; Cockpits, Hoods and Canopies; Adhesive Sealing and Glazing Compounds; Cabin

Atmosphere Control; Anti-G Systems and Leak Stoppers; Windscreen Clearing Systems; Anti- and De-icing Systems; Corrosion – Prevention and Remedies; and Non-Destructive Testing.

I could go on – don't worry, I won't – but I hope you get an impression of the breadth and depth of our studies. When I read of Modern Apprenticeships, such as those offered by Macdonalds, I just can't believe they are anything like the same. Somehow, even some of the modern engineering apprenticeships seem slight in comparison. I'm undoubtedly just being old fashioned and sniffy, but there it is.

Unlike many of my close friends back in Ludlow, I'd never had any interest in fiddling with cars or motorbikes, or any other aspect of engineering – none whatsoever. So joining the RAF as an engineering apprentice seems a tremendous gamble, both for the RAF, and for me. But, when they wouldn't have me as a pilot, training as an engineer seemed the next best thing, maybe better, because not only would I get close to the shiny machines I idolized from magazines, but deep inside, among the workings.

And luckily for both of us, I loved it.

I found all the trade-related subjects, theoretical and practical, tremendously interesting. And much to my surprise, and that of my friends at home, I could do the practical stuff. For whatever reason, I could work successfully on aircraft, in a way I couldn't on cars, and still can't.

Perhaps it was all to do with interest, but the structure and formality of aircraft engineering also suited me. Whereas you seemed to need some God-given knowledge to be able to work on a car – my friends just dived under the bonnet or chassis with little or no recourse to a manual - work on aircraft, in the RAF at least, is only undertaken as laid down in an Aircraft Publication.

To achieve the end result, you might still have to use no end of initiative – struggling to remove or insert items, or even manufacture them – but at least much of the path and the required end state were formally laid out.

And I enjoyed the basic engineering, taking a piece of metal and fashioning it into the required shape, drilling and tapping, reaming and milling. Much to my own surprise, I came top of the entry in this element of the course.

Even in 1974, some questioned whether we needed to be able to work with file and set square. Surely, in the era of modern aircraft, we'd be replacing items, not repairing them, or fashioning new ones from scratch? But I think the ability to carry out the most basic of engineering tasks, not only gave us a thorough grounding in our trades, but also a confidence in our abilities that was priceless. It may be that many of my contemporaries went to work on aircraft where these basic skills weren't needed, but I suspect I was one of many who had to use them for real, and much more often than I could have imagined.

With the fundamentals of metalwork under our belts, we moved on to aircraft engineering. It was all sensibly incremental. You learned the theory in the classroom and then transferred to the workshops, practising on the various aircraft and engines.

The workshops were a veritable treasure trove of old aircraft. These ranged from the positively ancient, like Piston Provosts, Vampires and Meteors, to the most recently retired, such as Javelins and Sea Vixens, and some that were, at that time, still in service, such as Hunters and Jet Provosts. We worked on their airframes and the hydraulic systems that operated their flying controls and undercarriages, and removed and refitted their engines.

The workshops were also an Aladdin's Cave, full of kit from the earliest years of aviation right up to bits from the recently cancelled TSR2. We spent much time working on old stuff, including rotary and in-line piston engines, again with people questioning the need in the jet era. But, once more, I was to find it invaluable.

Eventually, we graduated to the airfield and aircraft that actually moved, if you fixed them properly. Most were Jet Provosts, the jet I would fly in pilot training several years later. Certainly, this was the type from which we first removed and then refitted an engine.

I can still remember the tension when, having finished the job, we stood to one side and watched the instructor climb into the cockpit.

With our handiwork sitting just behind him, he pressed the start button. It was the first true inkling of the awesome responsibility of working on an aircraft someone else was going to fly. Although their was no intention of flying in this case, the fact that the engine started without blowing up was another great boost to our confidence.

Another high spot was a week-long visit to a front-line RAF station, in my case, Odiham, the home of the RAF's Puma battlefield helicopters. Here, I moved between sections, gaining experience of the working conditions and practices I'd encounter in the 'real' Air Force. I remember only three elements of the week with any clarity.

The first is working in the Blade Bay, where Puma rotor blades were serviced. The blades had rubber de-icing sleeves running along their leading edges. These could be inflated with pulses of high pressure air to prevent ice build up on the blades, especially important as the Pumas spent a lot of time exercising in Norway. The sleeves were attached with strong adhesive, and the smell was overpowering. I don't remember me or anyone else wearing any breathing protection, and I certainly had a headache by the evening.

Several years later when stories of teenagers sniffing glue started to hit the headlines, I thought back to that day and wondered how high I'd been by the end of it, and how high the rest of them probably were every day.

The second memory is of working alongside tradesmen completing routine servicings. I thoroughly enjoyed myself, even devising an improved method for the tricky task of inserting grommets round the base of Puma fuselages to stop moisture ingress. I discovered they went in easier if first soaked in silicone oil.

The final memory is of a short air test in a Puma. Having worked on them all week, it was great to launch into the air in one, if only briefly.

Back at Halton, the airfield became our simulator, representing life on an RAF squadron and station. Here, we brought together all the threads we'd learned: routine servicing, fault analysis, fault rectification and testing, and filling in the paperwork that went with all these tasks. We even got to start up and taxy the Jet Provosts ourselves, following the directions of our mates, waving their arms to practise their aircraft marshalling skills.

I'm biased of course, but I think it was a marvellous

education.

When we worked on the airfield, we travelled to work by bus. But, at 8 o'clock on every other working day of the three years at Halton, we marched three quarters of a mile or so down the hill from the Apprentice Wing, across the B4009 into Chestnut Avenue and on to either Workshops or Schools. And we did so behind our own Apprentice Pipe Band. At lunchtime, we marched back up the hill, then down again after lunch, and up again at 5 o'clock in the evening, all to the same accompaniment of mainly traditional Scottish tunes, such as Scottish Soldier.

Allowing for weekends, leave and detachments, and discounting ceremonial occasions, I must have marched to work behind that band some 2,000 times, covering well over 1,000 miles over the three years.

At the time of course, the pipes and drums came to be associated with this daily plod to work, often in bad weather. And after a night on the beer, the caterwauling could be absolute torture. But since leaving Halton, I find that the first note from a set of pipes makes my skin prickle and my heart race with pleasure.

Be it from a pipe band or a lone busker, I love it. During a holiday in Scotland with my young family, I found hearing the massed pipes and drums at the Edinburgh Tattoo a magical, near spiritual, experience.

Toward the end of my career, I had the privilege of attending the annual dinners of the three Scottish University Air Squadrons. One of the things that sets them apart from their English and Welsh counterparts is the tradition of piping in the port, the fortified wine used for after-dinner toasts.

On all three occasions, at the first sight and sound

of the piper, I struggled to control my emotions. Anyone observing me would probably have assumed I was merely caught up in the moment. And to a point, they would have been right. Such occasions were stirring and emotional. But I was also reliving the daily march up and down the hill at Halton 30 years earlier.

One of the routine duties arising from this march to work was the intriguingly named Dalek Drill.

Approaching the point where the parade route crossed the busy B4009 were road signs warning, 'STOP – CHILDREN AND TROOPS CROSSING.'

These were deemed insufficient to protect us from speeding vans and commuters, especially on dark winter days. So, as the column of marching apprentices approached the bottom of the hill, four members of the junior entry had to wheel two large, Dalek-like, objects with flashing lights into the road to form a physical barrier.

Placing the Daleks in front of impatient drivers could be quite hairy, and they could become visibly frustrated as first the band and then hundreds of apprentices marched between the small protective cordon. They didn't know how lucky they were. The congestion could have been much worse. As they drummed their fingers, a few hundred yards away, hundreds of personnel from the other side of the Station were marching or walking to work beneath the road, via an underpass.

Even when the winter of discontent was over, it wasn't easy for me to get to Ludlow and back.

Eventually, I established a pattern of travelling by train to Shrewsbury on a Friday night, arriving at about 9 o'clock. There, Nick would pick me up and drive me the 30 miles to Ludlow, where we'd head for a pub or, often, the Overton Grange Hotel, just to the south of the town.

Pub closing time then was 10.30pm every night except Saturday, when it was 11pm. Most landlords were strict about this, but not all. If you were already on the premises, you could often get a drink after hours, even be locked in for some real late night drinking if it was that sort of pub. The key was to get into the bar by about 10pm.

The travelling was very time-consuming, partly because the trains especially were unreliable, with frequent delays and cancellations. But I obviously found the few hours in Ludlow worth the hassle. I enjoyed seeing my family, and Nick, Andy and Simon, when he was home from university. On Saturday evenings, we invariably went to the pub, or pubs.

Ludlow also seemed to provide the opportunity to meet more girls, although I remained stubbornly 'single', while Nick, Simon and Andy all found long term girlfriends, and then wives. I was best man at Nick's wedding in May 1976, Simon's in July the same year, and Andy's a few years later, in September 1979.

Early on a Sunday afternoon, I'd catch the National Express bus from Ludlow to Aylesbury, via Leominster and Cheltenham, price £1.40. I'd then take a local bus to Halton or Wendover, and walk the couple of miles or so to the Apprentice Wing.

All bar one of the eleven route linings I completed were for visiting heads of state. I've lost the diaries covering most of the period, but one was for Queen Juliana of the Netherlands, and the last, in September 1976, was for the President of France, Valéry Giscard d'Estaing.

The exception was a state funeral. We practised for these on occasion, with the most likely candidate thought to be The Queen Mother. As you'll be only too aware, she well and truly dislocated any expectation of her demise in the 1970s, and I met her twice before her eventual death in 2002.

The state funeral at which we did perform followed the death of the Duke of Gloucester in June 1974. It took place in Windsor.

There were several differences between a funeral and a normal route lining. Much of the marching was in slow time, which is trickier and more tiring than marching in quick time, and we spent longer on the streets, about five hours rather than two or three. And, as the cortège passed, we had to rest on our arms reversed, which meant rotating our rifles and lowering them until the barrels rested on one of our shoes, then bowing our heads above the butts.

It's hard to convey how difficult it is to stand motionless for any length of time, especially for someone like me. I'm still a complete fidget, always twitching or hopping from foot to foot, but I was even worse in my late teens and early twenties. And we had to stand stock still, with no shuffling, flexing or grimacing, and no scratching of itches.

Just try and stand motionless in front of a clock for five minutes, one even, and I think you'll get an inkling of what it was like. Now, imagine doing it for most of five hours, standing in summer temperatures in a thick uniform, wearing a hat and holding a rifle, under the beady eyes of thousands of onlookers on the streets, maybe millions on television, but also your drill instructors and flight commanders, and, ultimately, if only for a brief time, the Royal Family.

To try and gain some relief, we were taught to tense and relax our muscles, and to rock gently back and forward on the balls of our feet, but I spent most of the time just yearning for the next drill movement to relieve the boredom, the agony even, of remaining still. I often think of this as I watch the young servicemen and women taking part in ceremonial now. There's always pain behind the pageantry.

In August 1974, I improved the time, if not the safety, of my journeys to and from Ludlow. Under Nick's guidance, I bought my first car, a light blue Ford Anglia, from an auction. It cost £40 and was a death trap, with a 1500cc engine in a standard body.

It had inefficient brakes and papier mâché wings. Seriously, if you squatted down and looked under the wheel arches, you could read the headlines for the day the newspaper had been covered with fibreglass resin, its upper surface smoothed and painted.

Unsurprisingly, no-one would insure the car until a standard 950cc engine was installed, at extra cost. This was an early introduction to the expense of car ownership. There was always a bill to pay, and I was forever on the brink of insolvency. From my letters, I was surprised at just how many times I borrowed money from my parents, and how long it took me to save up for car insurance and the like.

In April 1975, my finances weren't helped by an unbudgeted payment of £5.91 to Cherwell District Council, for *re-fixing of gate post and hanging of gate*.

The Anglia had nothing as posh as a fitted radio, so I used to balance a transistor on my RAF holdall on the passenger seat. Driving through the twisty village of Aynho near Banbury one Sunday evening, the bag and radio began to topple off. I lunged across to save them,

150

taking the steering wheel with me.

Stupid boy.

After a series of evermore eccentric swerves, I ended up on the verge and demolished a garden gate. The owners were remarkably understanding, and I was lucky no cars had been travelling in the opposite direction.

Six months before leaving Halton, I bought a newer car, a 1963 MG 1100 for £185. It was better than the Anglia, but not without its problems, including an undetectable hole that allowed rainwater to fill the passenger footwell. The only solution – without the unaffordable intervention of a garage - was to drill holes in the floor to let the water out.

This ploy was successful up to a point, but the inside of the car was always wet. One day, driving down the M69, the roof lining, so damp its adhesive had given up the ghost, fell down over my head. Luckily, I managed to fight it off and stop safely.

For several more months, I drove a car with no roof lining, and holes in the floor to let the rainwater out. When I started taking my future wife out in it, she was very impressed!

During the last 18 months at Halton, I used to spend at least some weekends with Simon and his girlfriend, Jane, in Leicester, where they were both students. The contrast between their lifestyle and mine was stark.

While, at 8 o'clock each weekday morning, I was marching to work behind the pipe band, they were enjoying what seemed to me to be the life of Riley, with long lie-ins, leisurely afternoons and wild nights. And while I was polishing the floors, walls and toilet pans of my barrack block, their shared student digs seemed to be totally relaxed, with little or no evidence of cleaning, or even washing up.

Like most people I guess, I've always said I wouldn't have lived my life any other way. But, when comparing lifestyles with Simon, I can't believe I didn't have doubts. And since, having spent much of my career working with undergraduates and graduates, I've often wondered how things would have turned out if I'd worked harder at school and gone down the university route.

But even back then, I knew I was living my dream of being in the RAF and working with aircraft, even if it was proving a bloody hard school. Later, when I eventually became a pilot, I felt even more content at the route I'd followed.

Although Simon eventually dropped out of university, I'm not sure he'd have changed anything either. He married Jane and went on to join the Police, enjoying a career almost as long as mine in the RAF. I often wonder if his career choice could be linked to an incident on August Bank Holiday Monday, 1975.

Late that night, Simon and I were in Ludlow, making our way home from the Queen's Head, a pub where he worked as a barman in his university vacations. At East Hamlet, a junction just outside the Dodmore Estate where we usually went our separate ways, we came upon a mini riot. In the orange glow of street lamps, a young man was trapped on the ground.

He was surrounded by a group of youths, all of whom seemed to be kicking him. We recognised some of them, including one particularly vicious character who was kicking the prone man's head as if it was a football. Two other groups of young men and women were on the periphery, exchanging violent threats and abuse.

I'd like to think Simon and I would have jumped to the victim's aid, but I don't think it would have been likely; there were just too many attackers and we'd have feared becoming victims ourselves. But we were saved from facing our cowardice when the Police arrived and the assailants began dispersing, running off in all directions.

At this point, we jumped into action, helping round up at least some of those involved. It was great fun, and, in the early hours of the next morning, we went on to make statements at Ludlow Police Station.

Such was the confusion on the night that I don't think we feared being identified and singled out for retribution, but six weeks later, we were asked to attend a Magistrates' Court as prosecution witnesses. Then, I at least began to think that we might have to watch our backs when we visited Ludlow in future. But, once again, we were saved when it was decided the prosecution case was strong enough without our evidence, and we were stood down before the hearing.

I still have the local newspaper report of the case. It seems it was an inter-family dispute, as a result of which several youths received fines ranging from £50 to £70, and were bound over to keep the peace for two years in the sum of £100.

I suspect that night may have led Simon to consider joining the Police.

In Leicester, his student house was in a long, Coronation Street-like terrace on an unadopted road of cobbles and potholes in the red light district. Opposite, were three houses of prostitutes, one of whom was famous, or infamous, having featured in the News of the World. I still have the cutting.

On return from the pub or a concert on a Saturday

night – I was lucky enough to see the Who in their pomp, and Eric Clapton – we used to creep upstairs and stare through a window at the comings and goings across the road. We'd watch men walk past the windows behind which the women sat bathed in red lighting, and try to work out what the signals they exchanged meant. We guessed they related to the menu of services on offer and the cost. If and when a deal was struck, we'd time the length of the man's stay, then work out the likely sum the women were earning in a night, a week, a month, a year.

Simon said they used to vary the price depending on the look of the potential client, and even turn some down. He also said he'd seen local dignitaries entering the houses.

Inevitably, there was tragedy behind what we perceived largely as comedy. After their pimps had been round, the women often sported black eyes. But it was all remarkably open, and they'd chat freely about their trade with the owner of the corner shop.

It was quite an eye-opener for a Shropshire lad.

At Halton, as well as the timetabled activities, we often had homework, revising for frequent tests and more formal exams. But we still had free time in the evenings and, for those that didn't go home at weekends, these two days also had to be filled. Much like a good boarding school or university, Halton offered plenty of extracurricular activities, anything from music – there were several pop groups and a brass band in addition to the pipe band – to things such as chess, stamp collecting and model-making.

There was also an amateur dramatic society, but I never pursued my childhood interest in acting. I did go on a theatre trip to London though, to a racy play called Pyjama Tops, starring a top shelf model called Fiona Richmond. The set was dominated by a glass-fronted swimming pool, effectively a large fish tank, and the script provided frequent opportunities for Miss Richmond and several other young women to strip and go for a swim.

I don't remember the plot.

Halton also had an annual air show, my first opportunity to see displays by military aircraft. All were impressive, but the highlight was the Red Arrows, as magnificent in their red Gnats then as they are in their red Hawks now. Seeing them produced a feeling of great pride. It still does. They've always exemplified what is best about the RAF.

At the time, of course, I had no idea that I'd get to know many of the Team's future pilots, even have a hand in teaching some of them to fly, or that I'd eventually take to the skies in one of their display practices.

As a Senior Apprentice during my final year, I had a room to myself, and I began to spend more of my free time in the barrack block, uninterrupted by the noise pollution of 14 other people. It was so much easier to listen to music – my favourite band was Yes – and to read – mainly science fiction still.

Not that communal living didn't have its benefits. It certainly exposed me to a wide variety of tastes. I was introduced to bands as different as Rainbow, Wings and The Real Thing, comedians like Blaster Bates and Billy Connelly, and books such as The Lord of the Rings. David Griffiths says he still thinks of me every time he plays the album Argus by Wishbone Ash, to which I introduced him, or did its frequent playing just brainwash him?

But, when not in the barrack block or the bar, at the Station cinema or the weekly discos, most of my free time was taken up with sport.

After seven years of enforced rugby at Ludlow Grammar, I relished the opportunity to play soccer again. I began attending training one evening a week, and was soon playing for the Station teams on Wednesday afternoons, usually the Second XI, but sometimes the Firsts. I played to left or right of midfield, where, blowing my own trumpet, my tenacity and fitness were my greatest assets.

At least one evening a week, I represented the Flight or Apprentice Wing in various competitions. My diary and letters mention outings to play badminton, basketball, cricket, cross country, hockey, 7-a-side rugby, soccer, softball, squash and volleyball.

I'd never even played hockey before, but my natural hand-eye coordination, and the positional sense gained from rugby and soccer, seemed to allow me to contribute without making too much of a fool of myself. And having thought it was a bit of a game for cissies, I soon discovered how hard a hockey ball was, and how much it hurt when it hit your shins, or the softer, fleshier, parts of your anatomy.

Some weeks, in addition to timetabled PT and soccer matches, I played sport every evening. Unsurprisingly, I was often bruised and sore, but the worst injuries were the previously mentioned broken finger, and skinned thighs and calves from sliding too enthusiastically toward softball bases.

One story from this period sums up Service life for me.

Seven or eight of us went to the gym one evening to play basketball for 7 Flight in one of the evening knock-out tournaments. We won the event, and were just about to leave the gym with our medals when we were approached by a very muscular physical training instructor.

Corporal Taff Davies had recently arrived at Halton and been disappointed to find there was no Station volleyball team. He decided to form one.

'You are now the Station volleyball team,' he informed us.

In any other walk of life, he might have been told where to go, but we just did as we were told. So, that was another two evenings a week, one for training and one for matches all over Buckinghamshire.

I took to the game immediately, and 18 months later, I and three other members of the Flight basketball team were playing volleyball for the county.

After Halton, I never played at this level again, but I continued to turn out for various station teams long after I'd stopped playing other sports. I played my last truly competitive game at the age of 36, and all because of that press-ganging nearly 20 years earlier.

Playing alongside us for Buckinghamshire was a prisoner from Grendon Underwood Prison. We were told he was a murderer. Whether this was a wind-up or not, I'm not sure. None of us had the balls to ask him. Whatever his crime, he used to arrive, play and depart under the watchful eye of two plain-clothes warders.

The prison team of which he was a member competed in the local volleyball league. They only played home matches of course, so we visited the prison a couple of times a season. It was one of the stranger places in which I've played.

On the way to the prison gym, the imposing main gate and several other doors would be slammed and locked behind us. The process always made us nervous, triggering the irrational fear that we were trapped, never to be released. The tension was still there as we stepped onto court.

Apart from the 'murderer', we had no idea what crimes the spectators and other members of the prison team had committed, or how they'd react if we got the better of them. As it turned out, this was never a problem, because we never came to terms with the playing conditions.

Most gyms have lofty ceilings, and we'd been trained to set the ball high into the air, so our 'spikers' could run in, jump, and slam it into the ground on the opponent's side of the net. But the prison gym ceiling was no more than 15 feet high, and we invariably set the ball into it, an immediate foul.

We were always trounced, and never had the opportunity to face the prisoners in a gym more to our advantage. On the other hand, we never had to find out how they'd deal with defeat.

I for one was always mightily relieved to get out of the place.

Two of my flight colleagues made it into the RAF volleyball squad, which played in the national league. With greater dedication, I might have done the same, but RAF training took place at weekends, and I enjoyed going home too much to take part in anything other than infrequent tournaments representing Halton.

In 1976, we played a 24 hour volleyball marathon at Stoke Mandeville Hospital to raise money for the UK amputee team bound for the Disabled Olympiad in Toronto, the forerunner of the Paralympics. Each player had to spend at least 16 hours on court, and the standard of play from all teams was high, with no quarter given, or expected.

Most of the amputee team seemed to be missing

more than one limb, in any combination of arms and legs. Those missing legs seemed to suffer most. After prolonged periods of play, their stumps became sweaty, leading to chafing where they mated with their prosthetic limb. This meant frequent changes of leg, and much black humour.

It's difficult not to sound patronising, but the courage and determination shown by all the amputees put our able-bodied efforts in the shade.

Once a year, we had an exchange sports day with the Army Apprentices of the Corps of Royal Electrical and Mechanical Engineers. The competition included encounters at almost every competitive sport, from Archery to Volleyball, and led to the award of a trophy for the overall winners. In 1974, the competition was held at the Army Apprentice's base at Arborfield, near Reading, in Berkshire.

I've already mentioned the contrast between the lifestyle of my friend Simon at Leicester University, and my own, harsher, conditions at Halton. Well, on my first visit to Arborfield, I was greeted with another contrast. We moaned about our barrack blocks, having our hair cut, the drill and the discipline. But, in comparison with the Army Apprentices, we were lucky.

They lived in long lines of corrugated iron Nissen Huts. I never saw inside one, but I can't believe the living conditions were as good as ours.

They also had to march everywhere, even in civilian clothes, and their hair was cut so short they reminded me of the skinheads that still plagued parts of the country. And there always seemed to be a corporal on hand to bawl at them, often for reasons that seemed obscure to us.

Their defaulters, of which there were many, were shaven-headed, stripped of belts and bootlaces, pushing wheelbarrows of rocks under the one-on-one supervision of red-faced NCOs, bundles of swearing malevolence, forehead veins throbbing like men on the verge of heart attacks as they shouted and threatened.

From the moment we arrived, we felt uneasy. We walked around in large groups, as if fearful of being separated from one another, never to be seen again. The unease turned to downright terror when we were shouted at for not walking smartly enough, even though we were in civvies. We feared arrest for breaching some minor rule of which we were ignorant, and being left to face Army justice while our friends returned to Halton.

I have to watch what I say during this era of political correctness and Jointery - jargon for closer and closer association between the three services - but I've always been very glad I joined the RAF rather than the Army. Both services are made up of fine individuals who are extremely good at what they do, but they're very different in character and outlook.

The Navy and RAF are, in many ways, similar; although, measuring their lifespan in centuries rather than decades, they'd put it the other way round. They also say that whereas they have traditions, we merely have bad habits!

Neither the Senior nor the Junior Service enjoys hardship. The Army does. They would walk through a comfortable hotel to sleep in a muddy hole in its garden. The RAF would stay in the hotel. Put another way, while the Army dig in, the RAF check in. For this, the Army detests us.

There are good reasons for the difference in

attitude, one being that they have to be prepared to live in muddy holes close to the enemy, so they prefer not to soften themselves by getting used to hotels. I understand.

But staying in muddy holes also saves pots of money, which is attractive to governments. They love Jointery. It almost invariably means Army control, which means we all sleep in muddy holes, saving on hotel bills. Okay, I exaggerate, but only slightly; at the best, it means we all live in tents.

My view is that if you send young men and women into harm's way, you have a duty to accommodate them decently whenever possible, and that may mean a hotel rather than a tent. This is especially true if you need them to be sufficiently rested to work on and fly aircraft with maximum safety.

I'm pretty sure the Army won the sports day at Arborfield in 1974, and the return leg at Halton in 1975. Back at Arborfield in 1976, however, when we were the senior entry and made up the bulk of the teams for most sports, we trounced them. This is the year of which I have most vivid memories.

The Army had run a series of recruitment adverts on television which Billy Connelly had parodied. *My name's Bob and I drive tanks. I earn £40 a week and I keep it all to meself 'cos I'm a selfish bastard,* or: *My name's George and I fire a rifle. I earn 30 quid a week, and I spend it all on Smarties. You can buy thahsands and thahsands of Smarties for 30 quid a week.*

We stocked up on Smarties and spent much of the day throwing them at the Army spectators. Infantile I know, and they generally looked bemused by the whole thing. But we thought we were hilarious.

We also thought the Army officers' dress and behaviour was hilarious.

Our officers dressed in smart jackets, ties, trousers and shoes of various styles and colours, with some in overcoats and rain jackets, also in various styles and colours. Not many beyond our own flight commanders were familiar to us, but they turned out, encouraged and supported us in a sporting way.

The Army officers on the other hand, were startlingly uniform in their civilian attire, favouring regimental blazers and ties, cavalry twill trousers, brown brogue shoes, camel hair coats and, the final flourish, little brown trilby hats.

They also had an exceedingly patronising, sometimes sneering, attitude to their apprentice sportsmen, goading them with stupid nicknames and berating them when they did anything wrong. Not quite the 'Jolly bad luck, old boy,' we'd expected.

Staying in a Parachute Regiment Officers' Mess in the mid-1980s, I chatted to a barman – in fact an ordinary soldier seconded to bar duties – and asked about some cuts on his face. He said he'd received them when he'd been thrown through a window for running out of one particular officer's favourite beer. The window had been shut at the time.

Later that same evening, the soldier was repeatedly belittled, not only by more officers, but by their girlfriends. The rank differential made it impossible for him to answer back or defend himself. Perhaps such behaviour was of its time, but I witnessed less dramatic examples several times during my career. It reminded me of my treatment on my first day at the Grammar School, and I always found it objectionable.

I represented Halton at two sports on the day. I think we lost at volleyball, but won at soccer, one of the showcase sports, and one of the last to take place and cement our victory. So we were in high spirits when we went to the presentation ceremony. All passed off with due decorum until the results had been announced and the trophy lifted.

In a cut glass accent, someone shouted, 'Three cheers for Colonel Tweet.'

The name would probably have been enough to raise the odd guffaw, but, as we waited for someone to shout Hip-hip, to which we were prepared to respond with our Hoorays, the Army all shouted, 'Hip-rah, Hip-rah, Hip-rah. On the 'rah,' the Army officers all raised their little hats in their right hands, beaming widely at the Colonel, who beamed proudly back at them.

It was too much. We fell about in raucous laughter, and threw our remaining Smarties.

Our officers tried to look stern, but the sight of their counterparts lifting their little hats had also proved too much for many of them. They turned their backs. But we could see their shoulders rolling.

Although I continued playing representative volleyball into my 30s, I stopped playing rugby in my early 20s, and soccer at 26 or 27 when, arriving on my Hercules squadron just as the Falklands War began, I was rarely available for training or matches. But I continued to play a wide range of sports in inter-Section competitions right up to my retirement at 50. By that time, I may have displayed more enthusiasm than skill, but I was rarely surplus to requirements.

The RAF was as committed as ever towards sport as a way of improving overall fitness and operational efficiency, and timetabled sport and fitness training continued to thrive. But it became increasingly difficult to entice people onto the sports fields after work. And perversely, a major part of the problem was the improvement in Service life.

When I lived in a 14-man room, or even after Halton, a 4-man room, I was only too glad to get out and find something to do, in my case, inter-Section sport. Now, most young airmen and women live in well-appointed single rooms with their own television and computer, etc. Why would they want to leave this comfortable environment to run around a cold gym or sports field?

I'm not advocating a return to multi-man rooms or compulsory cold showers, but the relative comfort of modern living conditions is a factor in the difficulty of raising sports teams.

On the plus side, it meant I invariably made the team.

I haven't played any organized sport since leaving the RAF. This is partly due to a hip problem which manifested itself after I'd run the London Marathon for the third time at the age of 47.

At Halton, any time not taken up with academic study or sport was devoted to drinking.

Others may have a different assessment, but in my eyes, my greatest weakness has been alcohol. I've rarely gambled, never beaten my wife, or anyone else come to that, but I have often drunk alcohol to excess. And it all started in earnest at Halton.

Our barrack block was opposite the NAAFI, a building containing a shop selling everything from food to electrical goods, a cafeteria and a large hall for the weekly disco or dance. It also had a bar.

The rules on underage drinking were strictly enforced in the NAAFI. Very few of my entry were over 18 years of age, but a roommate, Mike 'Sandy' Sanderson, and I were. Within a short time, we were drinking up to eight pints of beer a night. And, in my case at least, not draft beer, but bottles of Newcastle Brown Ale, a concoction reputed to go a long way towards filling the hospital wards in the city where it's brewed.

Perhaps we felt we had to make up for those in our entry denied the privilege of drinking. In my case, there was certainly an element of making up for my teenage years in Ludlow when, because of my youthful appearance, I'd been unable to drink in pubs with my mates. Whatever the reason, Sandy and I settled into a routine of drinking prodigious volumes of alcohol.

On the plus side, it left me with a lifelong friend.

Sandy was a great rugby player, and, as well as drinking with him in the NAAFI, I used to join with him at the Rugby Club in preference to spending time with my soccer teammates. We also used to spend two weeks of our summer leave together, Sandy visiting me for a week in Ludlow, and me visiting him for a week in Neyland, near Pembroke Dock in west Wales. Re-reading my letters, I was surprised to see how often he also accompanied me home for weekends in Ludlow.

After Halton, we were both posted to the same base in Lincolnshire, only being parted two and a half years later when I went off to train as an officer and a pilot. Three years after that, we met up again at Lyneham, where I was a Hercules co-pilot when Sandy arrived as a sergeant, but our differing work locations and lifestyles, and the demands of young families meant we met only infrequently. I was soon posted away and we never served on the same base again, although we remained Christmas card buddies.

Then, on a Friday evening in November 2005, soon after I'd retired to South Wales, we had a chance meeting on the streets of Cardiff. With wives, we were both going to an international rugby match in the Millennium Stadium. Before the same fixture in subsequent years, we'd meet for a meal and a drink or three.

By this time, Sandy was a Warrant Officer at Lyneham. Approaching retirement, he and his wife were debating whether to settle in Pembrokeshire or Cardiff. During their deliberations, they spent a weekend with us on Barry Island. To cut a long story short, they bought a house 500 yards from ours.

One of the proudest moments of my life was attending Sandy's retirement lunch in the Sergeants' Mess at Lyneham in May 2010.

Thirty seven years earlier at Halton, after a few months of heavy drinking, we began to realise it was becoming a problem. Every so often, we, or at least I, would switch to milk rather than beer, and one of my letters refers to the ribbing I received when taking milk into the bar. I wish I could say I drank more pints of milk than beer over the years, but it wouldn't be true.

I'm not sure it's the same now, but for much of my Service career, drink was seen as a means of bonding individuals and units together, and of relieving stress. Most courses started with a meet and greet in the bar, and a wind-down beer was a pleasant way to conclude almost any activity, including a hard day at the office or in the cockpit. I was a very happy supporter of this culture.

I was also an enthusiastic supporter of formal black tie events in the Officers' Mess, Dining-In Nights, Guest Nights, Summer Balls and Christmas Draws, occasions with the opportunity for hearty eating and, of course, drinking. But I was also a strong supporter of Happy Hours, a weekly gathering in the Officers' Mess bar at 5 o'clock on a Friday evening to wind down with colleagues and mull over the week's events.

Towards the end of my career, the increasing propensity for Servicemen and women to live outside the wire rather diminished Dining-In Nights and Happy Hours, as people either eschewed the events altogether, or took a quick soft drink before driving home. Very sensible, but I missed the 'crack' of those good old days when everyone stayed in the bar for several beers before walking home to their Married Quarter.

I've tended to distance myself from the Service since retirement, partly because I dread being the old fuddy duddy in the corner saying, 'things just aren't the same, young man.' But they're not. And, in the case of drink, that's probably a good thing.

Since leaving the RAF, I drink a fairly regular 20 units a week. I'm sure the fact that I know this speaks volumes. And yet, when I attend a social function and don't have to drive, I can still drink prodigiously.

I remember two occasions during my service when drink caught me out.

The first was in Denmark when four of us returned to our hotel after a night on the town. With no flying the next day, we settled down to put the world to rights while polishing off a bottle of whisky – and kept our chief flying instructor in the next room awake half the night. A few hours later, I resisted every attempt to wake me and was late for transport, an unforgivable crime in the RAF, and the only time I ever did it. I've rarely touched whisky or any other spirit since.

The second occasion was in Italy, where a nasty crack on the head requiring stitches was brought about by a wet marble floor, a large concrete flower pot and too much of a yellow liqueur called Limoncello, consumed during a stupid drinking game I should have been old enough and ugly enough to avoid.

On these two occasions, I know I made a fool of myself. There were probably other times when I thought I was being the life and soul of the party, but just came across as a drunken prat. For these, I heartily apologise. It won't happen again. Will it?

After that, I better try and establish some professional credentials again.

I ended up doing very well at Halton, certainly better than my school career had promised.

My annual reports say complimentary things about my performance, and my record of conduct was good, which I think is a true reflection; I'd been told to get my haircut a few times, but there'd been precious few other run-ins with authority.

At the halfway point, I'd done well in the Schools exams, coming seventh, and gaining an ONC in Engineering and a City and Guilds certificate for Aeronautical Engineering. And most importantly, I also did well in my Trade Training, gaining consistent high scores in tests and exams, and in my practical work. Overall, I came seventh out of the 100 or so remaining in the main branch of my entry; that is, discounting the Stroke As.

There, I said I was an inky swot.

On Wednesday the 27th of October, 1976, the 123rd Entry of Apprentice Technicians passed out of No 1 School of Technical Training. I received the Quinton Memorial Trophy.

Flight Lieutenant Quinton had been the pilot of an aircraft involved in a mid-air collision. Selflessly, he gave his parachute to an ATC cadet passenger, allowing the youngster to escape a crash in which he was killed. The Quinton Memorial Trophy was awarded to the best apprentice who'd been a cadet in the ATC.

We marched off the square as Junior Technicians in the Airframe and Propulsion trades. The Stroke As followed us six weeks later.

Although I would never have admitted it at the time, I enjoyed the rigidity and robustness of the regime at Halton. As well as a strong sense of camaraderie and pride in being an apprentice and a member of the RAF, I think it also instilled in me a growing self-reliance and self-discipline. I'm embarrassed at writing the words, but I think they're true.

And there was something about completing a demanding three year apprenticeship that prepared you for the long haul in the RAF, and in life. I'm sure that for some, even me, the three years contained many low points, but overall, I think the outcome was strongly positive.

I'm sure it was an expensive way to train young men, many of whom would go on to be commissioned as officers, spending less time than planned fulfilling the hands-on engineering function for which they'd spent three years preparing. The statistics show that about a third of all apprentices became officers at some stage, a few - two of our entry - straight from Halton, most, like me, later in their careers. The rest, those that stayed beyond their nine-year initial commitments, went on to become flight sergeants and warrant officers - the backbone of the Service.

Whether they stayed performing purely engineering tasks or not, I think ex-apprentices more than repaid the investment made in them, bringing to bear the skills, values and qualities their training had instilled to the benefit of the Service. My Halton training was still influential in the way I performed as a group captain 32 years later.

The modern system - training people only for the next task they'll perform - may save money in the short term, but, in my opinion, it misses the larger picture. There is more to a training system than its cost, and it should instil more than mere skill.

Of course, the problem is that the overall benefit of three years at Halton is unquantifiable, whereas the financial difference between the old and new systems is relatively easily measured. And I know from long experience that money is all that matters now, even in public service.

Politicians, senior civil servants and air marshals will always say they take more than the monetary issues into account when making decisions, but in my experience, when savings are highlighted, they're always taken, whatever the cost in others areas, such as welfare and morale.

Anyway, the bottom line is that I feel both I and the Service benefitted greatly from my apprentice training, and that something important was lost when the scheme was discontinued in 1993.

Chapter 6 – The Mighty Vulcan

After a few weeks' leave, I set out from Ludlow on what was to become a familiar car journey through Kidderminster, Birmingham and Leicester. Four miles north of Lincoln, I turned left through a set of large wrought iron gates. The turning was easy to spot: immediately before it, sat a Lancaster bomber. And beneath the bomber sat three large metal objects.

Two were easily recognisable as bombs, if very large bombs. They were examples of the Tallboy and Grand Slam, so called Earthquake bombs, used towards the end of the Second World War against high value targets, such as viaducts, bunkers and the German battleship, Tirpitz. The third object, directly beneath the nose of the Lancaster, looked like a large oil drum resting on its side. But this too was a bomb, a bouncing bomb.

On 16 May 1943, 19 Lancasters of 617 Squadron, each carrying one of these bombs, set out to attack German dams. Two of the dams, the Möhne and Eder, were breached, but nine of the Lancasters failed to return and 53 aircrew were killed. The development of the bomb, and the raid, were described in a 1951 book by Paul Brickhill, and immortalised in a 1955 film with the same title: The Dam Busters.

The base from which the raid had been launched, and onto which I was now driving, was RAF Scampton.

The book and film had been so influential in my childhood that I always felt a tremendous surge of pride as I drove past that Lancaster, something I did many hundreds of times over the years. But the feeling was never more pronounced than on that first occasion, when I was about to begin life as an airframe and propulsion fitter on the base where much of the movie had been filmed. I was 21.

Several others from my entry, including Sandy, were also posted to Scampton, and David Griffiths, my friend from the Stroke As, arrived six weeks later. His introduction to the unit proved that dislocation of expectation wasn't confined to training.

Being fresh out of Halton, they assumed he'd have a smart uniform and shoes, so he was sent straight off to join a guard of honour for the military funeral of a young airman killed in a road accident. Not the start he'd expected.

But I hadn't had the start I'd expected either. The Station operated four Vulcan squadrons: 27; 35; 230 Operational Conversion Unit, the squadron that trained Vulcan aircrew; and 617, who'd returned to Scampton after serving on several other bases since the Second World War. These squadrons were dispersed around the airfield, and I'd expected to be working on one, preparing the aircraft for flight and fixing them when they came back.

Instead, I was sent to one of four large, camouflage-green, hangars in the southeast quadrant of the airfield, the home of Mechanical Engineering Aircraft Squadron (MEAS), where I'd be carrying out in-depth servicing. Sounded more like factory work to me, but at least Sandy was posted to the same squadron, and we'd both be working on the mighty Vulcan. Or so I thought.

The Station also operated a positively ancient workhorse of the Berlin Airlift: the Handley Page Hastings. It was a large transport aircraft with a rounded nose sitting high above the ground, a fuselage that sloped down to a tailwheel at the rear, and two piston engines and their propellers on each wing. With a livery of white and light grey, a blue flash and red flourishes, it looked more like an airliner from the age of Empire than a military aircraft.

The last four Hastings' on the RAF inventory served on the Radar Flight of 230 Operational Conversion Unit, known as 1066 Flight - after the Battle of Hastings. They were used to teach Vulcan aircrew to operate the H2S radar equipment fitted in the nose of their bombers, but in a bulbous protrusion beneath the rear fuselage of the Hastings that added to its ungainly appearance. When not training Vulcan aircrew, they were used for maritime reconnaissance, or for transporting troops and sports teams around the UK and Europe.

They were retired from service on the 30th June 1977. Two are in aviation museums at Cosford and Newark, one is at Gatow in Berlin, and I'm not sure what happened to the fourth, although I think the SAS may have used it when training to free aircraft hostages.

Anyway, as you may have guessed, while Sandy began working on Vulcans, I became an airframe fitter on the Hastings team.

The MEAS hangar had a high ceiling and a floor the size and shape of a football pitch. It could hold three aircraft, so my Hastings could be sitting in front of, behind or in between two Vulcans, its bright colours and bulbous profile forming a vivid contrast with the sleek, green/grey, of the bombers.

Each aircraft, Vulcan or Hastings, was serviced by teams of airframe, propulsion, electrical, avionics, radar and armaments tradesmen. And they were all men, because Scampton was an all male base. When a female engineering officer arrived in 1977, it caused quite a stir in the national press.

The trades all had their own nicknames, some of which went back to the First World War. Airframe tradesmen were known as riggers, propulsion tradesmen as sooties, and both these trades were known as heavies. Electricians were known as leckies, avionics and radar tradesmen as fairies, and armourers as plumbers.

There was much good-natured banter between the different groups. We heavies were real tradesmen, working with meaty tools on bulky machinery, flowing with fluids you could see and touch, such as hydraulic and engine oil. Leckies and fairies were witch doctors, working with magical elements we labelled wiggly-amps. They trumpeted their superior intellect, saying we were too thick to understand electricity, let alone radio and radar waves. In my case, they were right, but we heavies enjoyed living up to our Neanderthal image. If a rigger was having trouble fixing something, or sensed an audience, he reached for a bigger hammer.

We all thought the plumbers were insane.

Having been convinced I'd drawn the short straw, I started work on my first Hastings. But once I'd overcome the image problem, the work proved challenging and, although I might not have admitted it at the time, fulfilling.

I learned so much in those first six months that it's hard to know where to start. For one thing, it provided immediate vindication for Halton's policy of giving us a strong grounding in basic engineering. There were few new components available for the Hastings, and I spent hours working pieces of metal into the required shape from scratch, something I'd have been ill-equipped to do if Halton had merely prepared me to change black boxes, as some had advocated.

Inevitably, it's the occasions when things went wrong that provide the strongest memories.

In my first week, I began work on a Hastings that had just been rolled into the hangar. Before getting into the meat of servicing it, we had to remove hundreds of access panels to get at the inner workings, and to collapse the main undercarriage legs. The combination of these two tasks almost led to my demise.

The main undercarriage legs of the Hastings protruded beneath each wing about ten feet out from the fuselage. When the aircraft landed on its two tractor-like mainwheels, air in the undercarriage legs was compressed against hydraulic oil to create a damping effect – like a car shock absorber - giving a smoother touchdown and, hopefully, preventing a bounce back into the air.

To work on the system, the air had to be released and the shock absorbers collapsed. But sometimes, even after the air had been let out, the shock absorbers refused to budge.

In a process that would give a modern health and safety official a heart attack, the solution was to walk a group of people out onto the wing, 15 feet above the ground, and have them jump up and down. If the undercarriage still refused to collapse, you just added more people until it did. And when it did, the wing dropped with a mighty lurch that threatened to throw everyone off.

Obviously, when this happened, it was important that no-one was underneath the aircraft.

Well, on this particular day, I was absorbed in removing panels from beneath the wing root. I can only think I was hidden from view, because no-one saw me and warned me what was happening. I could hear banging, and feel the aircraft rock gently every now and then, but I assumed that was normal - right up to the point where the wing dropped and hit me on the head.

I was extremely lucky. The wing had hit me at the bottom of its travel and the 20-ton hulk had merely caressed my hairline. If I'd been standing an inch higher, maybe half an inch, it would have been curtains.

I can't help thinking that those jumping on the wing were also pretty lucky to escape injury. Nowadays, an aircraft being serviced would be encased in a gantry to ensure that anyone who fell from the upper surfaces dropped only a short distance, not all the way to the floor. Back then, we merely walked around on the upper surfaces, or stood on ladders and hydraulic platforms that were pumped to the required height, often tens of feet. It was up to you to make sure you didn't fall off.

The Hastings had some particular danger spots, one of which was a panel in the floor just behind the cockpit. When it and a hatch above it were removed for servicing, it was possible to fall all the way to the ground, 20 feet or so if the aircraft was on its wheels, much higher if it was jacked into the air. Precautions were taken, but horror stories persisted of tradesmen bypassing every safety measure and falling to the ground, suffering everything from horrendous lower limb injuries to death.

As the new boy of course, I got all the worst jobs, two of which I remember very clearly. One involved the undercarriage again.

The Hastings used the same main undercarriage and wheels as the Lancaster, and, like the Lancaster, the mainwheels retracted into the inboard engine bays. Over time, these bays and their resident undercarriage legs became caked in a thick layer of engine oil and grease; to check the area for cracks, this layer had to be removed.

I was given an ill-fitting black rubber suit and wellingtons, goggles, a felt face mask, a dustbin of detergent, a long-handled, hard-bristled scrubbing brush and a set of steps. Thus armed, I spent more than a week scrubbing at the undercarriage and engine bays to clean away the oil and grease. In places, it was half an inch thick.

Most of the work was above my head, so pretty soon, my neck, back and arms began to ache. And of course, much of the detergent, oil and grease flowed into the neck and wrists of the ill-fitting rubber suit, where it mixed with the sweat I was generating on the inside. And, try as I might, it was impossible to keep the face masks dry, so I inhaled fumes and swallowed detergent, which gave me a sore throat.

Each night, I emerged from the undercarriage bay like a croaking, wrinkled, prune, much to the amusement of the others on the team, who'd suffered the same indignities in the past.

After a few days, I lost my voice. I didn't regain it until a week after using the detergent for the last time. Apart from this, I don't think there were any lasting effects. But in the early 2000s, a BBC Radio 4 programme ran an exposé on the health hazards of working long term with a detergent that sounded awfully like the one I'd used 24 years earlier. Thankfully, I'd only been exposed to its effects for a few days.

Barring cleaning out the cooked meat boiler in Mr Kennard's butchers shop, it was the worst job I'd ever had. That is, until the urinals.

Towards the back of the Hastings were some urinals. Because urine is very corrosive, the area around them was encased in rubber. However, not only are men notoriously bad shots at the best of times - ask anyone who cleans toilets – but we were convinced the pilots performed their aerobatic sequence whenever they spotted someone nipping down the back for a pee. Suffice to say, despite the rubber matting, urine seemed to seep through, and the metal beneath the urinals was always riddled with corrosion.

As the new boy, I spent days lying on my back in the cramped space beneath the floor of the urinals, filing away and repairing said corrosion. I tried very hard not to get any of the dust on my face, or in my mouth.

When not involved in the worst jobs in the world, much of the time as an airframe fitter was taken up with riveting.

Before the advent of modern composite materials, the various layers of aluminium making up an aircraft's skin were held together with rivets, smooth-sided metal pins, about the size and shape of small bolts. Large aircraft would have thousands, perhaps tens of thousands, spaced inches apart all over their airframes.

On jet aircraft, the heads of most rivets were flush with the skin to reduce drag. But on older, slower, aircraft, like the Hastings, most were mushroom headed, the domed portions standing proud of the outer skin, like thousands of drawing pin heads. And because one of the tasks of 1066 Flight was low level maritime reconnaissance, the rivets were exposed to highly corrosive, salty, sea air.

To spot damaged or corroded rivets on aircraft like the Vulcan, you pressed the area surrounding the flush-fitting heads to look for gaps, or the tell-tale seepage of blackened moisture.

On the Hastings, we were less subtle.

We grasped a wooden block the size and shape of a bar of kitchen soap, and, from nose to tail and wingtip to wingtip, scraped it along the long lines of protruding rivet heads. Those that were sound stood firm, the corroded ones, hundreds of them, flew off as the block hit, often with a resounding ping that reverberated around the hangar. The sound warned you of the task ahead: days, if not weeks replacing the damaged rivets.

With the body of the old rivets drilled out, new ones can be fitted to modern aircraft fairly quickly, using a special gun. On the Hastings, re-riveting was more basic, akin to that you'd find in a shipyard, albeit with smaller rivets. To begin the task, replacement rivets were pushed into their holes, passing through the several thin sheets of aluminium making up the aircraft skin. When the flat bottoms of the mushroom heads were flush with the outer sheet, the tail portions protruded from the inner sheet by about a quarter of an inch.

Positioned all over the aircraft, I and the other riggers would take up pneumatic hammers the size and shape of pistols, with air hoses running from the grips to an air pump. Into the barrel, we'd fit short bars with mushroom-shaped dimples in the end. Placing these over the rivet heads, we'd pull the triggers and the hammers would batter away, producing a cacophony of clattering that echoed round the hangar. Meanwhile, on the other side of the skin, metal blocks were held against the tail ends of the rivets, splaying them flat against the inner surfaces to hold the sheets together.

If your rivet was near an access panel, you could hold the pneumatic hammer and the block yourself. If not, someone else had to climb inside the fuselage, wing or tailplane, and hold the block against the tail end of the rivet while you hammered. This required good communication, teamwork and timing.

After a long day's riveting, I ended up with ringing ears, and numb and throbbing hands, symptoms similar to, if less dramatic than, the Miner's White Finger suffered by those operating larger pneumatic drills.

To the Army and Navy, the RAF often seems to have more than its fair share of NCOs, especially in the engineering trades. But the top-heaviness is not an effort to get one over on the other Services. It's a vital part of the RAF's safety culture.

At key stages in any work on an aircraft, it has to be inspected by a supervisor, usually an NCO, because only they have the experience and skill to judge whether the standard of workmanship is good enough. And if the work is on a critical component, such as the engine or flying controls, additional, independent, checks are needed. Again, these require NCOs with a high level of experience and skill.

So you sometimes needed almost as many chiefs as indians, an apposite term, because, to cope with the supervisory burden, the RAF's engineering trades had an extra rank, Chief Technician, between Sergeant and Flight Sergeant.

Another by-line of the safety culture was that my work was inspected several times each day, sometimes each hour. This meant I received immediate feedback if I wasn't producing the goods, although probably no more than grudging silence if my efforts were up to scratch.

The same is true for RAF aircrew, who receive constant assessment and feedback on their performance.

This navel gazing is another strong, yet necessary part of the RAF culture. The bottom line for me at Scampton was that I was constantly being assessed.

I usually passed muster, but I also made mistakes. Two spring to mind. The first earned me the biggest bollocking I think I've ever had.

Throughout training, I'd been taught always to treat propellers as if they were rotating. This is because it's not unheard of for a propeller to turn on its own because of some engine or electrical problem. And while there are stories of people walking through whirring propellers and surviving, there are many more where such encounters end in bloody death or disfigurement. Flight safety posters by Scarfe and other cartoonists rammed home the point, with graphic images of spattering blood and severed body parts.

I thought I'd taken all these messages on board. But one day, a few months after I'd arrived at Scampton, I walked past the large four-bladed propeller of a Hastings. In jovial mood, I gave the nearest blade an absent-minded tap. A nearby sergeant called me over and gave me a roasting of which the most seasoned drill instructor would have been proud.

In my defence, the propeller was in a purpose-made stand several yards from its parent engine, so there was no chance of it turning. But the sergeant was right. Treat every propeller as live. I deserved every syllable of his admonition, and walked away a very chastened young man. I never consciously walked within a propeller disc again, and took particular care to engender the same respect in the hundreds of students I taught to fly in propeller-driven aircraft.

Fifteen years later, as a squadron leader, when I became the staff officer responsible for one of our training bases, I was given a familiarisation flight in one of its aircraft, a Jet Provost Mk V. While strapping in, I suddenly realised that the civilian handing me my straps was the man who'd given me what for 15 years earlier. I quickly told him the story, and the effect it had had on me. As my aircraft taxied out, he was already telling one of his workmates. I guessed that many more would hear the story over the course of the day.

The other mistake was, in many ways, much more serious.

If we needed to work at height, we often stood on a wheeled platform that we hand-pumped to the required level. When pulling these platforms into position, you were meant to lower them to reduce the chance of hitting something. Well, one day, I was working on the rear edge of a Hastings wing, and I needed to move along a few feet. Because it was such a short distance, I decided not to lower the platform. Sure enough, as I moved it, its small wheels jumped over a cable and it lurched and it hit the rear of the wing, scraping an irreparable gouge in a yard-long metal tab.

I came clean, earning no more than a mild ticking off this time, but I'd learned another costly lesson, not least because, with the aircraft shortly to become obsolete, the item was no longer in stock. I had to manufacture a repair from scratch. Thank goodness for that Halton training again.

But, despite these mistakes, I think I came to grips with the work of an airframe fitter on the Hastings pretty quickly. I also think I earned the respect of my peers, all, that is, bar one.

Until our entry, one of the perks of training as an apprentice was that you passed out of Halton as a corporal, gaining your stripes after only three years in the RAF, and before you'd even set foot on the front line. Under our new terms of service, we had to spend a year as Junior Technicians and prove our worth before gaining promotion. Most of us succeeded in becoming corporals after this 'probationary' year.

But, in the late 1970s, four years to corporal still put us ahead of the vast majority of other airmen. Those who joined as mechanics could wait several years to be selected for fitter training, and several years more to gain their stripes. Airmen who joined as fitters could just gain promotion in four years, but most expected to wait at least a year longer.

As you can imagine, this could cause resentment. No-one was interested in the fact that I'd spent three years at Halton being kicked from pillar to post. And from their point of view, why should they show any sympathy, especially when they were often doing the same job. The only way to overcome the resentment was to prove you were as good as, or better than your fellow team members. In the main, I think I achieved this feat, facing only light-hearted banter after the first few days in the hangar.

But one corporal on my team, let's call him Jerry, had a simmering resentment against ex-apprentices that went beyond mere banter. In his early 30s, he'd come up 'the hard way' since joining as a mechanic, and felt himself long overdue promotion to sergeant. In my first few weeks, he took every opportunity to find fault and make life unpleasant. Luckily, he wasn't able to criticise too often, but he was still a bit of a dark cloud in my firmament for a while.

Jerry was a bully and, although he rarely stepped over the line when they were about, the senior NCOs had the measure of him. This explained why he hadn't been promoted. Also, I soon realised he was very unpopular, which blunted his power to make my life miserable. Two other things helped.

Firstly, he played soccer for the Station, and when I started to do the same, he seemed less inclined to bully a fellow sportsman.

Secondly, two months after my arrival, he got so riotously drunk at the section Christmas bash that he was sent home early. He refused all advice to walk to his married quarter on the Station, and set off unsteadily on his pushbike. A few hundred yards down the road, he was pulled over by the RAF Police, and, Jerry being Jerry, he refused to be reasonable, became obnoxious, and was arrested. When I left the party a few hours later, he was still in a cell in the Guardroom.

In the New Year, he was the subject of most of the banter, and what little power he'd had to make life unpleasant had evaporated.

On the domestic front, I was in a four-man room on the first floor of Cheshire Block, which overlooked the parade ground, more often used as the Station car park. The block was named after Group Captain Leonard Cheshire VC, a commanding officer of 617 Squadron during the War, and the man chosen as British observer of the atomic bomb dropped on Nagasaki in August 1945. He went on to found the Cheshire Homes organisation.

Even at Scampton, there were weekly bull nights followed by morning inspections, but, as long as the block was kept reasonably tidy, there was none of the excessive bullshit of the last three years at Swinderby and Halton, and no bedpacks. I could also walk the few hundred yards to work, rather than having to march. At the time, I didn't miss the pipes and drums one bit.

The Airmens' Mess, which had doubled as the aircrew briefing block in the Dam Busters film, was only 50 yards from Cheshire Block, so I didn't have far to walk for my meals. By this time, I was thoroughly used to and enjoyed the hearty British fare that was RAF food.

I have few recollections of the three men with whom I shared a room. A letter reminded me that one had smelly feet, and I remember that another had served at RAF Masirah, an airfield on an island in the Arabian Sea off Oman. I joked that meeting him was the nearest I was likely to get to foreign travel, as most overseas bases had been shut by Dennis Healey while I was in training at Halton.

The joke held true for several years, but I certainly made up for it after that.

I'm not sure what criteria led to Scampton and many other RAF bases being all male at the time. There were certainly WRAFs at the other Vulcan base, Waddington, just to the south of Lincoln. Perhaps it was to do with the availability of suitable accommodation, but I'm not sure this holds water.

When I returned to Scampton to train as a flying instructor in 1985, there were plenty of WRAFs, undertaking nearly all roles, including engineering. David Griffiths told me they'd moved in only six months after I'd left in 1979, and, with minimal infrastructure work, they'd taken over my old barrack block. The only visible change was the addition of net curtains at the windows, the identifying feature of every WRAF block in the RAF.

I suppose the lack of women should have made it a rather depressing place to be stationed, but the Apprentice Wing at Halton had also been all male, so I'm sure I wouldn't have given any thought to the lack of women at work. And anyway, some of the other bases nearby, such as Digby and the RAF hospital at Nocton Hall, were predominately female, and quite a few of their WRAFs used to attend our weekly dances, as did nurses from several of the local hospitals.

Just like the village discos in Shropshire, though, girls still danced in pairs or groups round their handbags. And if you wanted to dance with one, you still had to clump onto the dance floor to ask her, if you could get a mate to clump on with you and take her friend.

Just as at Halton, I turned to sport to prevent me spending all my time in the block or the bar. As already mentioned, I gained a place in the Station soccer squad, and then the Station volleyball team, which soaked up another couple of nights a week. I also began taking part in the many inter-section sporting competitions, again playing a large range of sports. In May 1978, I was selected to play volleyball for RAF Strike Command, but I have no recollection of playing any games for them.

Sandy was in another room in Cheshire Block, and he and I remained close friends, although, because we worked on different teams, and eventually on different squadrons, not as close as at Halton. He also tended to stay at Scampton at weekends, not least because he played rugby for Market Rasen, while I continued to go home.

In 1977, I too began playing rugby at weekends, for Ludlow IVth team. I have some newspaper cuttings from the time, one reporting that we'd beaten Malvern 33-0, with an old school friend of mine, Graham Barr, scoring four tries, and me scoring a try, a penalty and five conversions. This must have been the high point of my rugby career.

Sadly, Graham Barr was diagnosed with MS soon after this, and he died a few years later.

I was driving home in my increasingly unreliable MG 1100, and making frequent use of the Automobile Association to help me complete journeys. By the time I left Scampton, I must have spent time waiting for the AA in every lay-by between Lincoln and Ludlow. Sometimes, I had to leave the car to be fixed at a garage at one end of the journey or the other, and revert to travelling by train.

I often used to stop off in Leicester to see Simon and Jane, by this time, man and wife, and another of my childhood friends, Ian, was a driver at Scampton. He lived in Lincoln, and we used to spend the odd day together, until he was posted away. Finally, I spent at least some of the remaining time ten-pin bowling in the Station Bowl. Otherwise, I suspect I would have been found in the NAAFI bar, or listening to music in my room.

In April 1977, I switched from being a rigger - airframe fitter - on Hastings' to being a sootie - engine fitter - on Vulcans.

Originally manufactured by Avro, the Vulcan delta wing bomber is one of the most recognisable aircraft in world aviation. Looked on from above, it resembles an enormous moth, with a longish nose and shorter tail jutting fore and aft of wings shaped like an equilateral triangle. The statistics though, are very un-moth like. It has a length of just one inch under 100 feet, a wingspan of 111 feet, and a wing area of just under 4,000 square feet, almost enough for two tennis courts.

Some think the Vulcan beautiful, but, looking back now, when working in and around it, standing on and under those enormous wings, I was most struck by its aura of immense power and, sometimes, menace.

Although the Royal Navy's Polaris submarines had taken over the UK's strategic nuclear deterrent, Vulcans were still in the front line of the Cold War. Their mission was to fly at low level into the heart of the Soviet Bloc to drop up to twenty one 1,000 pound conventional bombs, or one tactical nuclear bomb. Hence the sense of menace.

I've always believed in the importance of talking to solve disputes, both domestic and international. But, I also believe you should have a big stick with which to defend yourself if diplomacy fails. So, unless nuclear weapons can be un-invented or neutralised, or eschewed by the whole world – with foolproof verification – I'm still in favour of Britain retaining a big stick, that is, its nuclear deterrent.

But only just.

In the current climate, I can't see us ever using such weapons, but I can envisage others doing so – Iran or Israel, India or Pakistan, or any number of terrorist groups – and I think the states at least would be marginally less likely to use them if they know others have them. I know this is too simplistic, because religious or ideological zealotry pays little heed to common sense or deterrence, but you'll probably be pleased to hear that I have neither the time nor the will to cover every angle of the nuclear debate here. I just think that, on balance, at the moment, we're better off with nuclear weapons than without.

In 1977, I don't think my reasoning would have been anywhere near as nuanced. We feared a nuclear attack from the Soviet Bloc, and it was my job to work on aircraft that might prevent that happening through deterrence, or allow us to retaliate if deterrence failed. I was prepared to do this despite the insanity of the Cold War doctrine of Mutually Assured Destruction, under which, if we were attacked with nuclear weapons, we'd retaliate and continue to do so, in the full knowledge that we'd be making great swathes of land uninhabitable, and killing vast numbers of people, if not all human life on the planet.

In the event of war, we assumed that the vast majority of the Vulcans we launched would be making a one-way journey, and that any managing to return would find nowhere to land.

As my career progressed and the sense of being on the verge of Armageddon faded, I continued to reason that I was a part of the British government's big stick, ready for all eventualities, large or small. The RAF was a deterrent, and, although many might disagree, I believed the strap-line that we were a force for good.

That is why the realisation that we'd been duped into the invasion of Iraq in 2003 was such a blow to me and many other Servicemen. Tony Blair and his cronies besmirched my 32 years of service.

Although my propulsion team worked mainly on Vulcans undergoing routine servicing, we also worked at short notice on aircraft with problems too labour-intensive or time-consuming for the squadrons to fix; these could be anything from a simple engine change, to more complex fault diagnosis and rectification. The variety made life less predictable than working on an airframe team, and my letters describe periods of hectic activity, when time passed quickly, but also periods, sometimes days at a time, when there was little work, and I was bored and fed up.

Throughout the period, I worked on fuel, oil, pressurisation, starter and extinguisher systems, as well as Airborne Auxiliary Power Units, small gas turbine engines that could be used to provide the aircraft with electrical power on the ground or, if necessary, in the air.

I also worked on the wing anti-icing systems that Uncle Charles had fitted in the aircraft when they were built at Woodford. But there's no doubt that my most vivid memories stem from removing and refitting the aircrafts' Bristol Siddeley Olympus engines, and especially ground running them afterwards to check that all was as it should be.

Olympus turbojet engines are knobbly silver cylinders, about four feet in diameter and 13 feet long. Partly covered in shiny pipes and a few box-like appendages, they fit, two each side, into tight bays at the Vulcan wing root, approximately 15 feet behind a four foot high air intake that extends about ten feet along the leading edge of each wing root.

Without falling into a lecture on jet engines, if you look in at the front of the Olympus, you see a ring of aerofoil shaped blades. Behind this first ring, are 12 more, of decreasing size, extending back about four feet to form the engine compressor. With the engine running, this rotates at high speed, drawing air in to be compressed progressively as it moves from ring to ring, front to back. The air then passes into a combustion chamber fitted around the centre of the engine. Here, it's mixed with fuel and burnt. This burning mixture expands rapidly, forcing back through two further rings of aerofoil-shaped blades: the turbine. Having turned the turbine, the hot air passes through an exhaust cone and 22 feet of jet pipe to stream out behind the aircraft.

I know the jet pipe is 22 feet long, because, after every flight or ground run, once the engine had cooled down a bit, I or one of the other sooties had to crawl up it to look for signs of damage or cracks at the rear of the engine. The pipe was only about a yard in diameter and crawling up it could be quite claustrophobic, especially at night.

Those nervous about flying should look away for a paragraph.

Among the things we had to check up the jet pipe was the exhaust cone at the back of the engine, just behind the turbine. As its name suggests, it was a cone with four or five thin vanes connecting it to the skin of the jet pipe. The cone and vanes were, if my memory serves me right, allowed to have 27 inches of cracks, as long as no one crack was more than ten inches long. I often saw cracks approaching this length. They were a startling sight, but someone had obviously decided they were within safe limits. Now the bit that could upset nervous flyers. I often wonder if the engines of commercial airliners have similar cracks. But hey, let's pretend I never brought it up!

You can carry on reading now.

As the turbine at the back of the engine turns, it powers the compressor and other engine components, such as hydraulic pumps to operate the flying controls and undercarriage, and alternators to generate electrical power. Air is also siphoned off throughout the engine to cool, heat or operate other systems, such as the air conditioning and anti-icing.

Each Olympus engine generates 20,000 pounds of thrust. Now, if pounds of thrust and the like mean as much to you as they do to me, another way of looking at it is that some of the Navy's largest and most powerful ships, such as Destroyers, are powered by two Olympus engines. The Vulcan, nowhere near as large and heavy, is powered by four.

This is why, for a relatively large aircraft, the Vulcan takes off in a remarkably short distance, climbs as high as 55,000 feet and barrels along at close to the speed of sound. It's also why the ground and your fillings shake when you stand beneath one with an engine or engines running. It's a visceral, never to be forgotten, experience.

I remember one ground run particularly vividly. It was a foggy day on the engine-running pan at the edge of the airfield, with nothing in sight beyond the great bulk of the Vulcan. As one of the engines was run up to higher power settings, a funnel of misty air started to spiral up from the ground beneath the air intake. It was like a little white dust devil, or the graphics of a television advert of the time for a detergent that cleaned like a white tornado. And as the engine was throttled up, the tornado grew until it reached all the way from the ground into the intake 20 feet above.

Afterwards, whenever I stood near a Vulcan with the engines running, I imagined that white tornado sucking up into the engine. It was a vivid reminder of why you should make sure the ground beneath a jet engine is clear of debris, and why you should never get too close to the air intake. At best, you could imagine someone losing a hat, or, more amusingly, a wig. At worst, the results could be much more startling and bloody.

I find it easy to remember the date of the Silver Jubilee of Queen Elizabeth II, because 7th June 1977 was the day I met my future wife, Geraldine. Although she was only a year younger than me, lived only a couple of miles from Ludlow, and had been to Ludlow Secondary Modern School before starting work in the town, I have no recollection of seeing her before that evening. For me at least, it was love at first sight.

On the evening of the Jubilee, she was out in Ludlow with a friend, Jan Brown, a girl with whom I'd been to school. I used this tenuous link as an excuse to strike up conversation, and then to follow them round for the rest of the night. I think we all got fairly tipsy, but whether Geraldine was won over by my drunken wit and repartee, or merely became fed up with my repeated requests to see her again, she finally agreed to a date.

I'm not sure she was any more impressed when she saw me next but, by a week later, when I'd returned to Scampton, we were exchanging letters, and continued to do so at the rate of one or two a week for the next couple of years. She must have seen something in me, because I tested her patience and tolerance on a fairly regular basis. I still do.

The weekend after we met, and probably the first time I took her out in the very impressive MG 1100 – roof lining then intact, but holes drilled in the floor on her side – I hit another vehicle.

On a narrow country lane, we met a Volkswagen Dormobile, a small camper van. It managed to stop, but I skidded on chippings and hit it, albeit at very low speed. The 1100 was undamaged, but the front panel of the Dormobile was dented, and my insurance paid out £90 for it to be fixed.

A more sensible young woman might have cut her

losses at that point, but Geraldine gave me another chance.

I have no doubt I made a fool of myself on numerous other occasions, but the next test of note occurred one Saturday afternoon in late October when I was playing rugby. A prop forward from Hereford put his elbow in my mouth, knocking out two of my front teeth, and loosening quite a few others. It was mid-way through the first half as I left the field, covered in blood.

Luckily, there was a dentist on the touchline. He said he'd sort me out, but not until he'd watched the rest of the match and had a pint afterwards. I wasn't in pain, and I was very grateful that he was willing to open his surgery on a Saturday evening to treat me, but even then, the delay seemed a bit odd. I suppose it just summed up the attitude to injuries in rugby.

I know Geraldine wasn't going out with me for my looks, but I still think she was remarkably loyal as I went round for several weeks with a large gap where two of my top front teeth should have been.

Belatedly, I had a gum shield made and went back to playing rugby, but a few more niggling injuries stopped me playing any sport for a while and made me consider the wisdom of continuing. My main sports were still soccer and volleyball, and I decided I couldn't jeopardise these for a bit of fun on a Saturday, so I hung up my rugby boots.

Geraldine was a shy, working class lass who worked in a bathroom shop. Her dad was head gardener for the Earl of Plymouth, a landowner with extensive estates in Shropshire and a large house near the village of Bromfield, two miles north of Ludlow.

In the late 19th and early 20th centuries, the Earl's forebears also had estates in South Wales. One had laid the foundation stone for Barry Docks, and many roads in the Vale of Glamorgan are titled Plymouth, or bear the family names of Windsor or Clive, while one of the family's homes, St Fagan's Castle and the adjacent land, which is now the Welsh Folk Museum, had been given to the nation in lieu of death duties.

Geraldine's mother also worked for the family as a cleaner and sometime waitress, and they lived in a large tied cottage next to a walled garden that her dad tended with the help of two or three other gardeners.

Geraldine remains shy. As to what class she is now, I'm not sure. Once I was commissioned, I always called us, or certainly me, an *in-betweeny*. Inside, I remained the same working class son of a dustman. And yet, as I became a pilot and rose through the ranks, I certainly became a professional, and then a senior manager. Apart from my accent, I could have claimed to be middle class, perhaps even towards the upper end of that category. And yet, I never felt part of the middle classes, and always thought of myself as an over-promoted corporal. Others probably thought the same.

Much like Pip in Great Expectations, I learnt what little I know about etiquette on the hoof, and I also know that someone of breeding can spot my lack of it a mile off. Some of the professional and social situations I encountered later in my career certainly made me feel out of my depth, but I always brazened my way through, ignoring the very few instances of snobbery I encountered. Geraldine often felt more uncomfortable, although she's always been the perfect lady in my eyes.

And now, although I've retired on a handsome pension, we live in a modest house and are not part of the County or dinner party set. I think we've reverted to being working class, albeit with some middle class habits, such as the tea we drink - Darjeeling. I'm less certain about where that leaves our children.

I think class is a fascinating topic, but I won't bang on about it any more here.

Every Vulcan due servicing was washed before it came into the hangar. This wasn't done with some sophisticated car wash-like machine, but by tradesmen like me who spent a week on the Aircraft Wash Team. A letter to Geraldine describes my re-acquaintance with a black rubber suit, scrubbing brush and dustbins of the since-banned detergent. It also provides another reminder of the approach to health and safety at the time.

To wash the upper surfaces of the Vulcan fuselage and wings, we climbed up, poured the detergent mix over them and swept it and any dirt off with brooms. As you can imagine, the surfaces were nowhere near flat. The fuselage domed a couple of feet above the wings and they sloped from 20 feet above ground level at the engine intakes, to about 10 feet at the trailing edges and tips. Skating around up there in your wellies was a precarious business, and although I never saw anyone fall off, I know it happened.

The same technique, minus the detergent, was used to clear snow. If it was allowed to build up, it could tip the aircraft onto its tail, so we slipped and slid around sweeping it off. Again, there was the odd casualty.

Another infrequent duty was being part of the Station Guard Force. This was a week of days or nights guarding the main gate to the Station. Armed with nothing but a torch, two of us would check the identities of everyone trying to gain entry, and deny access to anyone without the correct identity card or pass. If in doubt, or faced with an intruder, we could call for assistance from an NCO Guard Commander.

The main threats were thought to be the IRA, or Warsaw Pact agents trying to gain information – spies.

During each 12 hour shift, we shuffled between two hours on guard and two hours in the Guardroom as a mobile guard force, either resting or reacting to intruders attempting to break in anywhere around the perimeter. The mobile force was rarely called out, unless the Station was on Exercise.

Throughout much of the Cold War, the ability of RAF stations to fulfil their war role was tested by large teams of NATO officers in exercises called Tactical Evaluations, or Tacevals. The Taceval Team members would examine every aspect of the Station's planning, and the performance of its personnel, from the cooks to the aircrew, and the lowest ranks to the Station Commander.

And in between these major Tacevals, were exercises of varying scope and length, from small ones run within Station resources, to large ones not unlike a full Taceval, but carried out over several days by roving teams from various headquarters.

In October 1977, during a week when I was working nights on the Station Guard Force, we were subjected to a major exercise, whether by a full Taceval Team or an RAF Team, I can't recall, but it made for a very exciting and tiring few days.

For a start, we had to guard an additional gate giving access to the airfield, and we were armed with Self Loading Rifles, minus ammunition. The Team would test us by trying to gain entry though the gates, or to break in at other points around the Station perimeter.

When on the mobile guard force, we were incessantly being sent hither and thither to repel boarders, often made up of local Army or RAF Regiment units. They'd be firing blank rounds and setting off thunder flashes – large bangers.

Sometimes we were successful in holding them off, sometimes we weren't. If defeated, we could be given a piece of card explaining that we were dead, or that we'd been wounded, in which case the card would also outline our injuries. One of our colleagues would then have their first aid skills assessed. After a while, we'd miraculously be healed or resurrected and sent to deal with the next emergency.

We seemed to accept that there were groups of Fifth Columnists out there just waiting for the signal from Moscow to down tools and attack the perimeter of RAF Scampton. But you had to wonder how long the Station's limited manpower would have lasted in a war, when resurrection wouldn't have been an option.

During the day, when we were meant to be sleeping, we were forever having to react to air raid warnings or missing meals because the Mess had been blown up. One of my letters to Geraldine bemoans the fact that I kept being woken by Tannoy messages – we had speakers in the accommodation blocks as well as on poles at strategic points around the Station. In the letter, I also say that I'd just been left with a mouthful of toothpaste because they'd turned off the Station water supply.

The exercises were not without humour, although it wasn't always appreciated. On this one, I remember asking a casualty with a sign saying he'd lost both legs if I could have his boots. The assessor wasn't impressed, although the casualty seemed to find it funny.

Now that the Cold War has turned into a series of hot wars that leave large numbers of young men with horrendous injuries, including amputations, I find the joke less acceptable myself.

Another infrequent duty was a week on call as part of the Station snow clearance team, for some reason called Sno Flo. The Sno Flo team's job was primarily to keep the airfield open, clearing the runway and taxyways so our Vulcans could take off if the need arose. Station roads were of secondary importance.

Some of the team were ready just to wield shovels, but, as an engine fitter, I could also be detailed to operate a device called a Machine for Runway De-icing, or MRD.

MRDs were wheeled contraptions with two Derwent engines - from Meteor jet fighters – strapped to them. The jet pipes were modified to direct the exhaust gases at the ground to melt or blow away any ice. They looked like the pod racing machines in Star Wars Episode I, The Phantom Menace. Just as in the film, the operators sat between the engines. There were also single-engined MRDs where the operator sat in a little cabin above the engine, but it's the two-engined version that I remember most vividly.

MRDs weren't designed to move under their own steam, but were connected to the front of a fuel tanker. It was the tanker driver who pushed the machine and operator to where the ice had to be cleared, then pointed the jet exhausts in the right direction - hopefully.

MRDs rattled and shook in a very alarming manner. They looked and felt like death traps. Luckily, I only operated them in practices, but often saw them being driven about in the snow with some poor soul strapped into the hot seat. They were constantly breaking down, and my other job was to fix them when they did.

Even when they were working, MRDs could create more problems than they solved. For a start, they could damage the very surfaces they were trying to clear, lifting and blowing away ill-fitting or damaged blocks of concrete along with the ice. If the tanker driver went too slowly, you could melt the bitumen sealant between the concrete blocks of the runway or taxiway, and what could be done to tarmac or runway lights and signs didn't bear thinking about.

And finally, if the temperature was still below freezing, any water left behind the machine would re-freeze into a lethal sheet. At this point, if the MRD operator opened his throttles too widely, he could stop the tanker, even push it backwards. Not as funny as it sounds, especially for the tanker driver.

I'm not sure how many years MRDs were in use, but it's no surprise that airfields now prefer to use sweepers and chemicals to clear their surfaces.

During the three winters I was at Scampton, a great deal of snow fell, and it produced some strange effects. The airfield sits atop a ridge, running from south of Lincoln roughly northwards into Yorkshire. The predominately westerly winds used to whistle over the ridge and bite into you. It was bad enough in summer, but in winter, it could be like the Arctic.

Setting out across the airfield one morning in a heavy snowstorm, I walked straight into a wall of snow. It's the only time I've ever experienced what Polar explorers and mountaineers would recognise as a white out. There were no visual references at all, and I'd failed to see the drift, even though it reared up to several feet in front of me.

The next morning, the airfield was covered in balls of snow, like those children roll when preparing to build a snowman. There were hundreds of them, anything from a few inches to a few feet across, sitting at the end of trails in the otherwise virgin snow. Although I knew they'd been bowled along the airfield by the wind howling over the ridge, the lack of footprints made them an eerie, other-worldly sight in the middle of Lincolnshire.

On that occasion, Scampton had been cut off for several days, the A15 running past the gates having been covered by several feet of drifting snow. As a result, the Station was accommodating hundreds of trapped drivers, as well as airmen and civilian workers from the surrounding area who were unable to drive home.

The ex soccer referee and MP, Dennis Howell, had been christened Minister for Snow. Much to the delight of the Press, he was suffering the humiliation of being trapped on another RAF station, RAF Wittering, I think.

Eventually, the runways having been cleared, it was decided to send a fuel tanker with a snow plough on the front to clear the A15 into Lincoln, four miles to the south. The tanker set off, followed by trapped drivers and workers who wanted to head in that direction. At the first roundabout in Lincoln, it was apparent that the city's roads were clear, so the tanker turned round and headed back north, allowing the grateful drivers to continue their journeys.

But something that hadn't been considered was that drivers trapped in the city might follow the tanker as it travelled northward again. By the time it reached Scampton, it had quite a convoy behind it, and when it turned left through the Station gates, the drivers were confronted with a six-foot wall of snow barring any further progress north. Some at the back of the convoy managed to turn round and make it back to Lincoln before the snow blew over the road behind them, but many were trapped and ended up spending the night at Scampton.

The Station had merely swopped one group of lodgers for another!

That same winter, when I'd left MEAS and begun working on one of the squadrons, I collected a small Bedford minibus from the Mechanical Transport section and drove it gingerly on snow-covered ice towards the squadron dispersal. I spotted the Senior Engineering Officer, a squadron leader, walking to work and decided to stop and pick him up.

When I applied the brakes, the minibus did a graceful 360 degree pirouette, and came to a halt. Holding the steering wheel in expectation of a mighty roasting, I watched the Squadron Leader approaching.

He opened the minibus door, said, 'No thanks Ron, I'll walk!' shut it again and strode off.

No more was ever said. At the time, I was merely grateful for his forbearance, but having thought about it many times since, I think it was a fantastic example of good leadership.

He knew I wasn't the reckless type, that I'd be mortified at what I'd just done, and that I'd do my best not to do it again. So there was no message to be driven home, and any lecture would have served little purpose beyond asserting his authority and rubbing salt in my wounded pride. But that wouldn't have been enough to stop most people giving me a right royal dressing down. That he didn't take the opportunity spoke volumes about him. He earned my undying respect and loyalty.

Ever since, I've tried to follow his example. Not every mistake merits a bollocking. Some do, and some personalities or actions positively require it. But, in many cases, an understated response can be much more effective, even creating a bond between leader and subordinate that reaps rewards for both parties further down the line.

On the other hand, I accept that fear is a legitimate management tool, and I've seen plenty of examples of its use, with varying degrees of effectiveness. And I know that during my career, some of my superiors have thought my light touch leadership style a sign of weakness. All I can say is that I respond better and work harder for leaders like that squadron leader at Scampton than some of the martinets I've met. I suspect many others are the same, but I acknowledge that there is more than one way to skin a cat.

In August 1977, I applied for a commission. Following a catalogue of errors, it was 14 months before I attended the Officers and Aircrew Selection Centre (OASC) at Biggin Hill.

At the time, airmen like me had to pass through interviews with at least their flight, squadron and station commanders before their paperwork was sent to OASC. Any one of these officers, very few of whom were experts in selection, could turn you down, often because of some pre-conception or prejudice they held.

I was never turned down, but some of the officers interviewing me had some very wacky ideas, and gave some very misleading advice, most damagingly, that I was too old to apply as a pilot. As a result, I decided to apply to become an engineering officer.

Then, following a posting from MEAS to one of the

squadrons, my paperwork was lost and I had to re-start the whole process. During this application, I was advised, wrongly again, that my ONC in Engineering didn't qualify me for commissioning – as a serving airmen, it did. Sorting this out led to a further delay.

Many years later, the system was changed so that serving airmen and airwomen applied to OASC through Careers Information Offices in local towns, just like civilians. Although their superiors still provided reports to OASC, neither these, nor the potential inadequacies of Station administrative staff could delay applications, or prevent them being passed to the Selection Centre.

Many station commanders disliked this, feeling they were best placed to decide who on their station was most suitable to be commissioned. Some of them probably were, but others, most definitely, were not.

Some 25 years later, when I commanded OASC, there were regular pleas to revert to the old system. I resisted vigorously. Serving airmen and women deserve the same opportunity as a civilian, that is, to have their application dealt with in a timely and professional manner by experts in selection. The system wasn't changed during my time at the helm, but it may have been since. Several of the changes I instituted while running OASC failed to outlive my departure.

Anyway, having found out that my ONC was sufficient, that I was not too old to be aircrew, and having endured numerous additional interviews, my application for commissioning as a pilot finally left Scampton in early October 1978. I was given an appointment at OASC within a few weeks.

Work on the propulsion team in MEAS continued to

be spasmodic, with periods of hectic activity being followed by days with little work.

In September 1977, I decided to take O Level History to give me something other than sport to do in the evenings. So, one evening a week, I joined a small group being taught Modern European History by the Station Education Officer, an affable squadron leader.

I enjoyed the lessons and the accompanying reading and essay writing, and I suppose I should have been flattered that the squadron leader thought my first essay had been copied from a book. Eventually, from my performance in class, he realised that it was my own work.

In May 1978, I added a sixth O Level to my CV, a piffling achievement in comparison with the qualifications gained by my contemporaries at school, but it gave me a sense of achievement, and I'd enjoyed doing it.

On 27th October 1977, I was promoted to the rank of corporal and posted to 35 Squadron, sporting two chevrons on each arm of my uniform. I also moved into a single room in Cheshire Block, becoming responsible for the cleanliness of the four-man rooms on the top floor of the block, and for the behaviour of their occupants. I don't remember it as a particularly onerous duty, although my diary and some memos I've retained detail a flurry of cleaning for the annual inspection by the Air Officer Commanding in April 1978.

With a room of my own again, I became less averse to staying in the block. I acquired a stylish – for 1977 - white stereo deck and amplifiers from Simon, and, when I wasn't involved in sport, I used to lie on my bed listening to albums - still by old favourites such as

Yes and Wishbone Ash, but also new ones, such as The Jam. While listening, I was now likely to be reading military history, drinking milk and eating chocolate digestive biscuits by the packet – without putting on weight!

Sandy was also promoted and he and I ended up on different squadrons, which made it more difficult to stay in touch.

One element that made keeping up with friends difficult was shift work. As a tradesman on 35 Squadron, I worked alternate weeks of day and night shifts. Except for the odd working weekend, days were from 8am until 5pm Monday to Friday, and nights from 5pm until 8am the next day; although, depending on the flying programme, the number of aircraft on the line and their serviceability, we generally finished in the early hours of the morning.

Working this pattern, I met few people on the opposite shift of my own squadron, let alone those working elsewhere on the Station, where shift patterns could vary widely. Since arriving at Scampton, David Griffiths had been on 27 Squadron working fortnightly shifts of days and nights; I'd barely seen him. Now, Sandy joined 27, while David was posted to MEAS.

Sandy also moved into a house in Lincoln with some lads from his new squadron, before meeting his future wife, Lyn. So, inevitably, we saw less of one another, although we remained good friends, still meeting up when not working nights, even if only at the weekly disco in the NAAFI.

I found working a week of days followed by a week of nights very wearing. Perhaps it's easier if you work nights continuously rather than flip-flopping, but I don't envy any night shift worker who, like me, finds it difficult sleeping during the day.

The squadrons at Scampton were scattered around the airfield, occupying dispersals - clusters of parking bays, or pans – on which the Vulcan bombers sat exposed to the elements. I can't remember exactly how many aircraft were on each squadron, but, with one or two on routine servicing in MEAS, there were usually between four and six 'on The Line' at any one time. This number could be depleted further when aircraft deployed overseas or to other bases in the UK.

On the 35 Squadron dispersal - Foxtrot - we Linies worked from a cluster of low-rise brick buildings and Portakabins close to the aircraft.

I'd been looking forward to becoming a Linie. For a start, joining 35 Squadron was the opportunity for me to demonstrate my full potential as a dual trade technician, that is, as an airframe and an engine fitter. I had a woolly hat with RIGGER stitched on the front and SOOTIE on the back. Whenever I moved from an airframe to an engine job, and vice versa, I'd turn the hat round. But the Vulcan was such an enormous airframe that I spent the majority of my time with the word RIGGER to the fore.

The airframe jobs were many and varied, from changing cockpit windows – complex layers of glass and perspex totalling over an inch in thickness - to re-fitting the brake parachute that was deployed from a bay behind the tail to help the aircraft stop after landing, especially on shorter runways. But I seemed to spend most of my time on a ladder or platform in the nosewheel bay, working on the hydraulic panel, a dense, Heath Robinson, forest of interweaving white pipes and valves, through which most of the aircraft hydraulic systems passed.

The area was prone to leaks, and we Riggers had to

reach into the forest to remove and refit components, then twist thin wire between nuts and unions to prevent them coming undone – a method widely used in the aircraft industry known as wire locking. During the subsequent pressure testing, we took frequent showers in hydraulic fluid, OM15, a sticky red goo, either because the original leak had not been fixed, or a new one had sprung.

As a corporal, I had greater responsibility, supervising the work of other tradesmen, although I wasn't cleared to over-sign their work until I'd served a probation period of about 6 months.

I enjoyed it on The Line. There was a real buzz about preparing the Vulcans for flight; meeting the five aircrew as they came out; watching them climb up the ladder into their aircraft; working beneath it as they started up and taxyed out; seeing that distinctive shape launch into the air, the brown exhaust plumes from its four dirty engines remaining in sight long after the aircraft itself had disappeared in the distance.

And then, several hours later, waiting on the pan, spotting the same brown plumes approaching from the far south west, before the aircraft itself appeared in its distinctive nose-high attitude, flying a long straight in approach to land; praying that the crew didn't cause extra work by streaming the brake chute, and swearing when they did; watching it taxy in to the pan again; seeing the aircrew emerge; sitting across from them in the Debrief Hut, discussing any faults; and helping them write descriptions that would dictate our tasks beyond the routine after flight checks.

There was a camaraderie that rarely seemed to exist in the more mundane environment of the hangar. There was also a heightened sense of responsibility.

When I completed or over-signed a job, I knew men would climb into and fly the aircraft I'd just worked on, placing an ultimate trust in my skill as a tradesman or supervisor. It was a raw form of responsibility, the like of which I never experienced again, even when I was responsible for an organization of 1500 people operating 120 aircraft at 14 airfields.

Of course, I'm sure I wouldn't have articulated it in this way back then, but I felt the responsibility deeply, especially on the rare occasions when, just over 18 months out of Halton, with my sergeant on leave, I was airframe or engine trade manager, responsible for oversigning the work of all the men of that trade working on The Line.

When I became a pilot myself and mentioned my time at Scampton to ex-Vulcan aircrew, they'd immediately ask, 'Oh, do you remember old Johnny, or Fred or Pete?' any one of their aircrew buddies from that time. And, of course, the answer was invariably, 'No'.

Unlike a fighter squadron with relatively small numbers of aircrew and groundcrew, Vulcan squadrons were large and impersonal. When not flying, the aircrew spent their time in offices along the side of one of the hangars to the south east of the airfield. Apart from infrequent beer calls involving both sets of personnel, we generally met only for the few minutes before and after flight, when business rather than social chit chat was the norm.

Time was also limited by the short distances Vulcan aircrew walked. They were brought to the aircraft in mini-buses that parked as close to the aircraft steps as possible. And, after flight, they were met by another mini-bus, which most boarded to be driven the few yards to the Debrief Hut. Finally, after debriefing, they were driven away again, with barely any interaction between us.

I joked that if I was successful in becoming aircrew, I'd never have to walk again. When I eventually became a Hercules pilot, I discovered that I hadn't been far off. We really were bussed around almost everywhere, rarely having to walk more than a few yards.

I often wondered what the young tradesmen who watched me getting in and out of the ever-attendant mini-buses thought of me.

In September 1978, I started a Higher National Certificate course in engineering at Lincoln College. It was day release, which meant attending the College every Wednesday for two years. The first year syllabus included Maths, Engineering Measurement, Mechanical Technology and Materials.

From the outset, I found it very demanding, and much less fun than the ONC, or the history O Level I'd just taken. But it was a necessary evil. If I failed to become a pilot, it would bolster any future attempt to become an engineering officer and, whether my aspirations for a commission were successful or not, it would improve my worth as a tradesman.

The College also had a volleyball team, which I joined. They played in a local league, and this occupied another weekday evening.

After my promotion, I discovered the delights of being Orderly Corporal, a duty performed alongside an Orderly Sergeant, an Orderly Officer – a junior officer - and a Duty Executive – a senior officer of squadron leader rank or higher. They were 24-hour duties that, in my case, came around once every few months.

The duty staff were rarely called upon during working hours, when the Station was run by the normal hierarchy. But, from 5pm to 8am, when Station staff stood down, we took over to carry out a few routine duties and field any problems that cropped up; basically, ensuring the smooth running of the Station overnight.

The Orderly Sergeant and I spent the night in the Guardroom, while the Orderly Officer and the Duty Executive were on call. My routine duties included booking keys in and out, patrolling certain buildings, including the NAAFI to make sure it was shut up on time, and staying awake all night to look after the Guardroom while the Orderly Sergeant, Orderly Officer and Duty Executive slept.

I never became an Orderly Sergeant, but I was an Orderly Officer and a Duty Exec many times. When I put my head down, I always thought of the Orderly Corporal, denied the same luxury.

One of the first and last routine duties of the Orderly Sergeant and Orderly Officer is lowering and raising the Station Ensign, a light blue flag with an RAF Roundel in the centre and the Union Flag in the top left hand corner. It flies on a flagpole outside the Station Headquarters on all RAF stations, and is the subject of two low key ceremonies daily: Ensign raising early in the morning, and lowering in the evening.

To begin the raising ceremony, the Orderly Sergeant blows a whistle, the signal for all vehicles in the vicinity to brake to a halt, and all pedestrians to stop and face the Ensign, officers saluting. He then pulls a rope to raise the Ensign, hopefully with the Union Flag uppermost, while the Orderly Officer salutes. With the Ensign safely atop the pole, the

Sergeant blows his whistle twice, clearing everyone to continue on their way.

The lowering ceremony in the evening is similar, with the Ensign being taken into the Guardroom for safe keeping overnight.

Later in my career, as Orderly Officer, I managed to create quite a stir around the Ensign raising. It must have been about 1987, because I was a flight lieutenant flying instructor at RAF Abingdon.

Soon after 7am, I was in the Guardroom chatting to the Orderly Sergeant, when the Station Padre, a squadron leader, came in. He explained that a warrant officer who'd worked on the Station for 11 years had died after a courageous battle with illness, and suggested flying the Ensign at half mast. This seemed an entirely appropriate sign of respect to a long and faithful servant of the RAF and the Station, so I agreed and we swotted up on how to do it.

At 7.30, the Padre and I stood to attention outside the Station Headquarters and saluted as the Orderly Sergeant raised the Ensign to the top of the pole then lowered it to the halfway point. Satisfied, I went to the Officers' Mess for breakfast.

In a quiet dining room full of other officers, I spotted the Officer Commanding Administrative Wing, a silver-haired female wing commander with a ferocious reputation, and the nickname Wicked Witch of the North. I decided to go over and tell her what we'd done, just in case she was surprised to see the Ensign at half mast when she walked to work. I suppose I expected an expression of gratitude for letting her know.

Turning puce and shattering the calm of breakfast in her fury, she yelled, 'Put it up again. Now!'

As soon as she said it, I realised I'd goofed.

How many times in my career had I seen the Ensign at half mast? Very few, if at all. And if it was done every time a prominent member of the Station or the RAF passed away, it would rarely have been at the top of its pole.

I scuttled away and the Orderly Sergeant and I righted the Ensign, although probably not before several hundred people had seen it and wondered which member of the Royal Family had died.

From this event, I learned that putting the Ensign at half mast was the prerogative of the Queen, not the Orderly Officer. But I also learnt not to trust Padres, or anyone else coming in at short notice with bright ideas, even if they did out-rank me.

To be fair to the Padre, he hadn't been in the Service long. His rank gave him the authority to complete his pastoral duties, and was not an indication of his experience as an RAF officer, or his knowledge of military tradition. It was I who should have known better.

I don't remember the Wicked Witch of the North following up on her initial swift bollocking, and once I'd wiped the egg off my face, the episode formed the basis of a good barroom story for the rest of my career.

In 1978, The UK was still in the grip of the IRA bombing campaign. Any suspicious package had to be treated as a bomb and the area around it evacuated and cordoned off.

One evening when I was Orderly Corporal, a mysterious package was found in Supply Squadron. The Squadron was evacuated and I helped establish a cordon that would keep everyone about 250 yards from the building.

The suspect package had been discovered when

unloading the Early Bird, a lorry that toured RAF stations delivering urgently required items of equipment. It was a cardboard box about a foot cubed with no labels to indicate where it had come from, where it was destined for, or what it was. It now sat in a clear area of the loading bay about ten yards behind the lorry.

The probability was that the box's labels had either not been put on, or had fallen off as it was manhandled or bounced around in the lorry. Nonetheless, once reported as a suspicious package, it had to be treated as such, disrupting the life of the Station, the lorry driver and other stations awaiting items on his lorry. We phoned the bomb disposal people and awaited their arrival.

We waited, and waited. But they were experiencing a particularly busy night and there was no estimate of when they'd arrive. The Orderly Officer and Orderly Sergeant decided to go and have a closer look.

I'd recently completed my annual Ground Defence refresher training. One of the lessons had been about improvised explosive devices and their effect. It included a gruesome film emphasising how much damage could be done by devices containing even small amounts of explosives. With the graphic images of severed limbs fresh in our minds, the bomb disposal instructor explained how he'd seen people walk up to quite large suspect packages and give them a prod with a toe. As they did so, he said, they invariably leant back at 45 degrees, as if this was going to save them if the thing went off.

Well, this night, I watched from behind a wall as the Orderly Sergeant edged up to the box and gave it a nudge with his toe, all the while leaning back at an improbable 45 degree angle. Of course, if it had gone off, it would have been terrible. But it didn't, and I couldn't help smiling at how accurate the bomb disposal instructor had been in his description of human nature.

The box was opened and the labels inside identified it as destined for Scampton. After several hours' disruption, life went on.

When working in the MEAS hangar, only rarely did I think about the ramifications of what I was doing; that is, servicing aircraft that could one day take off and drop conventional or nuclear bombs on another country. Even on 35 Squadron, when seeing off several aircraft a day, I seldom thought about the destruction they could unleash.

The event that was guaranteed to bring all this to mind was an exercise, either one organised by the Station, or a full-blown Taceval.

In MEAS, exercises had meant working extra hours to get the aircraft out of the hangar and onto the squadrons as quickly as possible. And during the one exercise in which I'd been on the Guard Force, it had been about protecting the Station from attack. Exercises on The Line brought home that the Squadron's sole purpose was to send its aircraft to war.

When Taceval Teams wanted merely to test the Station's response to attack, the exercises could be called at short notice, or no notice. But when they wanted to test our full war role, we knew they were coming.

In the days leading up to the Team's arrival, intelligence would describe escalating tension between NATO and the Warsaw Pact. And when they arrived, the situation would become critical, with the Station moving to a war footing. For major exercises, this could involve the Vulcan force deploying to a number of other bases, making it a more difficult target. I deployed twice, once to RAF Finningly, near Doncaster – now Robin Hood International Airport – and once to RAF Leeming in North Yorkshire.

Whether we deployed or not, the Taceval Team would slowly unfold its carefully constructed exercise scenario. This would probably lead up through ground attacks, such as those I'd faced when on Station Guard, to air attacks, with increasing emphasis on the possibility of nuclear, biological or chemical weapons being unleashed.

Authenticity was added when pairs or 4-ships of Buccaneers or Phantoms roared across the airfield at ultra low level - no more than tens of feet – simulating air raids. During this phase, we'd spend many hours in our NBC suits and respirators, uncomfortable at the best of times, but doubly so when running around with a rifle, or working on aircraft.

For safety reasons, there were limits on the engineering tasks we could perform in our NBC suits and respirators, and I seem to remember that this saved us engineers from having to wear the full kit all the time.

As the exercise escalated, we'd move our Vulcans to parking bays at the ends of the main runway called Operational Readiness Platforms, or ORPs. Other squadrons would do the same. We'd be protected by armed guards and scores of RAF Policemen, many with Alsatian dogs. While we completed our airframe or engine tasks, the plumbers would simulate arming the aircraft with nuclear weapons, and we'd start to hear Tannoy messages, different in content and tone to those that had gone before.

'This is the Bomber Controller for Scampton-based

aircraft only, Readiness State One Five.'

We'd beaver about to ensure the aircraft were ready to take off in 15 minutes.

By now, the exercise scenario had probably unfolded to the point where nuclear weapons had been launched against this country, or we'd actually been attacked with them. So we were working on aircraft that, in the real case, would be retaliating in kind.

Looking at our Vulcans perched at the end of the runway, even the least sensitive must have realized the enormity of what we were doing.

I certainly had a feeling of being involved in something momentous, and of increased responsibility. But it manifested itself, not in a wish to be somewhere else, avoiding the issue, but in a desire to make sure I did everything right; or, to put it another way, a determination not to screw up. After all, launching these aircraft was what I'd been trained for, and I should imagine the aircrew preparing to climb into them were feeling the same tension, only heightened in their case.

We could stay at a particular readiness state for several hours, but eventually a deep male voice would boom out of the Tannoy again.

'This is the Bomber Controller for Scampton-based aircraft only, Readiness State One Zero.'

Ten minutes readiness.

At some point, the five aircrew, pilot, co-pilot, nav radar, nav plotter and air electronics operator, would be driven over to sit next to their aircraft. And then, with the tension mounting, the Readiness State would eventually reach Zero Two.

Everything would now be prepared. The aircraft were fuelled and armed, and they were plugged into ground electrical power through umbilicals that would pull out as they moved off.

We sat back and waited, jumping at every routine call on the Tannoy, until, finally, 'This is the Bomber Controller for Scampton-based aircraft only, Scramble! Scramble! Scramble! I say again, this is the Bomber Controller for Scampton-based aircraft only, Scramble! Scramble! Scramble!'

Long before the Controller had repeated his message, the aircrew were out of their vehicles and racing to the aircraft. We positioned ourselves beneath our Vulcan to make sure all was well. One by one, the crew climbed the ladder in front of the nosewheel and disappeared inside, the ladder being pulled up and the hatch shut.

In what seemed a matter of seconds, we'd hear four loud and distinctive squeals, 'Poww, poww, poww, poww,' rising in pitch and volume until melded into one cacophonous scream.

All four engines had been started using high pressure gas from an internal rapid start system. Very quickly, the engines spooled up, the noise rising in intensity until the ground shook. But still the shrieking and shaking increased, until, suddenly, the brakes were released and the aircraft shot forward onto the runway.

The mighty jet exhausts now swept over the pan, and woe-betide the person who'd neglected to keep a safe distance, or, in the case of those of us that had to be too close for comfort, failed to dive behind some immovable object.

I once saw an RAF Policeman and his dog blown base over apex by the exhaust of a scrambling Vulcan. The dog handler had wrongly assumed that 50 yards would be sufficient distance between him and the rear of the aircraft. Man and dog looked decidedly dazed as they lifted themselves from the coils of barbed wire that eventually arrested their tumbling flight. Luckily, only their pride had been hurt.

In another few seconds, all four, five, six or more aircraft would be on the runway, the noise unbearable, the vibration earthquake-like. The first would be airborne in a remarkably short distance, the others leaping into the air behind it, climbing in pursuit at an improbably steep angle, the mucky brown plumes from their jet pipes lingering on the runway.

We'd sit back and watch them go, waiting for our heads to clear and our hearing to return before starting to tidy up after their violent departure. I for one, would be contemplating that, in the real case, they'd be unlikely to return. Those that reached their targets and avoided being caught up in the explosions they unleashed, would be lucky to survive the return journey, and perhaps equally lucky to find somewhere to land in the nuclear desert created during their flight time. I have to confess that, at the time, my thoughts were with the crews, rather than the millions of innocents that might have been killed.

Sixteen years later, as a squadron leader working in the Ministry of Defence, I organised and attended a set of talks with the Polish MOD in Warsaw. The talks were memorable for a number of reasons that I'll cover in a later volume, but staying with the current theme, one conversation stood out.

After a formal dinner, we retired to an ante-room for coffee. I sat with the UK Defence Attaché in Poland, a group captain and ex-Vulcan navigator. He and I had already talked about our very different experiences of the aircraft earlier in our careers. But, on this occasion, he was in conversation with a Polish Air Force brigadier-general, an ex-Mig 15 fighter pilot. They were discussing their respective Cold War missions.

The Polish Brigadier-general, a short, roly-poly man with slicked back black hair, spoke in jovial manner. 'We knew the routes you were going to fly on the way to your targets, and we'd have shot you down.'

'Aha,' said our Defence Attaché, a short, dapper man of about 50 years of age, 'You only knew the routes we wanted you to know. We were going to follow different ones. I'm sorry General, but we'd have got through.'

'There you are wrong my friend,' said the Brigadier. 'We knew *all* your routes and, I assure you, we'd have shot you *all* down.'

The two carried on in the same vein, laughing heartily and agreeing to differ.

I sat back and wondered which of them would have been right, and thanked providence that we never had to find out. But also, I pondered what an incredible conversation I was privy to, taking place only a few years since the two men had been sworn enemies on opposite sides of The Iron Curtain.

Back at Scampton or the dispersed base, the exercises usually ended shortly after the aircraft had scrambled. Sometimes, they'd fly off to drop small conventional practice bombs on bombing ranges round the UK coast, while on other occasions they merely took off, completed a circuit of the airfield and landed again. And sometimes, they didn't even fly, merely taxying down the runway and returning to their dispersals.

On 17 May 1978, my diary indicates that one of these taxying scrambles was especially memorable. It involved 13 Vulcans, and although they didn't get airborne, the sight, sound and smell of them starting up and streaming down the runway to return to their dispersals were unforgettable.

While I was on 35 Squadron, my new commissioning application was working its way through the system. I had interviews with the Junior Engineering Officer, the Senior Engineering Officer, the Squadron Commander, the Station Commander and a panel of officers from the Station. Finally, I was booked to attend OASC at Biggin Hill for the pilot selection process in late October 1978.

I took some ribbing from my workmates for wanting to be a Rodney, or a Zob, two of our more polite nicknames for officers. But most people were supportive, even if it did mean 'having my brains removed and my pockets sewn up', more airman terms for officers' lack of intellect and cash, especially when there was a need to buy anything, like a round of beer.

I've met and worked with many airmen who would probably have made much better officers than me, but who never applied for a commission. The reasons were many and varied, from something as simple as not being prepared to face the inevitable ribbing, to deeply held feelings of inverted snobbery. But a large number had a genuine fear of moving from a life of hands-on work on a squadron or station to one of paperwork and management in a headquarters.

Although airmen face more paperwork and management responsibility as they move up the non-commissioned ranks, they tend to stay on the front line. Officers, however, tend to move into headquarters jobs, a transition that doesn't always meet their aspirations. Fear of being promoted and dragged from the cockpit is one of the major reasons pilots leave the RAF to join the airlines, where they can just concentrate on flying.

I didn't want to leave the cockpit when I was promoted, but found that I enjoyed most of the managerial and policy jobs into which I moved, and I never wanted to be an airline pilot.

It takes all sorts. In 1978, I just wanted a commission, as a pilot if I could manage it, as an engineer if not.

On my third visit to the Officers and Aircrew Selection Centre, I was more nervous than I'd been on the two previous occasions, six and five years earlier. Then, I'd been taking a speculative punt at becoming a pilot, the second time, knowing that I wasn't going to gain the necessary A Levels anyway.

Now, as a 23½-year old serving airman, my six O Levels and ONC in Engineering were sufficient to qualify me, and I really wanted to succeed. In the five years since my last visit, I don't think I'd set out to change my personality, or taken on any airs and graces, but even I wouldn't have classed myself as the street urchin I was in my teens.

Luckily, I'd changed in other areas as well. I can't describe these without blowing my own trumpet to a certain extent, so forgive me, but I was more mature and responsible, filled much of my spare time with academic effort and physical activity, and knew and could express what I wanted from life.

I'd also swotted up on current affairs – I could say Ndabaningi Sithole and Mangosuthu Buthelezi without stumbling – and was prepared to discuss world, domestic and military affairs.

So, on 21st October 1978, I arrived at Biggin Hill. I passed pilot aptitude and the medical again, and performed well enough in the interview to move on to Part 2 of the selection process. Here, I know I was more confident in the discussion and problem-solving exercises, and I participated fully and enjoyed the leadership exercises in the hangar, even if I didn't complete my own – something to do with planks and shark-infested custard again. I was very aware that I mustn't come across as a bossy corporal, although, in truth, I wasn't one of those anyway.

But, as I've explained before, I was also well aware that OASC had no guaranteed pass mark. If I'd failed to impress, that was it, but even if I'd done incredibly well, I knew I still might not be selected. It was no good coming 11th if there were only ten places.

I returned to work at Scampton and waited for my results to come through.

My first flying training sortie was in a tiny piston-engined Chipmunk. Halfway through our flight, the instructor asked me how much fuel we had left. I looked down at the little round fuel gauges on each wing root. Both needles pointed to the figure six.

'Twelve thousand pounds, sir,' I chirped, to hoots of laughter from the rear cockpit.

The correct answer was, of course, 12 gallons. But, over the previous few years, I'd become used to aircraft fuel being measured in tens of thousands of pounds, not tens of gallons or less.

I never ceased to be amazed at how much aviation fuel, Avtur, a Vulcan could hold: a total of 74,000 pounds, over 9,000 gallons, in seven large tanks – two on each side of the fuselage and five in each wing; and up to nearly 20,000 pounds, 2,000 gallons, in removable tanks in the bomb bay.

We seemed to spend a lot of time on 35 Squadron, either putting fuel in our Vulcans to prepare them for flight, or taking it out to prepare them for servicing, or because the aircrew had decided they needed a lighter fuel load than originally planned.

It was a complicated business. My diaries for 1978 and 79 have a table in the front, detailing the fuel required in each tank to make up a set fuel load, from 10%, 7,400 pounds, rising in 5% percent increments to 95%, then to the normal maximum, 98%, 72,600 pounds, which allowed room for the fuel to expand with increasing temperature without venting overboard. We rarely fuelled to 100%.

For refuelling or defuelling, a fuel bowser positioned itself to the side of the pan, the driver monitoring the fuel flow through a large bore hose that connected to the underside of the Vulcan. I sat in the cockpit and pulled out a fold away panel from between the pilots' ejection seats. It was covered in switches that operated fuel pumps and valves in individual tanks. The tanks had to be filled or emptied in a set order, or you risked the centre of gravity moving so far aft that the aircraft tilted back to rest on its tail, something I saw only once, thankfully, on another squadron.

In the air, it was the co-pilots job to operate this panel to keep the engines fed and the fuel load in balance.

To enter a Vulcan, the crew climbed up a ladder and through a rectangular hatch beneath the fuselage, just in front of the nosewheel. Once inside, the two pilots carried on up another narrow ladder to sit side by side on their ejection seats beneath the domed cockpit. One of the three rear crew - two navigators and an air electronics operator – having telescoped and stowed the entrance ladder to one side, closed the hatch. These three then turned their backs on the pilots and, just behind the hatch, stepped onto a small platform, on which they sat side by side at a desk, facing backwards at a wall of instruments and radar scopes.

Some way behind this wall was the bomb bay – inaccessible to the crew, unlike in the James Bond film, Thunderball, where there was a door between the crew compartment and the nuclear weapons in the bomb bay!

Close to the hatch, was a sixth seat, which could be occupied by a passenger or an NCO called a Crew Chief, an engineer who flew with the aircraft when it was due to land anywhere other than its home base.

Only the pilots sat on ejection seats. To get out in an emergency, they had the option of pulling a yellow and black handle on the seat between their legs, or a similar one above their heads. Pulling either would blast the heavy canopy away, then fire them and their seat into the airflow. Separation from the seats was automatic, after which they could float down on their parachutes.

The rest of the crew had no such luxury.

To save costs during the development of the Vulcan, it had been decided not to provide the rear crew with an automatic means of escape, even though it was technically feasible. Instead, the rear crew were provided with assister cushions which inflated to help lift them out of their seats against the g forces likely to be experienced in a stricken aircraft. The Crew Chief or passenger lacked even this minimal level of support.

Once out of their seats, the rear crew had to step down to the hatch and pull a handle to blow it open against the pressure of the airflow. Then, one by one, they had to slide down the hatch and clear of the aircraft – avoiding bashing into the nosewheel if the undercarriage was down. Once clear, their parachutes were operated automatically by a static line attached to the aircraft. If this failed, they could pull the ripcord themselves like a conventional parachutist.

As you can imagine, in an emergency, with the aircraft doing heaven knows what, none of this was likely to be straightforward.

The nightmare scenarios were emergencies where there was insufficient time for the rear crew to get out before the aircraft broke up or hit the ground, or where, even if they managed to get out, the aircraft was too low for their parachutes to open.

The history of the Vulcan was peppered with accidents where the front crew ejected and survived, and the rear crew died in the ensuing crash. But there were also instances where the front crew seem to have stayed in the cockpit to die, rather than eject and leave their comrades to face death alone.

It's possible that there was one such instance just after I'd joined 35 Squadron.

After a low level flypast when practising for the Chicago Air Show, the Vulcan display crew from 617 Squadron crashed into a rubbish dump adjacent to the display airfield. There was speculation that the front crew had fatally delayed their ejections in an attempt to right the aircraft and save the men down the back.

Over the life of the Vulcan, all deaths where the rear crew could have been saved, or the front crew fatally delayed their ejections, make the decision not to provide everyone on the aircraft with an automatic means of escape appear pretty cynical and penny-pinching. And yet, from my own managerial jobs, I know that financial constraints mean not all safety recommendations are implemented.

Following the Chicago accident, the Vulcan display

commitment for that year was taken over by my squadron commander, Wing Commander Roger Sweatman, and his crew. A few weeks later, I and the other groundcrew were watching them practice over Scampton airfield.

Following a low level wing over similar to that that had led to the fatalities in Chicago, their Vulcan's starboard wingtip seemed to come perilously close to the ground. We might have dismissed it as an illusion caused by our distance from the display line, had not the crew climbed out ashen faced after landing. As far as I know, the rest of the display season passed off without incident.

Thirteen years later, Roger Sweatman was a retired group captain, the Regional Commandant of the Air Training Corps in Wales, and based at RAF St Athan, near Cardiff. I arrived at the same base as a squadron leader flying instructor, the new Officer Commanding the University of Wales Air Squadron.

Of course, I remembered my ex-squadron commander as soon as I met him. He didn't remember me, but why should he? I'd been one of many airmen on a large squadron. But once he'd made the connection, we got on well and he helped me with what could have been one of the trickier parts of my new position.

The bulk of the 60 or so students on my Air Squadron were reservists, and that made me a member of the Territorial, Auxiliary and Volunteer Reserve Association for Wales, TAVRA. This august body looked after all the reserve Army, Navy and RAF units in Wales, including my Air Squadron. Inevitably, because of the predominance of Territorial Army units, TAVRA was dominated by colonels and brigadiers. Several seemed to have titles, up to and including an earl.

Roger Sweatman was supremely confident in this environment, and, during TAVRA meetings and dinners, usually in the Officers' Mess of some Army barracks, he took me under his wing. He taught me not to be daunted by rank or accent, and he greatly improved my confidence in such circles. I knew that most of the great and good could tell immediately that I was 'from the lower decks,' as the Navy would put it, but I learnt not to worry about such things, and all the more quickly for his help.

I also learnt that the uneven stitching on a gentleman's suit was not a sign of shoddy workmanship, but a way of displaying that it was handmade, unlike my Marks & Spencer example with its uniform seams.

A few months after we'd been re-acquainted, he died in a Chipmunk crash just over 100 yards from my office.

I'd dropped in on one of the last days of the Squadron's summer leave to catch up on paperwork. Geraldine was with me and, surprisingly, neither of us heard the crash, or the emergency vehicles rushing to it.

About an hour or so later, driving away to do some shopping, we heard on the car radio that the Commandant of the University of Wales Air Cadets had died in an air crash. This title, a mixture of mine and Roger's, was sufficiently confusing to make me grateful Geraldine was sitting next to me. Had she not been, I know the poorly prepared news flash would have made her think it was me.

A few days later, among the many letters received by the Station, was one regretting my death.

Partly as a result of this episode, and others I've

witnessed, I have very strong views on the reaction of the Press to accidents, civilian as well as military. Unless it can be demonstrated that an announcement is in the public interest, rather than of interest to the public, the Press should not publicise accidents until the next of kin of all the deceased have been informed, at which point they can say that this has been done.

This obviously becomes very difficult when any passer-by can post details on the internet, and especially in the case of large scale accidents, such as those involving airliners or trains. But whenever possible, I believe responsible news outlets should adhere to the principle of non-disclosure. Too often, announcements are made which cause distress to anyone who has a loved one or friend who could have been involved.

I missed Roger Sweatman, not for the selfish reason that he was no longer around to look after me at TAVRA gatherings, but because I'd enjoyed his company. I was a pall bearer at his funeral.

I flew in a Vulcan only once. In the run up, I was given a medical and fitted with a flying suit, helmet and oxygen mask. During flight, if there'd been an emergency that required the crew to evacuate the aircraft, I would almost undoubtedly have been helped out by one of the rear crew. But I had to be capable of getting out by myself, so I was also sent off to the Vulcan Rear Crew Escape Trainer.

Sitting in a magnolia-painted room, it was a Vulcan front end, propped high enough above a floor covered in thick mats for the crew hatch to be opened.

I climbed in and closed the hatch. Then, I unstrapped again, pulled the emergency handle to blow open the hatch, slid out onto the mats and pretended to pull my parachute ripcord. Piece of cake.

In fact, too easy.

In January 1977, a crew had had to escape a burning Vulcan at about 10,000 feet over Spilsby, east Lincolnshire. One of the rear crew attempted to open the hatch, but to no avail. A second tried and the hatch blew open. Unfortunately, the first man was now standing on it. He fell out, but not clear, and was left dangling, head down, on the hatch. They pulled him back in and threw him out again, this time with sufficient force to clear the aircraft and allow his static line to operate his parachute.

The reason he'd failed to open the hatch was that he'd been pulling the handle in one swift movement, as he had done countless times in the Escape Trainer. But, on the aircraft, the groove the handle followed had a gate – a dogleg - halfway down that had to be negotiated before carrying on to the emergency position. Over years of use, the gate in the Escape Trainer had worn away, allowing the handle to be pulled straight to the emergency position in one movement.

Of such simple things are calamities, or in the Spilsby case, near calamities, made.

The handle in the Escape Trainer was fixed not long after my flight, but I was well briefed on the difference between it and the one in the aircraft. As an aside, Sandy became responsible for the upkeep of the Trainer soon after I left Scampton.

At 10pm on a stormy night in September 1978, I took off in a 27 Squadron Vulcan for a maritime reconnaissance sortie. We were airborne for six hours and spent most of it at 37,000 feet patrolling the North Atlantic over the Faeroes Iceland Gap to the north west of Scotland.

I should, of course, say what a marvellous experience it was. But the truth is that although the build up was good fun, the actual flight was anything but. I sat on the sixth seat, in the dark, with no window, and a crew who kept their backs to me and maintained a stony silence.

Now, it may be that their weight of work, task focus and normal intercom discipline left little time to engage with a passenger. But, to be truthful, they seemed not to be very busy, just sullen. I honestly think they'd had a row or something. Even the crew member detailed to look after me rarely spoke, and no-one seemed keen to address the few questions I plucked up the courage to ask when they seemed to have time to spare.

So, basically, I sat in a dark metal tube with five sulky men for six hours. And to make matters worse, the aircraft was flying in and out of the jetstream, a high level wind that can, and did, cause turbulence. I'm not sure whether it would have been classed as severe turbulence by an experienced aviator, but the constant lurches were bad enough to make me use my little blue and white sick bag several times.

I'd expected the flight to provide the final motivation for my visit to Biggin Hill the following month. But it had just the opposite effect. For the hours and days after landing, I questioned why on earth I wanted to become a pilot when, firstly, I was prone to airsickness, and secondly, this lot so obviously disliked what they were doing.

I never did find out what had made them so grumpy.

In the end, on the advice of the Vulcan pilot with whom I played volleyball, I decided to discount the experience. He convinced me that six hours rattling about in a darkened dustbin was no way to judge your susceptibility to airsickness, and that the crew really were just a miserable bunch of so and sos. Even so, it knocked my enthusiasm and confidence for a while.

Years later, of course, I found that flying wasn't always a bed of roses, and that not all aircrew were the outgoing and friendly types depicted in films. But, on the plus side, I was rarely airsick, and characters as grumpy as those on my Vulcan flight turned out to be fairly thin on the ground, on the Hercules force anyway.

Geraldine and I became an item. I used to travel home for weekends as often as I could, with the few occasions when work prevented this causing great anguish, if my letters and diaries are anything to go by.

In the summer of 1978, we had seven nights in a hotel in Tenby - £57 per person per week, plus an extra £7 for a room with a shower. It was a very enjoyable week in a part of the country I knew well from a teenage holiday with Andy, Nick and Simon, and from visits with Sandy during our exchange weeks when on leave from Halton.

One night, Geraldine and I visited Sandy's family, and returned to the hotel so late we were locked out and had to wake the owner to let us in. Luckily, he wasn't the inspiration for Basil Fawlty, even giving us tickets to a one-man show on the life of Dylan Thomas when he heard we'd been to a local performance of Under Milk Wood.

And, in the autumn of the same year, we spent four nights in London, visiting nearly all the large museums and galleries, and seeing many of the other major tourist sites.

On the first night, we saw Close Encounters of the Third Kind in the Odeon on Leicester Square. With its enormous screen and surround sound, it provided a totally different experience to any other cinema we'd ever visited.

On the next two nights, we saw Donald Sinden in Shut Your Eyes and Think of England at the Apollo Theatre, and Dave Allen, the stand-up comedian, at the Vaudeville. These experiences fuelled a life-long passion for the theatre. On the final night, we had what I describe in my diary as a 'beautiful meal', at a Garfunkels restaurant, the height of sophistication for us then.

During this period, I think it would be true to say I was a fairly happy-go-lucky and contented character, prone to jumping and clicking my heels as I walked down the street with Geraldine. Life was good.

The little MG 1100 continued to let me down, though. During 1978, it needed a new voltage regulator, battery, front brakes, clutch, exhaust manifold, exhaust, engine mountings, and welding on the rear sub-frame and front wing. And then, on 15th November 1978, while I was inside playing volleyball, it was stolen from outside Lincoln College.

It turned up six days later behind a block of flats in Leeds. A friend from Scampton gave me a lift to collect it. Like many in the same situation I should imagine, I wished it had never been found. It was a wreck – or more of a wreck than it had been before being stolen. Judging from the silver necklace in a little blue packet the Police found on the floor, it had been used in a robbery, during which the exhaust had been knocked off and the sump and engine damaged.

I had it fixed, but it failed to regain its previous low standards, and I took out my first ever bank loan, £800, and bought a second-hand Wolsely 1300. My woeful inability to tell the difference between a decent car and a dud continued, as the 1300 needed a new engine one month after I'd bought it!

The day after the 1100 was stolen, I found out I'd been successful at Biggin Hill, and was to be posted to the Officer Cadet Training Unit at RAF Henlow on 15th April 1979, just less than five months away. The Unit's 16-week course had to be passed before I could reach my true goal, training as a pilot.

In the run up to Henlow, I became much more serious about fitness. In addition to the usual weekly sport, my diary mentions frequent runs, the start of a habit that led to three London Marathons 20 years later. I still run every other morning, but the wear and tear of all that sport has left me with a hip problem that limits me to a maximum of five kilometres at a time. I'd like to run further, but, alongside daily walks, 5k is enough to give me my endorphin high and keep me sane.

In February 1979, I was posted a few hundred yards to 617 Squadron, where I spent most of my time working as an airframe fitter, again on alternating weeks of nights and days, with the odd working weekend and a major exercise, during which the Squadron dispersed to RAF Leeming in North Yorkshire.

Although it was only for two months, I'm proud to say I served on 617. After the Dam Busters raid, they'd been given the motto, 'Après Moi le Déluge' – after me the flood – words originally attributed to Louis XV, or maybe his mistress, Madame Pompadour, and seen as prophetic when the French Revolution erupted several years later.

When I joined the Squadron, the motto had been unofficially updated to 'Après Moi Buster!' It summed up their spiky attitude. They had great esprit de corps.

Over my two and a half years at Scampton, I'd met and worked with some marvellous people, few of whom I would ever meet again. Almost to a man, they'd given freely of their knowledge and experience to help me become a better airman. And, blowing my own trumpet again, I think that, in the main, I'd taken heed of their advice and was developing into a good tradesman and supervisor.

So why on earth was I throwing it all away in a deluded attempt to become an officer and a pilot? I'd heard that many airmen failed the officer training course, and often because their faces just didn't fit. In the jargon of their suspension reports, 'Corporal Scroggins failed to make the transition between junior NCO and officer.'

How I, the son of a dustman, was going to make that transition was anybody's guess.

Chapter 7 – Officer Training

My first full day at the Officer Cadet Training Unit at RAF Henlow confirmed all my worst fears.

I found myself alongside 19 other serving airmen destined for 16 weeks on Number 334 Officer Cadet Training course, one of the last to pass through Henlow before all officer training moved to RAF Cranwell. We were joining 71 young men and women who'd already been under training for two weeks, having enlisted from civilian life.

Some of the reasons we airmen started later were undoubtedly sound. We were saved periods sitting around kicking our heels as the civilians received items of uniform and basic military knowledge we already possessed. And we avoided some of the harsher treatment they undoubtedly suffered as they learned the rudiments of drill and bullshit we already knew.

But, on the debit side, it set us apart, denying us the opportunity to bond with our fellow officer cadets from the outset. It also fed the paranoia about status to which some of us were already prone.

We spent much of our first day receiving information about the course, and being issued with text books and items of kit. Then, in the evening, we were given a talk on the changes in dress, manner and lifestyle that would be required if we were to make the transition from airman to officer.

The flight lieutenant giving the talk, a flight commander on the Squadron we were to join, had a cut glass accent and a haughty manner. He reminded me of the Army officers I'd seen at the sports weekends at Arborfield.

'From now on,' he began, 'you will be expected to

dress conservatively, in smart jacket and slacks, except in extreme warm weather, when one may, if absolutely necessary, remove one's jacket. If, God forbid, it also proves necessary to remove one's tie, say to work on one's car, one should at least wear a cravat.'

It seemed that on no account should an officer display his bare throat, especially not in the presence of an airman.

Did sight of an officer's throat make airmen homicidal? If so, was I immune, or had I just never been confronted with such a sight before?

Over the course of the briefing, the flight commander made it clear that we were currently a lower life form. They'd do their best to beat us into shape, but some would prove beyond redemption, lacking the breeding, manner and intellect to succeed as officers.

At that moment, I hated him and all he stood for.

Whether the briefing was intended to elicit such a reaction, I never found out, but it led one of our number to withdraw from training as soon as it had finished. Like all of us, he'd felt insulted, but, unlike the rest of us, he wasn't prepared to hang around and be part of what this particular flight commander was peddling.

My sympathies went with him. I thought he'd shown great integrity, but, like the others I guess, I wasn't prepared to follow him and throw everything in for what might, after all, be a deliberately provocative test.

The flight commander in question turned out to be a stuffed shirt who probably believed everything he said. And perhaps he was right. Perhaps officers should always dress and behave as he'd suggested, and perhaps they shouldn't commission those of us from the lower orders.

Luckily, although I met many officers with cut glass accents during my career, I met few in the RAF willing to express such views, and those that did generally received the ribbing they deserved from their peers.

The next morning, with the new rank of Officer Cadet, I joined J Flight of Blue Squadron, one of ten flights: A to K. Each flight should have received two ex-airmen; although, after the talk the previous evening, one received only one 'hairy', as we were sometimes called.

I still have a squadron nominal roll. It lists the flights and the names of the officer cadets on each. A Flight had ten members, the remainder nine. In addition to the 19 ex-airmen, the 91 members of Blue Squadron included 11 women, training for commissions in what, until 1994, remained a separate part of the Service, the Women's Royal Air Force; and five from foreign air forces, two from Nigeria and three from the Sultanate of Oman. J Flight, however, was all male and all British.

I find my copy of the document quite sinister. Many of the names have been scored through – by me - with red ink, a gesture that could mean only one of three things, none of them good for the individuals concerned. They'd either withdrawn from training; been re-coursed to repeat some or all of the course on another squadron; or been suspended - the dreaded chop – that is, sent back to civilian life or to resume their careers as airmen.

Most flights have one, two or three names crossed out, but one has five. In total, there are 24 red lines, and no flight completed the course intact.

Three of the names in the J Flight column are red-lined. One was chopped so soon after my arrival that I have no recollection of him. The second and third lasted until mid-course, with one of them being chopped in the most callous, and to my mind, unnecessary manner.

So, discounting the J Flight member chopped very early on, for about the first half of the course, we were a group of eight. And we were another disparate bunch.

Two were straight from school. The first, Darryl, was a slim, dark-haired, athletic young man of medium height, who was trying to become a pilot. He was one of the few on Blue Squadron who could beat me at the mile and a half run, one of the major measures used to assess our fitness. Over the 16 weeks, I improved my time from eight minutes 40 seconds to eight minutes nine. Darryl could run the distance in just under eight minutes, and another chap – an ex-apprentice – could do it in just over seven.

A year or so later, Darryl and I completed our advanced flying training together, before spending a further 3 years on the same Hercules squadron.

The second school leaver, a slight, golden-haired boy, hoped to become an RAF Regiment officer.

Members of the RAF Regiment are known as Rock Apes. The name originated when they were serving in Aden in the early 1950s. One evening, two of their officers set out to shoot some of the local baboons, known as rock apes. Seeing movement in the gloom, one officer shot, not a baboon, but his companion.

The victim recovered, but there was an inquiry at which the marksman said he'd fired because he thought his colleague was a rock ape. The story whistled round the RAF and, ever since, all RAF Regiment members have been known as Rock Apes.

Because of his diminutive stature, however, our second school-leaver was nicknamed Pebble – that is, a little Rock. I can't even remember his real name

The Regiment training that followed Henlow was notoriously tough. With some justification, RAF Regiment members see themselves as an elite to stand alongside Marine Commandos and members of the Parachute Regiment, and they're the smartest foot soldiers in the world, witness the ceremonial drill of the Queen's Colour Squadron.

To say that Pebble didn't look the part is an understatement. And the early weeks of the course seemed to underline his unsuitability. He was terribly unfit and his slight frame was prone to injury. But, he was one of the most determined individuals I've ever met, walking for miles with bloodied blisters the size of pound coins on each heel. He pushed himself to exhaustion on every exercise.

Perhaps this strong determination was what the selection centre at Biggin Hill had spotted, because he didn't seem to have much else going for him. But, in the end, they were right. Pebble went on to succeed at Henlow and in his subsequent RAF Regiment training.

The third member of the Flight, David, was a graduate of medium height and build. I can't recall what college he'd attended or what degree he'd attained, and I don't remember much else about him, only that he completed the course and went on to train as a navigator.

The fourth, let's call him Tom, was one of those chopped. He was tall, slim, fair haired and baby-faced, with a butter-wouldn't-melt demeanour. In his early 20s, he'd spent a few years in employment. I can't remember what he'd done, but I doubt he'd done it very well, because he had an uncanny ability to disappear when hard work was in the offing.

Mike, the name we'll give the other suspendee, was an ex-Civil Servant in his late 20s. He was tall and dark-haired, had a pock-marked complexion, and, in build and movement, resembled Herman Munster.

Perhaps, in other circumstances, he may have displayed a more open manner, even humour, but his inability to cope with almost any aspect of the training at Henlow quickly took its toll. He retreated into a dour shell from which he rarely emerged. From the outset, he seemed out of his depth, and I thought him unlikely to succeed.

I know from my own time running the Officers and Aircrew Selection Centre that those conducting officer training are always critical of the people sent to them by the selectors. All I can say is that, although OASC is widely recognised as one of the best selection centres in the world, it only assesses candidates over a three day period. Errors are made, statistically, not too many, but enough to upset the trainers.

But even giving OASC the benefit of the doubt, it was hard to see what they saw in Mike. His selection could hardly be seen as anything other than a dreadful mistake.

Tom was a very different kettle of fish. Behind his laziness, he had abilities, and these would undoubtedly have been to the fore at Biggin Hill. Even so, such types usually reveal the chink in their armour at some stage of the selection process. Tom obviously didn't.

To compound matters, in the 1970s, OASC made no assessment of fitness, even though the officer training course was relatively short and very physical, offering little opportunity to improve if you were unfit at the outset.

Some who may have had the potential to be fine leaders in other circumstances were unable to cope with the leadership exercises solely because of their lack of fitness. They became so exhausted they were unable to think, let alone cope with the physical demands laid on them. If their underlying leadership potential was recognised, they might be re-coursed to allow extra time to get fit; otherwise, they'd be chopped, a real waste.

In my time running OASC, we assessed fitness with a shuttle-run test. I set great store on this, doing the test with most groups of candidates that passed through our hands. But it was only a brief assessment, and not always a strong indication of the stamina required to succeed in officer training. In recognition of this, those selected received further assessments and advice on fitness as their officer training course approached.

In the second decade of the 21st Century, selection is much more focused on fitness, and the officer training course is twice as long, partly to allow time for a progressive improvement in this area.

Back in 1979, time to improve was not the issue for Mike. He was just one of those individuals who lack the aptitude for physical activity, not just running, but almost anything. He was so poorly coordinated that even walking looked laboured, and his foot drill was appalling. On leadership exercises, his whole body seemed to close down after quite short distances. Unfortunately, his brain did the same, and this led to a downward spiral that left him unable to perform adequately in other areas, such as public speaking, or briefing subordinates.

All in all, he was a disaster. He didn't fit in. And yet, for some reason, he lasted well into the course.

The sixth member of J Flight was a great character. Tall and heavily built with a Saddam Hussein moustache and an infectious laugh, Dave was a 32-year old comprehensive school teacher, desperately keen to become an education officer. I'm not sure what had led him to seek a military career, because he seemed completely ignorant of what the course was likely to demand of him.

As an example, in the two weeks before my arrival, the Physical Training Instructors - PTIs – had taken the Squadron on the first of many gruelling long distance runs. At the end, with everyone lined up in threes, breathing heavily, some doubled up, coughing and heaving, one of the PTIs asked, 'Right, put your hand up if you didn't enjoy that.'

Now, those with any understanding of the military, and especially military training and PTIs, would know that this was a tongue-in-cheek question for which no response was required, or expected.

Dave put his hand up. And, of course, he was made to do the run again.

He wasn't thick, and he learned his lessons, but, throughout the course, he continued to make mistakes based on an over-literal interpretation of rules or criticisms. The mistakes had ramifications that were often painful, but, to onlookers, nearly always hilarious.

I met Dave again only once, a few years after Henlow, by which time he was involved in the design of training courses for those working on and flying Nimrod maritime reconnaissance aircraft. Over the 30 minutes we were together, we were both reduced to tears of laughter recounting the various experiences we'd shared at Henlow. It would be the same if we met again now, over 30 years later.

The seventh member of the Flight, Glen, was the other ex-airman. Of medium height and build, with receding dark hair and a moustache, he was a 35-year old ex-flight sergeant Air Loadmaster, a helicopter crewman. Most recently, he'd been a winchman on Search and Rescue helicopters, earning a Queen's Commendation for Valuable Service in the Air for his bravery in rescuing injured sailors, walkers and climbers.

After gaining his commission, he hoped to return to the search and rescue role. I'm not sure it worked out, though, because I have a vague recollection of him being an Air Traffic Controller when we met several years later.

At the start of Henlow, Glen and many of the other ex-senior NCOs were very serious, stern even. They seemed to find it hard to relate to and sympathise with the younger members of their flights, or even the older ones who were less experienced in the ways of the Service. The communal living – a flight to a room in barrack blocks – and the early emphasis on drill and bullshit were hard to bear.

Worse, some of them weren't as fit as they once were, and they'd forgotten some of the skills learned in their own basic training. They were also unused to being criticised for their dress and deportment, or suffering for the deficiencies of others. And they absolutely hated being shouted at by young corporals and officers, even when the abuse wasn't directed at them personally.

The problem was that their previous experience of such treatment had been a long way in the past, and they'd become accustomed to receiving a degree of respect and deference based on their age and seniority. Although they'd known that trying to become an officer would re-expose them to the rigours of basic training, the reality still proved a shock to the system.

I, on the other hand, felt in a privileged position.

It wasn't so long since I'd spent three years at Halton, up to my neck in bullshit, marching up and down, saluting anything that moved, polishing anything that didn't, and being shouted at loudly and often. So, while I didn't enjoy the abuse of the Henlow staff during drill, or room and kit inspections, it didn't bother me as much as it did some of the others. And, as a 24-year old sportsman, I was young and fit enough to cope with the more extreme physical aspects of the course.

I was also young enough to remember what it was like to try and learn from scratch how to march, or to polish your boots and brasses, and I was more than happy to pass on what expertise I had in these areas to those who were struggling. This was a major reason why the spread of age and experience on flights was so important. We all had something to offer. Some of the older ex-airmen just took a while to re-learn this lesson.

It wasn't that long before we were all benefiting from Glen's knowledge and experience, and before his humour asserted itself.

Over the 16 weeks of the course, it was fascinating to see the youngsters become more mature, and the oldies less so, swopping some of their sternness for youthful enthusiasm. In Glen's case, he changed from someone who found it hard to take the unlikely scenarios of the early exercises seriously, to someone who became totally immersed in the later ones, even when they were no less realistic.

In an attack on an enemy position toward the end of the course, he ran out of blank ammunition.

Undaunted, he imagined a bayonet on the end of his rifle and set about stabbing the defenders. Fearing he might have someone's eye out, the directing staff were forced to confiscate his rifle. I'll never forget Glen's face as it was taken away; he looked like a sulky teenager.

My nominal roll also has a list of the Squadron staff, including a squadron commander, a training and an education officer, ten flight commanders, an RAF Regiment flight sergeant and a small staff of Regiment NCOs to supervise our drill and ground defence training.

J Flight was commanded by Flight Lieutenant Roger Kinzett, a dark-haired man of medium height and build in his early 30s. We were his first flight, and I think he was a very good role model.

Unfortunately, in my opinion, the same could not be said of all his peers.

Even as I was helping less experienced flight members cope with the bull of the early weeks, I had trouble with one aspect myself.

The last thing you needed on a course with many hours of foot-slogging was a new pair of boots. But while working under the mighty Vulcan at Scampton, my trusty old pair had received regular dousings in hydraulic and engine oil. While this hadn't prevented me polishing them to a standard acceptable for working on the line, now the toecaps had to gleam, the oil meant they just wouldn't shine without smearing.

The RAF Regiment drill instructors were sympathetic, the flight commanders less so. This was a strange feature of Henlow.

At Swinderby and Halton, the NCOs had been the

bullies, shouting and haranguing, while the officers had generally hovered above such behaviour, speaking in gentler tones and appearing more reasonable.

On Blue Squadron at Henlow, these roles were reversed.

The officers were the bullies, the NCOs more measured and approachable. Our first Regiment flight sergeant was moved on when, to our eyes, he'd become too sympathetic towards us, too eager to take the role of prisoners' friend. Perhaps he'd become disquieted by the behaviour of some of the flight commanders; as the course progressed, I certainly did.

But, at this early stage, it meant that, although the NCOs were prepared to give me time to address the problem with my boots, the officers weren't. I needed a quick fix. One evening, on the advice of the NCOs, I waved the toecaps of my boots over a candle, burnt off all the polish and tried to evaporate the oil without permanently damaging the leather. I then spent several hours with cotton wool and polish attempting to produce an acceptable shine.

I'm glad to say it worked, and although I was never truly happy with the result, the toecaps shone well enough to pass muster on inspections. And, in contrast to the officers, I was grateful to the NCOs for their pragmatic approach. Most importantly, I didn't have to break in a new pair of boots.

Henlow placed a tremendous emphasis on physical fitness. My diary still tends to concentrate on this aspect, detailing daily PT and sport, long runs and longer walks, including a 20-mile slog on the first Saturday. There was little let-up throughout the 16 weeks, but I really enjoyed it and finished the course fitter than I'd ever been, or would be again.

But, as you'd expect, there was also plenty of time in the classroom, studying subjects including Air Force Law, RAF history and customs, the history of war, and written and oral communications. There was a strong emphasis on public speaking, leading to five and ten minute talks later in the course. We also covered the theory of ground defence training, before moving outside for the more practical aspects, including shooting and the basics of nuclear, biological and chemical protection, which for me, of course, was revision.

And having been told at Swinderby that we'd only be forced to inhale CS gas once during our careers, we ex-airmen found we had to do it again at Henlow, and in pretty much the same way.

I should imagine I wasn't the only one concerned about etiquette, especially after the talk on the first night of the course, but I remember only one lesson on the subject. We stood in front of a table in the Officers' Mess that had been laid for dinner, and were taught not to touch the silver before the meal, to use the cutlery from the outside in, and to pass the port decanter to the left. Even I knew there was more to it than that, so I remained under-confident in this, to my mind, vital area.

Eventually, I discovered that as long as you were reasonably house-trained and didn't eat your peas with your knife, your behaviour would generally be acceptable. I also came to realise that those with breeding could spot my lack of it a mile off, but I seemed to manage in most situations, including dining with Royalty.

As you might expect, much of the syllabus was given

over to the teaching of leadership, moving from theory in the classroom to increasingly complex practical exercises in the great outdoors. The major tests were to be an 8-Day Camp at the course mid-point, and a 6-day tactical Camp at the end.

The qualities required of a leader were listed as: sense of duty, loyalty, integrity, presence, upright bearing, smart appearance, physical fitness and good social conduct. Armed with these qualities, when given a task, a leader should be able to make a plan, allocate work and resources appropriately, ensure quality and check performance. As a task progressed, the leader should be able to communicate, delegate, motivate, foster team spirit, set standards, maintain discipline and make adjustments where necessary.

They should also have the skill to perform their own primary function to a high standard – ie, be a good pilot, engineer or administrator.

Under the model of functional leadership taught at the time, a leader had to juggle three sets of needs: those of the task, those of the group and those of the individuals within the group. In military situations, completion of the task nearly always has primacy, but a good leader should, wherever possible, also strive to meet the often conflicting needs of the group and its individuals.

In reality, I've known leaders who didn't give a stuff about the team or the individual, as long as the job was done, or appeared to have been done, and they received the kudos for it. But, at Henlow, they at least tried to fashion you into an ideal leader.

I was selected to lead my flight's first leadership exercise away from the classroom. It was not unlike the selection exercises at Biggin Hill, only on a slightly larger scale. We had an hour to bridge a chasm - a ten foot gap between two sunken wartime shelters - with heavy pine poles and ropes.

Whether any science went into my selection for this honour, I'll never know, but my diary states baldly that I *'messed up'*.

I forgot everything learnt in the classroom about standing back and delegating tasks to the other seven flight members, controlling them and setting and monitoring standards. Instead, I tried to do everything myself, lifting every pole and pulling every rope. It was a disaster. But when the exercise ended, it got worse.

We moved a few yards away from the equipment. Six of the Flight sat in a semi-circle in front of Flight Lieutenant Kinzett. To his left, looking at the reams of notes he'd made, sat the member nominated to observe my performance and comment on it. Totally knackered after all my exertions, I walked to the Flight Commander's right hand side and slumped down.

As I did so, every muscle relaxed and I let out a tremendous fart.

Well, that was that. Since my arrival, I'd been worried about my airman status and lack of breeding, and it had finally caught me out. No need to debrief the exercise. My public humiliation was complete. Time to pack my bags.

Most of the Flight struggled to keep straight faces, but Dave just collapsed in gales of laughter. After a few moments' hesitation, the rest joined him.

I looked at Flight Lieutenant Kinzett.

He wasn't without humour, but it was still early in the course, and we'd seen more of his stern face than any softer side. I could tell he was struggling, deciding, I presumed, whether to ignore what had just happened, or to use it as the final example of my unsuitability for a commission in Her Majesty's Royal Air Force.

I waited for what seemed an age before his head fell back and he laughed heartily.

I still didn't know whether to laugh or cry, but I chose laughter. It was the right choice. Once order had been restored, my rubbish attempt at leadership was torn to shreds, but the fart was never mentioned again, at least not by Flight Lieutenant Kinzett.

This style of public debrief, sitting on the grass immediately an exercise was completed, although painful for the person having their performance dissected, was an excellent idea. It continued throughout the course, and we all learned by discussing each other's mistakes, with perhaps the person nominated as observer learning more than anyone else.

After more simple leadership exercises like mine, we moved on to longer and more complex scenarios, covering greater distances and carrying heavier loads and more equipment.

We might have to walk or run five miles to locate a crashed aircraft, rescue its atomic bomb, keeping at least a yard from its radioactive container, and then carry it another five miles to a place of safety. For other exercises, the bomb could be a secret radio or top secret plans, and there could be enemy forces to dodge, partisans to meet, casualties to carry, even a traitor within the team.

And then, just at the point you thought you'd finished, there was dislocation of expectation, a further time and energy-sapping task to complete, delaying meals and rest.

At the start of each exercise, the designated leader was called aside, given the scenario and allowed a few moments to digest the information and formulate a plan, even if only in outline. He then called over the rest of the Flight and, using the mnemonic SMEAC, briefed them on the Situation; the Mission; the Execution, that is his plan; asked if there were Any questions; and finally, Checked understanding.

Hopefully, the rest of the Flight would be on the leader's side throughout, working hard and providing helpful hints and suggestions, anything from, 'Why don't you try a different knot?' to, 'I thought we should be walking a little more to the left.'

The better leaders could assess new information quickly, re-brief if necessary, and acknowledge the help they'd received. But not all leaders were prepared to accept help. Some ploughed on with their original plan, even when its inadequacies became apparent, while some that accepted help, failed to acknowledge it, and sought to take all the credit themselves.

And, scandalous as it seems, we soon realised that some of our peers were unwilling to help others, preferring to see them fail in the hope that it reflected better on their own efforts. Some even seemed willing to stoop to sabotage, although this would have been almost impossible to prove.

Perhaps for this reason, we sometimes had guest leaders or subordinates from other flights – someone who may have been struggling, even being let down by their own group, and who needed to be assessed in a different one.

From the people available for any particular exercise, the leader allocated duties, usually nominating a second in command; a navigator; people to look after the various items of equipment; someone to monitor compliance with the rules to avoid penalties for getting too close to something radioactive or poisonous; and finally, someone to count paces, assisting the navigator by noting the distances we were covering.

We soon came to know who was good at navigating, carrying extra weight, or running extra miles, and who was trustworthy and able to work unsupervised. We also came to know the reverse, those who couldn't read a map or run far, or would feign injury or tiredness to avoid work, and those who just couldn't be trusted.

Armed with this knowledge, leaders tended to allocate the same people to the same duties, unless the Flight Commander intervened because he wanted to see someone in a particular role, such as second in command or navigator. In the case of Mike, the Flight Commander had to intervene quite often. Such was his ineptitude that he was usually selected to count paces, even when there was no particular need for it.

I think I gained a reputation for reliability in most roles, but mainly for stamina. I was often sent off on tasks involving extra mileage.

My leadership skills improved, but I still had a tendency to attempt too much myself, even setting off to cover extra distance during my own leads, leaving the Flight leaderless until I returned. Sometimes this turned out to be the right decision, but sometimes it didn't.

Early on 25th May, after several weeks of leadership training in and around Henlow, Blue Squadron set off in a convoy of coaches and trucks for 8-Day Camp at Stanford Training Area (STANTA), a large military training area in Norfolk.

I was selected as the first Camp Commandant. This meant planning the move from Henlow to STANTA;

supervising the loading of all the equipment - mainly on the previous day; 'establishing' Wretham B Camp - a large Nissen-hutted complex – when we arrived; and making it ready for an inspection and an Ensign ceremony at noon.

Being made Camp Commandant was an indication that the Directing Staff wanted to have a closer look at me. This was either because I was doing very well, or very poorly. In hindsight, I was doing well, but I wasn't confident enough to assume that at the time. I was still working all out to try and make the grade.

All went well until the erection of the flagpole for the Ensign ceremony. For some reason that escapes me, this took several attempts, a process that the notebook I kept during the eight days describes as, a *bit gash*.

Overall, I received a pretty good debrief for my first major leadership role; even if Flight Lieutenant Kinzett seemed overly disappointed about the Ensign ceremony. Only at the end of the course did I gain more of an insight into why this should be.

I'd also been given a high profile role back at Henlow, that of Messing Representative on the Squadron Entertainments Committee. This meant organising the catering aspects of every social function during the course, no small task as these included a cocktail party, a barbecue, a mid-course party, formal dinners at the two deployed Camps, a Graduation Dining-In Night; and a Graduation Lunch and Graduation Ball, both catering for several hundred people.

Over the course of these functions, I had to liaise with Mess Managers, chefs and stewards on every aspect, from menus to seating plans, and I learnt a great deal about how to work with airmen in my new capacity as a potential officer. I also learnt to cope with the inevitable crises caused by weather, supply failures, or unexpected or missing guests.

As you'd imagine for Norfolk, STANTA was reasonably flat, but it was also densely wooded, dotted with numerous streams and pools and criss-crossed with countless tracks. It was mainly used by Army units, and we were often surrounded by gun battles.

Over the course of the eight days, we covered greater distances than we'd become accustomed to thus far, and faced longer periods of physical exertion. My notebook often says *wet*, or *wet and miserable*. This was only partly because the weather was appalling for much of the week. We also got soaked during a number of river crossings.

The daily routine was Reveille at 6am; breakfast and kit cleaning until a parade and inspection at 7.40; leadership exercises all day followed by an evening meal and a short break; and then more leadership exercises, generally from 8.30pm until midnight, sometimes later.

The Army's gun battles were especially impressive at night, with flares and tracer rounds lighting the sky. On nights when they weren't playing, it was totally dark and eerily silent.

On one such night, Mike led one of the more memorable night exercises. In pitch blackness under the canopy of trees, he lost the one and only torch we'd been allocated. We were reduced to lighting matches to read the map, and shambling between checkpoints crocodile style to avoid losing one another.

Mike seemed totally at sea, at one point, holding up his arm and saying, 'Follow my watch,' as if we could all see its faintly luminous face from several yards away. Not for the first time, we didn't know whether to laugh or cry.

He continued to make a hash of everything when leading. And no matter how much we tried to help, we usually ended up covering extra mileage because of his inadequacies. Even in subordinate positions, his low level of fitness meant we were always in danger of finishing exercises late. And sorry to say, he tried our patience too often for us to feel any real sympathy.

He wasn't the only one struggling, though.

After his first attempt at leadership on 8-Day Camp, Dave had been criticised for being too soft and democratic. He was told to adopt a sharper, more military, leadership style for his next lead. This turned out to be a dash into enemy territory to locate a partisan and retrieve buried gold.

The first inkling of how much Dave had taken the advice to heart came when we arrived at a small river. He decided we should wade across it.

Someone spotted a bridge 50 yards upstream and pointed it out to him, but he refused to change his plan. He even forbade us to take off our boots, puttees and socks and roll up our trousers. It would take too much time.

The water only came up to our knees, but we, including Flight Lieutenant Kinzett, who waded across with us, were a very wet and unhappy group when we reached the other side, especially as we'd watched another group walk across the bridge.

As we trudged off, Dave, worried that the enemy might hear us, added insult to injury by telling us to stop squelching!

I thought the Flight Commander was going to give him a piece of his mind, but he thought better of it and decided, squelching apart, to suffer in silence like the rest of us.

A few kilometres later, he added a complicating factor that explained why we'd been lugging a stretcher for the last few hours. He told us Mike had been shot and would have to be carried.

Now, as well as being the slowest in the Flight – which was why he was often chosen as the casualty – Mike was also one of the heaviest. And don't believe what you see in films, where slightly-built men carry stretchers at speed over long distances. Carrying a casualty is slow, backbreaking, blister-inducing work. And with the observer excluded, Dave in dictator mode, refusing to let the navigator help, there were only four of us to share the burden.

Harried by our impatient leader, we'd been struggling for a few kilometres when we came to a gate. They were usually locked and Dave told us to lift the stretcher over. But when the navigator pushed, the gate swung open, so we walked through with the stretcher.

We'd gone no more than a few yards when an angry voice called out. While telling us off for disobeying his orders, Dave made us retrace our steps through the gate, close it and lift the stretcher over.

Now, as I've said, he was a very clever guy, and, in the cold light of day, he'd have been just as incredulous at his behaviour as the rest of us. But such was the pressure he'd put himself under, such was his will to become the leader the RAF wanted him to be, that he'd lost all sense of proportion. And, on this particular lead, it got worse.

When we reached a large clearing in the pine woods, the place Dave thought the partisan was meant to be, we found only dog walkers, none of whom looked like Fifth Columnists. He panicked.

Dressed in dishevelled, damp and dirty combat clothing, with staring eyes and drooping moustache, he ran up to randomly-chosen dog walkers and screamed, 'Mousetrap.'

Men bristled and little old ladies flinched as he confronted them, then ran off when it became apparent that the password meant nothing to them. He'd scared several folk half to death before Flight Lieutenant Kinzett managed to rein him in.

Due to a navigational error, we were still about a kilometre short of our destination. But Dave was not to be daunted by such trivia. He decided we didn't need an exact location, or a partisan. We'd just start digging. Choosing a random spot in the middle of several acres of tufted grass, he set to with a spade and encouraged us to do the same.

Only the Flight Commander's intervention saved us from a night digging up large areas of the training area.

You'll have to take my word for it that Dave wasn't as mad as he sounds. Henlow did things like that to you, and like all of us, he had to find the balance between democracy and autocracy required for different situations of military leadership. It was just that, more than any of us, he explored both extremes before eventually settling into a style that was acceptable, and that worked.

Glen too had trouble, but he had to move in the opposite direction, from out and out autocrat to something more inclusive. My notes as observer on one of his early exercises indicate a complete lack of sensitivity and empathy, with comments like: *short with people, inferred they were shirking, completely insensitive,* and, *deriding effort.* Again, Glen got there in the end.

I led only two other exercises after my stint as Camp Commandant. I have little memory of them, but my notebook records some negative comments, *too polite, failed to keep discipline or standards*, as well as more positive ones, such as, *quite good* and *completed*. The exercise I remember most vividly, though, was led by Tom.

He'd already led two exercises. My notes for both say we ran much of the way because of his shortcomings, but still failed to finish within the allotted time. Before his third attempt, Flight Lieutenant Kinzett pulled me aside and told me I was to be a traitor and do all I could to disrupt the task.

The method I chose, stealing the map, was very unsubtle, but should have been effective. Unfortunately, I ran out of patience, grabbed it on impulse and ran off when Darryl, the only person who could catch me, was close by. He apprehended me in fairly short order.

Flight Lieutenant Kinzett was very disappointed. He made it plain that I'd let him down, and I had. It's funny that this is one of only two episodes during the course that I recall on a fairly regular basis. The other is the treatment of Mike. It soured my memory of officer training and, over the years, I've tried to draw lessons from it where I could.

Mike had been like a fish out of water for much of the course leading up to 8-Day Camp, and I have no idea why he hadn't been suspended before this point. It would have been better for all concerned, because the exercises over the Camp period had further highlighted his unsuitability, and in the cruellest possible way. His mental and physical anguish were plain for all to see.

And yet, still he wasn't chopped.

For some reason, they seemed set on breaking him completely. Whether this was out of pure malice, or in order to justify his suspension, I'll never know, but he received the worst treatment I witnessed during my 32 years in the RAF.

One of the final exercises at STANTA was a long and demanding assault course. Before attempting it, we were walked around the obstacles. This was done partly to demonstrate the best way to attempt them, but also to ramp up the air of tension and intimidation.

Many of the obstacles were high, most of the low ones wet, and the rest had the potential to leave you wet if you failed to jump, swing or balance your way across them. All had to be completed as a team and against the clock.

Every flight had its weaker members, but Mike was likely to be among the weakest for an exercise like this. And so it proved. But we dragged, pushed and threw him around the course and completed it without, if I recall correctly, coming last. I loved it. Soon after finishing, soaked and covered in mud, we were told to race for the buses, parked some way off.

Mike was already completely exhausted, and inevitably fell so far behind that we were all on the buses as he lumbered up, struggling with his characteristic ungainly gait. As he neared our bus, several flight commanders leaned out of the door and shouted at him, making it plain how utterly useless they thought he was. Then, they told the driver to move off.

Mike staggered after us, his face crumpled in pain, but we drove away, the flight commanders still screaming abuse. I don't know how he made it back to camp. I suspect he was eventually picked up by one of the staff Land Rovers.

I think we were more outraged at his treatment than he was, but he'd been thoroughly broken and we were unable to gee him back up in the few hours we had left at STANTA. I have no recollection of seeing him again, either after we returned to Henlow, or later in my career, so I assume he went back to civilian life rather than being re-coursed to another squadron.

I've tried not to over-dramatise the event, and perhaps I've mis-remembered some of it, but it made such a strong impression on me that I recall it whenever I think of Henlow.

Not all the flight commanders were involved, but I can't help feeling that one of the others should have stepped in and stopped what was happening. Not easy when the more experienced were the worst offenders, and when anyone intervening would have had to have done so in front of a bus load of officer cadets. But it should have been done.

I'm sure there were hidden pressures to being a flight commander on such a demanding course, but it was as if they came to adopt a prison guard mentality, like those in 1960s psychological experiments that punished people excessively with electric shocks. Whatever the reason, some of them acted very oddly.

Earlier on 8-Day Camp, one had made his flight walk into a swamp up to their waists. This seemed to be for no other reason than to impress his fellow flight commanders. Others seemed to delight in dishing out extreme physical exercise, again for little or no discernible reason other than that they could. We wondered if they were involved in some bizarre, sadistic, contest.

And I don't think my disapproval is because I

wasn't prepared to be given a hard time, to be pushed, physically and mentally. I expected dislocation of expectation to be used freely, and it was, with many extra miles walked and unexpected loads carried. No, the behaviour of some flight commanders was just cruel and un-officer-like, with examples throughout the course that culminated in their treatment of Mike.

Although still unsavoury, it would have been easier to understand if the NCOs had been the ones dishing out the irrational discipline, but the officers? It all harked back to my early concerns that the roles of NCOs and officers at Henlow seemed to have been reversed.

At the least, I think it should have been possible to suspend Mike without making him fail so dramatically, and at such personal cost. If we officer cadets could all see it, the staff should certainly have been able to do so.

The other thing that concerned me, and had done since the toffee-nosed briefing on the first night, was the impression given by some flight commanders that all non-commissioned airmen were slovenly dimwits out to create trouble.

Now, it has to be said that I'd met some slovenly dimwits and troublemakers during my own service. And parts of the syllabus, notably Air Force Law, had to prepare us to face the sort of airman who'd get riotously drunk and throw up behind the piano – a Technicolor Yawn in the language of the RAF justice system, by the way.

But I'd met precious few folk like this, and I believed that the flight commanders were giving their charges, and especially those with no service experience, an unduly pessimistic impression of airmen that would hinder rather than help them once they graduated. I also felt that the anti-airmen views of some flight commanders were based on nothing more than snobbery.

As usual, I've probably over-stated my case, and perhaps I have some basic misconception of what Henlow was trying to achieve. However, when a new officer training course was introduced at Cranwell in the mid-Noughties, it aimed to distance the flight commanders from the harsher elements of training and discipline that should be the domain of the NCOs, and to allow them to project themselves as positive role models for the potential officers on their flights. In my opinion, it was a change that was long overdue.

Instructors often complain that it's impossible to chop trainees, and that when they try to do so, those responsible for the suspension decision, or for reviewing it, tend to give the trainee the benefit of the doubt. I've seen the problem from most angles: as a trainee, as the instructor writing the suspension recommendation, as the supervisor responsible for the decision and as the reviewing authority. Inevitably, I have strong views on the issue.

It may be that sometimes the 'system' is too soft, too reluctant to suspend. After all, training is expensive and suspending trainees is wasteful, especially at the latter end of training. But, in my experience, failure to gain suspensions is often the fault of the instructors and their supervisors, rather than the system. They simply fail to produce a persuasive audit trail of poor performance that leads logically to a suspension decision.

Sometimes, to avoid knocking a trainee's confidence, instructors choose not to be too critical of poor performance. This may be for the best possible of motives, but it can be misguided. What is required from the outset is honest appraisal, putting early failings in writing, while convincing the trainee that they can still turn things around. If the trainee improves, as they often do, all well and good. If not, there's a long and accurate audit trail outlining their failings.

At other times, sadly, instructors can be too lazy to write thorough reports, or lack the skill with a pen to explain failings in a clear and persuasive manner.

Whether through misguided softness, laziness or lack of writing skill, when a suspension recommendation lacks a trail of substantiating evidence, the supervisor is almost duty bound to overturn it, to give the trainee more time to prove his or her worth. And if the supervisor blindly supports their staff and errs on the side of suspension, the reviewing authority will be duty bound to overturn the decision anyway.

Back at Henlow, I can't believe Flight Lieutenant Kinzett hadn't been flagging up Mike's failings – he was very good at pointing up mine - so I have no explanation for his treatment. It was a sorry episode.

Eight-Day Camp ended with a concert, a revue of songs and sketches by the flights, and a dining-in night, which I'd arranged. After returning to Henlow, we had a couple of days off. I went home to Shropshire, where I spent most of the time with Geraldine. We'd been going out for nearly a year.

At the beginning of June, the survivors of 8-Day Camp moved into single rooms in another barrack block, a step closer to moving into an Officers' Mess. With Tom and Mike gone, J Flight was down to six.

My diary continues to detail plenty of sport and Mess Committee meetings, but also mentions a half hour flight in a Chipmunk – *Great* – and a mid-course interview – *Good*. From Scampton, Sandy wrote to tell me he and Lyn were getting married, and Geraldine and I went to their wedding in Neyland the following year.

The academic studies continued, as did practical leadership training, but now with the emphasis on leading a small section of infantry. I really enjoyed this, running around with a rifle, learning to lay ambushes or attack enemy positions. I was being paid for playing the games I'd loved as a child, and I was wearing and carrying the correct kit, including a real gun and blank ammunition that made a loud bang.

I organised a mid-course cocktail party. Official guests stayed until 9pm, at which point, Squadron members went on to have a cold buffet and a disco until two in the morning. My diary states merely that it *seemed to go well.*

Mid-way through June, we began practising for the graduation parade of the senior course, Red Squadron, who were six weeks ahead of us. We were their support squadron, which meant marching onto the parade square before them; standing around looking pretty for their friends and families; staying in the background as they marched on, did some drill and received their prizes; listening to a tedious speech from the Reviewing Officer; watching them march off and into the Officers' Mess as newly commissioned officers; then, marching off the square ourselves.

All in all, the build up to the parade was a bind, and only one detail of the rehearsals remains crystal clear in my mind.

When the members of our course entertainments

committee had been chosen at the beginning of the course, we'd been given a chat by the officer cadet running the same committee on Red Squadron. A very assured young man in his late teens told us what events his committee had organised and how they were going to make sure they happened as planned.

Although he was several years younger than me, and only a few weeks ahead in his training, he was every inch an officer. If there was some secret ingredient that marked out future air marshals, he seemed to have it.

A couple of months later, it came as no surprise that he was the parade commander for Red Squadron's graduation, or that he was awarded the Sword of Honour for outstanding performance on the course.

I met him again several years later, when we were both flight lieutenant flying instructors. This time I was surprised, firstly that he was still the same rank as me, and secondly, at how disillusioned he'd become.

He said it was as if the Sword of Honour had come with a curse. Although he'd gone on to do extremely well in flying training, becoming a Jaguar pilot and fast jet instructor, he never quite seemed to live up to that early promise, in other's eyes at least. I'm pretty sure he left the RAF to become an airline pilot soon after our meeting.

Perhaps the burden of expectation laid at Henlow had proved too much.

In the run up to the parade where he received his Sword, I also received a very minor pat on the back. I was chosen to open the car doors for the VIP guests. In truth, it was nothing more than recognition of my expertise at shoe cleaning, but it saved me having to stand on the parade square for hours during the later rehearsals and the parade itself.

During the 16 weeks at Henlow, I didn't get to go home that often. Even when not working a full weekend, we often had only Sundays free, which made it impractical to travel to Shropshire and back. When I did go home, I spent most of my time with Geraldine. I even began staying the night in the spare room at her parent's house.

The lack of a spare room in my parent's house made the opposite arrangement impractical, and sharing a room would have been out of the question - at either house.

Looking back, although, technically, I'd left the family home when I'd joined the RAF nearly six years earlier, this was the point when, emotionally, I moved out, and the strong bond with my parents and brother began to loosen. My old bedroom was still there, but I rarely slept in it.

Mum's health was okay and Dad was still working. Brian was living with them and had settled down to work at a local newsagent: Abbott's, which became Yeo's, something of a Ludlow institution until it closed in late 2011.

On 1st July, the surviving members of Blue Squadron moved into the Cadet Officers' Mess. Although it wasn't a full Officers' Mess, and we didn't receive the same privileges as Station officers - having our beds made, rooms and shoes cleaned, and steward service in the dining room - it was an indication that we were on course to graduate. It also gave us a valuable introduction to the geography and traditions of Officers' Messes.

Apart from the grander buildings, like the Rothschild Mansion at Halton, most RAF stations have

Officers' Messes of similar construction and layout. They tend to have an imposing red brick frontage with large, white-framed windows, behind which are the public rooms, as they're called. To either side are two-storey wings, also of red brick, containing accommodation - rooms and suites - for those officers who live in.

These 'living-in' officers pay for their accommodation and meals. But all officers, whether living in or out of a Mess, pay towards the upkeep of its building and facilities. These standing charges are paid every month, whether you set foot through the door or not. Running up to my retirement in 2005, I paid standing charges of about £30 per month.

Except when far from home on training courses or detachments, I didn't live in Messes after I married in 1980. So, my normal Mess bill consisted of the standing charges, my bar bill if I drank in the Mess, and the cost of any functions I attended.

Until the introduction of standing orders and direct debits, Mess bills had to be paid by cheque by the 10th of the following month. Failure to pay was one of the most heinous crimes an officer could commit, and would lead to a round of interviews with senior officers of escalating rank until the bill was paid. Bouncing a Mess bill cheque was an even worse crime.

Officers have the privilege of buying drinks on credit. The system may have changed since my retirement, but up until then, every Mess member had a bar book. Any drinks you ordered were written in the book by the white coated bar steward, who then handed you the book to sign. It meant you didn't need to carry cash in the Mess – one of the things that led airmen to believe that officers never carried money.

It was very convenient, but it also made it very easy

to rack up a large bar bill without realising it, especially if you were a piss-head like me. It was also the major reason some officers ended up *with insufficient funds to honour their Mess bills*. To avoid such surprises, I always paid for drinks in cash.

During my 27 years as an officer, I never missed a deadline for paying my Mess bill.

What follows is a whirlwind tour of a generic Officers' Mess, and a brief explanation of some of its customs.

On passing through large double glass doors in the centre of the frontage of the Mess, you usually enter an imposing, carpeted, entrance hall. It will probably contain a trophy cabinet or two and be hung with a picture of the Sovereign and his or her consort; numerous paintings of Station aircraft past and present; scrolls bestowing the Station with the freedom of local towns; and honour boards of past and present Station Commanders and Presidents of the Mess Committee, PMCs.

The PMC is usually a squadron leader or wing commander, and is responsible for both the day to day running of the Mess and its Committee, and for organising, and then sitting at the head of the table and orchestrating most formal Mess functions. PMC is one of the most demanding secondary duties on a station, a good one if you're looking for promotion - if all goes well, of course.

I was PMC twice. During one of these appointments, my Mess burned down. But that's a story for later.

The entrance hall will also contain a highly polished table bearing two equally polished wooden name plates, one giving the Station Commander's rank, initials, surname and post nominals – OBE, DFC, that sort of thing, the other, the PMC's. It's an RAF tradition that the Station Commander and PMC can leave their hats adjacent to their name plates. Other officers, no matter how high ranking, have to hang their hats in the cloakroom.

Somewhere near the entrance will be Mess Reception. It's here that new arrivals to a Station, or those departing, sign the Warning In and Warning Out Books. On a symbolic level, writing in these leather-bound books signals your arrival or departure, while on a practical level, it tells the Mess staff how many people to cater for, and how many rooms are required.

Attached to the wall will be a wooden mail rack with numerous pigeonholes for letters or notes. On a small station, each officer, whether living in or out of the Mess, could have a personal pigeonhole, but, more usually, they're allocated alphabetically.

During my service, some living out officers preferred to have their mail delivered to these pigeonholes rather than their home address. Sometimes the reason was innocuous, sometimes a matter of speculation. Occasionally, there was a scandalous reason that was open knowledge. I'll leave you to guess the possibilities.

To one side of the entrance hall, along a corridor lined with paintings, will be the bar, toilets and cloakrooms, as well as snooker and television rooms, and some offices; at the end of the corridor will be a door to one of the accommodation wings. To the other side of the entrance hall, along another picture-lined corridor will be the entrances to the Ante- and Dining Rooms.

The Ante-room is usually large, and furnished with a number of coffee tables, each surrounded by four or five comfortable armchairs. A table to the side will hold a selection of neatly folded newspapers and periodicals, and, at 5 o'clock each evening, another table will be loaded with tea, toast and jams for living-in Mess members.

Early in my career, there would have been a separate, similarly furnished, Ladies Room, the only room in which women other than WRAF officers were allowed, except during formal functions.

Unless they were flower arranging or on some other official business, wives certainly didn't go into the Mess without their husbands; that would have been very bad form. This tradition must have died out sometime in the early 80s, but some officers and, more usually, their wives, continued to frown on women being given free run of the Mess.

Most Officers' Messes hold a dozen formal functions a year, of which ten are Dining-In or Guest Nights, the others being a Summer Ball and, probably, a Christmas Draw.

During Dining-In Nights, newly arrived officers are introduced to the Mess, and those departing are bade farewell. In my early years as an officer, attendance was mandatory. Later, it became voluntary, and I invariably volunteered.

A couple of functions a year are Guest Nights, during which, as the name implies, officers can be accompanied by their partners or other guests. When most officers were male, and most couples were married, they were called Ladies' Guest Nights.

For both types of function, officers dress in their Mess Kit; for males, an RAF blue uniform of trousers, short jacket with gold rank braid at the cuffs, sleeveless waistcoat, white soft-fronted evening shirt and black, self tie, bow tie. In the days when such traditions were religiously upheld, the penalty for being discovered wearing a pre-tied or elasticated bow tie would be public humiliation and a bottle of port, even, in some Messes, a round of port for all your fellow diners.

For many years, the Mess Kit of female officers has been very similar, the only difference being the option of wearing a long RAF blue skirt rather than trousers. Before that, though, WRAFs had to wear a long, tightly fitting, royal blue dress, known disparagingly as a 'boob tube', because of its figure-hugging qualities.

Civilian male guests should wear black tie, and female guests, long dresses. An old rule that female shoulders should be covered has fallen into abeyance.

Before Guest and Dining-In nights, the Ante-room is cleared of furniture and used for pre-dinner drinks, proffered on silver trays by the Mess staff. The only choices used to be sweet or dry sherry, but, toward the end of my career, gin and tonic or orange juice became the norm. Out of habit, I often hankered for, and sometimes asked for sherry. I didn't always get it, though, often, if you can believe it, because the Mess no longer stocked sherry!

Anyway, on entering the Ante-room before a Dining-In Night – at 7.30 for 8 – each officer introduces themselves briefly to the PMC, not the Station Commander, before moving away to let others do the same. In the days when dinners were mandatory, this allowed the PMC to identify those attending – and any absentees.

Officers then join their mates and stand around chatting and drinking, remembering at some point to check the seating plan for the meal. This is usually displayed on a large easel at one end of the room.

The plan has a top table, along the upper length of which are 20 or so names, those of the senior officers and guests attending the meal. Running down from this table are several others, known as legs, either side of which are the names of the junior officers. Having identified where they're sitting, officers return to their groups and continue chatting.

The most junior officer on the Station, known – whether male or female - as Mr Vice, sits at the end of the central leg, looking along the table at the PMC, sitting in the centre of the top table.

At Ladies Guest Nights, husbands and wives can be seated close to one another, perhaps on opposite sides of the table, but never side by side, and when I became a senior officer and Geraldine and I sat at the top table, we could often be separated by its entire length.

Approaching 8pm, I would go for a pee, because leaving the dinner table was another heinous crime, usually leading to a fine of a bottle or a round of port. This rule was very rigidly enforced during my early years, with no breaks during a three-hour Dining-in Night.

I've been growing an enlarged prostate for a long time and used to dehydrate myself leading up to dinners, but I could still be in agony by the end of the evening.

At Ladies Guest Nights, very much in deference to the ladies, you understand, there was a comfort break – ease springs – after the Loyal Toast and before the speeches. Later in my career, much to my personal relief, it became routine to have comfort breaks at all dinners. Some old hands still refused to leave the table, showing their manliness by sticking to the old traditions. Bully for them.

At 8pm, dinner is signalled, generally by a trumpet call, after which the Mess Manager steps forward, bangs a gavel and announces, 'Ladies and gentlemen, dinner is served'.

At this point, junior officers leading, everyone files out of the Ante-room and into the Dining Room, where a band or chamber orchestra will be playing. On most stations, there are likely to be over a hundred diners.

If ladies are present, checking the seating plan before the meal is particularly important, because you're expected to escort the lady sitting on your right to the Dining Room. Before leaving the Ante-Room, you offer her your left arm, so that your sword arm is free, and set off.

Throughout my career, this used to cause all sorts of confusion, with people not only trying to remember which lady on which arm, but trying to locate someone they may never have met before. When I became a senior officer, and therefore one of the last to leave the Ante-room, there would always be a jumble of junior officers and ladies trying to pair off, and often, one poor lady left behind looking forlorn, until someone, usually her husband, came back for her.

And no, RAF officers didn't wear swords to dinner. In fact, they wore them only very occasionally on ceremonial parades. I never wore one after Henlow.

Officers' Mess Dining Rooms tend to be thickly carpeted, high-ceilinged and imposing, hung with large pictures of Station aircraft past and present. For most routine meals, eight to twelve officers sit on padded dining chairs at large, highly polished tables, arranged wide apart in a herring-bone pattern. Some elements of breakfast, such as cereal, could be self-service, but most meals were ordered from a steward who would then deliver the dish to your table. It was basically restaurant silver service for every meal.

For Dining-In Nights, the room would be transformed, with tables being pushed together to form the top table and legs, and all groaning with shining Mess silver and cutlery, gleaming glasses and extravagant candelabras bristling with brightly glowing candles.

I loved entering RAF Dining Rooms on such occasions, but have to admit that both my most memorable meals were eaten in Navy shore establishments: HMS Drake in Plymouth and The Painted Hall at Greenwich.

I'm now going to try and describe the format of an RAF Dining-In Night. Inevitably, I will make errors in etiquette, for which I apologise, and the etiquette in various Army Messes and Royal Navy Wardrooms would have wide variations.

Each officer, having studied the seating plan in the Ante-room, makes for their seat, or delivers the lady they're accompanying to hers, checking the nameplate to make sure they've found the right place. They then stand behind their chairs chatting to their neighbours as the senior officers file in to the accompaniment of the band.

As the top table diners settle behind their chairs, a hush begins to descend. The PMC looks around, perhaps allowing a straggler to escort a forgotten lady to her seat and dash to his own, before banging a gavel. The remaining chatter ceases and the PMC sets the evening in motion by asking the Padre to say Grace.

Grace is generally a straightforward part of the meal, although some Padres are very adept at coming up with amusing, even profane, versions of the standard wordings. It can be more dangerous when no Padre is present, and a lay member of the Mess has to be dragooned to open the proceedings.

When I was PMC at a University of Wales Air Squadron Ladies Guest Night, I asked one of my few Welsh students to say Grace. It wasn't until he finished with, 'gogogoch', that many in the room realised they'd been bowing their heads to the name of the famous railway station on Anglesey. Luckily, there were no external guests to be offended, and I took the jape in the mischievous way it had been intended.

With Grace over, the diners pull out their chairs, or the chairs of the lady guest next to them, and sit down. This too sounds fairly straightforward. But, on Stations with large numbers of young officers in groups with strong corporate identities and rivalries, such as different training courses or flying squadrons, this is where the high jinks can start. There are several possibilities.

A favourite prank is attaching a rival group's cutlery to their chairs with thin thread, so that when the chairs are pulled out, knives, forks and spoons clatter to the floor. Another is seeding the rivals' napkins with flour or talc, so that when they're shaken free of their folds, the targets are covered in white powder.

Station Commanders and PMCs can either get angry at this early tomfoolery, thus enhancing the power of the prank, or shrug and join in the general laughter. They're more likely to be grumpy when the joke is inflicted on the top table, which I've seen on several occasions.

With everyone seated, the Mess Manager, standing behind the PMC, nods to the small army of waiting staff. They begin serving the first course, while the band or chamber orchestra strikes up its first piece of the evening. Menus placed around the tables forewarn of, not only the meal, but what music is to be played and what toasts are to be made.

When everyone has been served their starter, the Mess Manager tells the PMC, who begins to eat. No-one should have touched their cutlery before the PMC. Again, on a nod from the Mess Manager, the waiting staff move along the tables offering a choice of red or white wine. And when the Mess Manager is happy that everyone has finished eating, the staff clear away the first course.

The other courses, three, or four if there's a sorbet between the first and second course, are handled in the same way, with wine being served as the meal progresses.

The main course, usually meat, two veg and gravy, can take quite a while to serve, with all the elements being dished up separately, even the gravy, spooned on to the diners' plates from gravy boats by the staff. But still, no-one should start eating until everyone has been served and the PMC reaches for his cutlery. As a result, some diners' meals are lukewarm, if not downright cold, by the time they come to eat them.

Most of the waiting staff are very adept at their duties, and I often admired the skill with which they served a range of vegetables, scooping them from the serving salver without losing peas, potatoes or sprouts. But I've also witnessed new waiting staff shaking with terror as they try to do the same, their serving spoon and fork clanking together as if they were playing the spoons.

Some never reappear from the kitchens after their first attempt, especially if they've dropped something in some poor diner's lap. Others quickly conquer their nerves and go on to serve for many years. The ladies who first served me at dinners at RAF St Athan in the early 1990s are still serving me at University of Wales Air Squadron events to which I'm invited over 20 years later.

Throughout the meal, the band or chamber orchestra plays. I've often felt sorry for the musicians. With everyone chatting to their neighbours or shouting across the table, it can seem as if they're being ignored, receiving only a polite ripple of applause at the end of each piece to reward their efforts. But I think most diners enjoy the music, and no matter what the standard of band, I always felt it added immeasurably to the occasion.

I add only one caveat. Some brass bands seem to contain musicians determined that you should hear and appreciate their individual contribution above all others. They play at full volume, as if to entertain a crowd of seaside merrymakers on a windy promenade, rather than a relatively small group of diners in an enclosed space. Those closest to the band, and anyone with deteriorating hearing – all aircrew for a start - can find it impossible to hold a conversation with their nearest neighbours, let alone those across the table. But, even on these occasions, it's impossible not to admire the enthusiasm of the players.

Any pranks beyond flying cutlery or powdered napkins are meant to be banished until after the loyal toast, but this truce is not always observed.

If some poor unfortunate can't control his bladder – it's always a he – he's meant to walk to the top table and ask the PMC if he can be excused, then walk out and back under the full gaze of the whole Mess. Although embarrassing, his honesty should spare him from any retribution beyond withering looks.

But, if he seeks to sneak to the loo unnoticed by the PMC, it invariably ends badly. While he's out of the room, his chair will be stolen. The merriment as he crawls back in and looks for it is certain to alert the PMC, and a round of port is a foregone conclusion.

A method of avoiding such a fine that I've never witnessed, thank goodness, is to make use of an empty wine bottle taken from the Mess staff. I'm sorry, I shouldn't have mentioned that.

And on occasions, invariably on flying Stations, groups of diners can join together to move their tables around the room in a surreal, seated, ballet. Immensely childish, and only really funny to those doing it, but there it is. A sensible diner on such a table has a difficult decision to make: be a killjoy and end up sitting in the middle of the dining room in glorious isolation as your table moves away, or go with the flow. Most choose to go with the flow, and I have to admit to being on a roving table whilst in advanced flying training at RAF Finningley in 1981.

As long as the table or tables are moved back into position fairly swiftly, the PMC and Station Commander usually greet the prank with little more than a world-weary shake of the head.

During the final course, the staff used to pass along the tables and take orders for after-dinner drinks - brandy or liqueurs – but this tradition seemed to die out about the same time as the smoking ban banished after-dinner cigars.

When the final course is over, the tables are cleared of place mats, napkins, and all drinks glasses bar those for the port. In another jolly jape, diners can tie their napkins together so that the staff member ends up pulling one long string of napkins. They generally just roll their eyes and get on with it, undoubtedly the best response.

With the table cleared of all bar the silver, candles and port glasses, the staff wipe off any crumbs and position the port glasses in front of the diners. They then reappear from the kitchens bearing glass decanters of port, often to the accompaniment of a piper in Scottish Messes. At a nod from the Mess Manager, the decanters, stoppers in place, are positioned around the tables, with one each in front of the PMC and Mr Vice, who is about to come into his or her own.

The PMC removes the stopper from his or her decanter and Mr Vice follows suit, the other stoppers being removed by Mess staff. The PMC charges their glass and passes the decanter to the diner to their left. The other diners with decanters in front of them do the same. At Ladies Guest Nights, diners may also fill the glass of the lady to their left, before the decanter is passed on.

In RAF Messes, the decanters are not meant to touch the table until all the glasses have been charged, whereas in Navy Wardrooms, the decanters are slid along the tables.

There can often be another little game now, with some diners, usually, but not always, the younger ones, trying to fill their glasses until the meniscus of the port is bulging above the top of the glass. Any hoots of derision at this point will be because someone's glass has been over-filled, the final drops brimming over onto the table.

Much to my shame, I once did this inadvertently when sitting at the top table of a formal dinner at the end of a conference in a hotel. It was a combination of too much wine and a distracting conversation with a fellow diner, and was compounded by the table being covered in a white tablecloth. Whatever the reason, I left a blossoming red stain on the white surface. It was not one of my finest moments.

In a Navy Wardroom, everyone may remain seated for the toasts, a tradition that dates back to the lack of headroom on ancient warships. At an RAF function, once everyone's glass is charged, the PMC bangs the gavel for the second time in the evening. Standing to attention, he or she says, 'Mr Vice, The Queen.'

At this point, Mr Vice stands to attention and, under the gaze of every diner, says, 'Ladies and Gentlemen, The Queen.'

Everyone stands. And now there is a trap for the over-eager or those unfamiliar with the correct protocol. The temptation is to reach straight for your glass and raise it, but you'll be embarrassed, because the band is about to play the first verse of the National Anthem. Only when the music stops do you reach for your glass, raise it and say, 'The Queen', before taking a sip of port, setting the glass down again, and resuming your seat.

There's usually someone who can't resist saying, 'Gawd bless her' before taking their sip of port. This is generally frowned upon. About the only allowable variation on the Loyal Toast is to be found in Lancashire, where the toast and reply may be, 'The Queen, The Duke of Lancaster.'

Depending on the occasion, the PMC may now have to bang the gavel for several more toasts. For instance, where foreign guests are present, there could be a toast to their head of state: The President of the United States of America, or the President of The Republic of Kenya. Again, the band will have rehearsed the first verse of the relevant national anthem, and diners will have to stand to attention and wait for this to be played before raising their glasses.

The first verse of some anthems can be long, and full of confusing pauses. This can have two effects, the first, diners reaching for their port because they've mistaken a pause for the end of the anthem, can lead to the second, fits of the giggles, usually, but again not always, from the younger and less experienced diners. And the tunes of some national anthems just seem to sound funny, which can cause a problem for even the most seasoned diner.

Of course, it's never acceptable to giggle at someone else's national anthem. It's an insult, and one that some countries take better than others.

My advice to avoid the giggles was to look straight ahead at the wallpaper and not strike eye contact with anyone across the table, especially friends, and especially if they've mistakenly reached for their glass. Even then, I have to admit I haven't always been successful.

If there are representatives of several countries dining, there is a catch-all toast, 'The heads of foreign and Commonwealth nations here represented'. This can be quite a mouthful for Mr Vice, but, I should imagine, a welcome relief for the band.

People are always trying to get Mr Vices drunk, or trick them into some faux pas. And, of course, if they succumb to drinking too heavily, the more they drink, the more likely they are to wumble their mords. There are stories of Mr Vices being so drunk they collapse and have to be carried from the Dining Room before the toasts, or being too drunk to stand when the toasts are reached. Thankfully, I've never witnessed either of these.

One thing I noticed becoming more prevalent over the years was Mr Vices being encouraged to make the pause between, 'Ladies and Gentlemen,' and, 'The Queen', as long as possible, with some diners running a book on the time gap. Sometimes, the pause could go on for a very long time indeed, becoming evermore embarrassing, especially with guests present.

When I was PMC or the senior host at a dinner, I always briefed my Mr Vice very carefully on the behaviour I expected. I was never let down.

Finally, a couple of the Mr Vice stories I've been told over the years.

The first involves a Ladies' Guest Night at an overseas base with no band, but a large number of diners. Someone managed to convince Mr Vice that he'd have to fill in for the lack of music during The Loyal Toast. As they reached for their port glasses after hearing Mr Vice say, 'Ladies and Gentlemen, The Queen', the diners were amused when a thin, reedy, voice launched into the National Anthem.

The second story happened after the Loyal Toast at a Mess where the French windows were blown open by a gust of wind. The PMC banged his gavel and said, 'Mr Vice, the French windows', at which point the inebriated Mr Vice stood up, raised his glass and said, 'Ladies and Gentlemen, the French windows.'

Both the University Air Squadrons I commanded, Wales and London, had royal connections. The Prince of Wales was the Chancellor of the University of Wales, and the Princess Royal was Honorary Air Commodore of the Universities of London Air Squadron. At the respective dinners, the royal connections are toasted immediately after the loyal toast, the music preceding the Welsh toast being God Bless the Prince of Wales.

Later in the evening, speakers may end their speeches with their own formal toasts - Departing Guests, The Squadron, RAF Little Soddit in the Marsh, or whatever. But, immediately after the initial toasts, the PMC is joined by the chef and the bandmaster or leader of the chamber orchestra. They're given a glass of port and seated to spend a few minutes speaking to the PMC and the senior guest, after which they rise and leave the room to a hearty round of applause.

For all dinners in recent years, the PMC will now bang the gavel again and announce a ten-minute administrative break, at which point diners can briefly leave the room, some to ease their bladders, some to have a quick drag on a cigarette. During this pause, coffee is served and, in olden days, the liqueurs or brandy ordered earlier in the proceedings used to appear. The port decanters continue to be passed along the tables for people to charge their glasses.

At the end of the ten minute break, with everyone seated again, the PMC stands to bang the gavel and introduce the first of several speakers. For a Dining-In or Guest Night, the main speaker will be the Station Commander. For dinners to mark other occasions, there could be speeches from one or more visiting guest.

Whatever the occasion, the first speaker will invariably open by thanking the band and the Mess staff, who receive a generous round of applause, which they're unlikely to hear because most of them will already have left the building.

The nature of the ensuing speeches depends on the occasion. A Station Commander will probably be saying farewell to several officers who are leaving the Station on posting or retirement. In fine military tradition, he starts with the junior departee and moves through the rest in rising order of rank until arriving at the most senior. He reads snippets on each that have usually been provided by their colleagues, the more funny and scandalous the better.

Some Station Commanders are excellent at this; others are awful.

The Station Commander of one Station on which I served, insisted on peppering his speeches with obscene jokes, even at Ladies Guest Nights. He seemed to remain oblivious of the grimaces and groans from diners, or perhaps he mistook them for appreciation of his comedic talent.

After each dinner, I assumed someone would speak candidly to him and make him see sense. But, at the next, off he would go again, giving everyone a fit of the vapours. The worst story revolved around finding his teenage son masturbating in his room. It went on for ages, with everyone hoping the floor would open to swallow either them or the Station Commander.

You can only hope his poor son never found out what his father said, or that none of the diners told their offspring, the lad's schoolmates and friends.

With the loyal toast out of the way, behaviour can become louder and, at events without external guests, more outrageous. At the least, heckling can be expected. But I've also seen Station Commanders having to contend with pyrotechnics, water pistol fights and, on one occasion, a live chicken, clucking up and down the top table. I'm sure other pranks will come to mind as I continue to unfold the story of my career.

Further speeches come from visiting dignitaries,

such as university vice chancellors at University Air Squadron dinners, or visiting senior officers. I've heard some awful speeches over the years, but I've also heard some truly inspiring and/or rib-ticklingly funny ones; notably, from the then Vicar of Swansea at a St David's Day dinner at RAF St Athan; and, a few months later, at the University of Wales Air Squadron Annual Dinner, from Air Chief Marshal Sir Peter Harding, who went on to become the Chief of the Defence Staff, before being retired after a well-publicised affair with Lady Bienvenida Buck.

With the speeches and toasts exhausted, the PMC bangs the gavel for the final time, signalling the move from the Dining Room to the Bar. All stand and allow the top table diners to leave the room before most follow them.

I say most, because Mr Vice now moves into the PMC's seat, to be joined by his or her mates, usually to polish off the port, if there's any left.

Most dinners finish by 10.30 or 11pm. But the night could be far from over, for me at least. Having consumed sherry, wine, port and maybe a liqueur, I'd now drink beer until the bar shut at one or two in the morning, and even beyond that if a group of us had decided to make a night of it and had stacked up several more beers. I walked home with the dawn on several occasions.

It's hard to find anything to say in my defence, but I'll give it a go. It was early in my career, and no more than one Friday night a month. When more officers began to live off base and became reluctant to stay on a Friday night, dinners started to be held on a Thursday. At that point, I had to moderate my behaviour, but I like to think I'd already done so with the arrival of my children.

And, although she never bullied me, just the presence of Geraldine at a Guest Night used to provide a restraining influence. We still used to stay late though, at Summer Balls, until champagne breakfast at about five in the morning.

Not all the time after Dining-In Nights was spent drinking. Especially on training bases and those with a large number of aircrew, there could be bar games. Scenes in films like The Dam Busters and Angels One Five give a flavour of such events, many of which take place in the Ante-room.

The games included Mess Rugby, a free for all with two teams trying to touch down some item of clothing or mess furniture at the opposition's end of the Ante-room. It could be extremely violent, and often led to injuries from clashes with other players, the wall or, on one occasion that still makes me grimace, a large, cast iron, central heating radiator.

On another occasion, at the instigation of a very senior officer, we were playing with a pillow. Inevitably, it burst, covering the contestants and the Ante-room in its contents. You just wouldn't believe how many feathers a well-stuffed pillow contains.

Because of the risk of injury, I think Mess Rugby has now been outlawed, although it was still being played at some University Air Squadron dinners in the early 2000s.

Another standard is broomstick tug of war, a contest, as the name suggests, between two teams vying for ownership of a broomstick held by the front member of each team. Behind these front men, the rest of the team sit on the carpet, resplendent in their Mess kit, arms locked round each others waists. On a signal, they sway from side to side, trying to pull the broomstick and the other team across the room, and/or wrest the broomstick from the other team's front man. Of course, everything depends on the grip of the front men, and some people become legends for never letting go of the broomstick, even when they and their team are being pulled all around the room.

Another game is the broomstick relay. Two teams stand at one end of the Ante-room. The first runner on each holds a broomstick vertically, puts his forehead on it and, shuffles round it ten times, before letting go and setting out to cross the room. Completely disorientated, they stagger away, bouncing off or narrowly missing the other team's runner and the walls. If and when they reach the far end, they turn to stagger back and tag the next member of their team. It can be very funny, but inevitably leads to more injuries.

The final game I'll mention is deck landings, another potentially dangerous game. A row of tables is laid out and participants run up and launch themselves with enough impetus to slide the length of the tables and into a pile of seat cushions, gaining kudos for style, or the lack of it, and distance travelled.

Before he joined my Hercules squadron, a colleague had spent several months having his face reconstructed after a game of deck landings. During the run up, he'd tripped and smashed his jaw into the front edge of the first table.

Health and safety has attempted to consign many of these games to history. And common sense would seem to dictate that this would be no bad thing. But young men being young men, it wouldn't surprise me if these or equally idiotic, dangerous and hilarious games are still being played today.

That was a much longer diversion into Mess life than I'd intended, and it's time to return to Henlow, when, for me, all the excitement and high jinks of Dining-In Nights was in the future.

In the summer of 1979, I seemed to have enough excitement to be going on with. People were still being chopped or re-coursed, and we were about to undertake our Flight Project, an event that seemed to hold special dangers, in my imagination at least.

Over a three day period, we had to take on a challenging project. Some flights chose canoeing or hill walking expeditions, others more community or charity-based activities. It was a major milestone on the course, especially for the person chosen to lead, which, in our flight, was Dave.

Through links at home in the Midlands, he'd organised a long weekend during which we were to lay a badminton court at a retreat for city kids who'd either gone off the rails, or were in danger of doing so. By pure coincidence, the retreat was a few miles from Ludlow. Dave tasked me with organising our Saturday night out on the town.

The centre was an isolated house set in its own grounds. It wasn't particularly grand, having about half a dozen bedrooms, a few, sparsely furnished reception rooms and a large country kitchen. That weekend, it was home to a trio of twenty-something social workers and a handful of young lads from Birmingham. The youngsters ranged from 12 to 15 years of age, and seemed archetypal street urchins in the Artful Dodger mould, only with Brummie rather than Cockney accents.

I think we slept in tents in the garden.

The work of levelling and preparing the ground for the badminton court and laying the turf was backbreaking, but it went well and was finished before we departed on the Sunday lunchtime. However, I gained the impression that the court was unlikely to be used, or looked after. Neither the social workers nor the lads looked at all sporty. Both groups seemed to spend most of their time lolling about smoking roll-up cigarettes, provided, even to the 12-year old, by the social workers, and drinking cider and beer, at least that's what they did on the Friday evening, the only one we spent with them.

Perhaps, in the second decade of the 21st Century, we're used to such scenes, having seen them in reality television shows about unruly teenagers. But back in the late 70s, the social workers' lack of responsibility and authority, and the resulting lack of deference or respect from the teenagers, came as a real shock, to me at least. There seemed no way the lives of these kids could be turned around by this bunch of adults; their lack of standards and discipline made them hopeless role models.

But I too had been truanting and smoking at the age of 13, and yet, somehow, I'd avoided sinking into petty criminality or worse. In my case, I think I was probably saved by the example of my parents and those who supervised me in the Air Training Corps. Hopefully, these lads would come through as well, but I wasn't sure where their role models or opportunities would come from. If this retreat was meant to provide the impetus, I feared for their futures.

This sounds really patronising. Perhaps it was only by gaining the confidence of the youngsters that the adults could make progress, and I'd witnessed an early stage of the process, when providing cigarettes and booze was the easiest way of striking a rapport, before moving on to change outlooks, if not lives. I hoped so.

I wasn't looking forward to the Saturday night on the town in Ludlow. Although I hadn't hidden my background as a dustman's son from my flight or flight commander, I hadn't particularly flaunted it either. And I'd grown up with some real characters. Meeting them was likely to be quite an eye-opener for Flight Lieutenant Kinzett, especially as they'd be only too keen to tell him stories from my ne'er do well youth.

Sure enough, as the evening progressed from an Indian meal into a pub crawl, we came upon some of the folk I'd quietly dreaded meeting. And, as I'd feared, drink taken, a few of them button-holed the Flight Commander. But strangely, they spoke about me, my family and what I was attempting to do with an affection and pride that was quite touching.

What Flight Lieutenant Kinzett really thought of some of them, I can only guess, but the experience didn't lead to my instant suspension, as I'd feared it might.

A few months after this weekend, Geraldine and I drove to the country house to look at the badminton court. The strips of turf we'd so painstakingly laid were brown, shrivelled and curled up at the edges. I was sure the court had never been used, and never would be.

Back at Henlow, the second week of July was fairly routine. It included leadership exercises, Air Force Law lectures and role play, Ground Defence exercises, General Service Knowledge exams and sport.

For me, it also included a meeting to work on the detail of our Graduation Lunch and Ball. These were events I very much hoped to attend, although, even at this relatively late stage, I sometimes doubted I would.

I also had to plan for the party to be held on the day, three weeks hence, when we'd find out whether or not we were to graduate; it was known as Black Tuesday.

On Sunday 15th July, we left for another major milestone, our 6-Day Leadership Camp, again at the Stanford Training Area (STANTA) in Norfolk. Our flights had been broken up or amalgamated to make small sections of infantry about ten strong.

Working 18 and 19 hour days, we roamed back and forth over the training area to complete various tasks. This time, we were armed with Self-Loading Rifles. These were fitted with yellow adaptors over the muzzles - blank firing attachments - and we were issued with large amounts of blank ammunition for exercises involving assaults on enemy positions, laying ambushes, rescuing downed airmen, blowing up bridges and the like. The enemy was all around and there were frequent gun battles.

I loved every minute.

Each task had a different leader. I don't remember any of my leads, but do remember that I had very few over the course of the six days, something which, in hindsight, probably meant they were content with my performance and wanted to put the spotlight on others whose future was less assured. I don't remember thinking this at the time, though.

In the few hours we had each night to put our heads down, it was either under canvas; in parateepees – shelters made from parachutes draped from trees or over wooden frames; or under our ponchos or capes – draped over a length of parachute cord stretched between two trees. We were always so tired that, by and large, we slept where we fell, and July in southern England was a good time of year to be living under the sky. January would have been a whole different proposition.

We lived on Compo rations, hearty tinned and dried meals that came in boxes holding enough food for a week, with a different menu each day, and plenty of treats, such as sweets and chocolate. We cooked the meals in mess tins placed over small metal stoves fuelled by firelighter-type blocks of a substance called Hexamine. The stoves looked insubstantial, but worked well.

I enjoyed Compo meals, foods such as tinned bacon, sausages, powdered egg, oatmeal biscuits, stews, boiled baby's heads – tinned steak and kidney puddings - tinned vegetables, hearty puddings, bread and jam and the makings for gallons of tea and coffee. We seemed to spend a lot of time preparing and clearing up after meals, and our mess tins and other equipment were regularly inspected for cleanliness.

For me, 6-Day Camp provided two memorable highlights.

The first occurred during a race against time over several miles to reach a clearing in pine woods where we were to find our food for the next few days. Speed was of the essence. The enemy – all the other sections – were on the same mission and would steal our supplies if they arrived first, so we pressed on as fast as the tactical situation allowed.

When, after several skirmishes, we reached our designated point on the edge of the clearing, we were told to wait for a set time and signal. As far as we could see, the clearing, about one kilometre square, was empty.

As the time approached, I heard the beat of aircraft engines. The sound came closer, my excitement rising with its volume, until, running in towards the clearing at low level appeared an RAF C-130 Hercules, a large, camouflaged, four-engined transport aircraft. I guessed what was about to happen and my excitement continued to rise.

Sure enough, as the Hercules flew over the clearing, a line of large boxes appeared from its rear cargo doors, closely followed by billowing parachutes, under which the boxes floated down into the centre of the clearing.

My excitement was tinged with pride at the professionalism of the men flying the aircraft. They belonged to the Service in which I wanted to become a pilot, and they'd just dropped their cargo bang on the button. There was pride also in the fact that this incredible demonstration had been laid on for our training.

We'd been told many times how important we were to the future of the Royal Air Force, but I tended to take such guff with a large pinch of salt. Now, this supply drop seemed to underline the truth of the message. We were striving to become part of a large organization, but an important part, important enough to justify the expense of laying on an air drop as part of our training.

And, of course, standing on the edge of the clearing that evening, I had no way of knowing I was destined to spend over three years as a Hercules pilot.

Anyway, as the supplies hit the ground, a whistle blew and, from all around the clearing, groups of camouflaged figures appeared from under the trees. With the flight commanders shouting encouragement, we charged off to try and retrieve our share of the supplies. I outstripped most of the others and was one of the first to arrive at the boxes, entering into an almighty gun battle, firing off my blank ammunition at any members of opposing flights who came near my prize. It was great fun and eventually we made off with our box.

Afterwards, Flight Lieutenant Kinzett called me over. Here we go, I thought, a pat on the back at least, maybe even a medal. But no, he gave me the biggest bollocking I received at Henlow.

Although fitted with a blank firing attachment and firing blank ammunition, the burst of air emitted from the barrel of our rifles could still be dangerous at very close range. I'd become carried away in the heat of the gun battle, and I didn't doubt that I'd been reckless in defence of our Compo rations, firing at anything and everything. Unlike Glen, they didn't confiscate my rifle, but I felt very chastened as I walked back to the others.

Years later, though, it's the excitement not the ticking off that I remember most vividly.

On another occasion, we had to lay out a helicopter landing site in a clearing. It was the sort of thing we'd had to do in other exercises, so it raised no expectation of anything happening beyond the task itself. Imagine then, our surprise and excitement when a Puma helicopter appeared overhead and landed next to us.

Following a hasty briefing for an assault on an enemy position, we climbed aboard.

I'd flown in a Puma during my week of work experience at RAF Odiham, but that flight was nothing like the one around STANTA training area. It remains one of the most memorable flights in a long flying career.

I sat opposite the large door in the side of the helicopter, which remained open as we skimmed over the countryside, banking steeply round buildings and trees, staying low enough to avoid detection by enemy eyes – or radars in a more sophisticated battlefield environment. At times it felt as if I could reach down and brush my hand through the foliage of the treetops. It was incredibly exhilarating.

Of course, it was an everyday experience for the crew of the helicopter – pilot, co-pilot and loadmaster – but it gave me the strong impression that the excitement of rotary wing flying was a very well-kept secret. Subsequent flights at RAF Shawbury and in Jordan confirmed this view. Later in my career, when I had to tell young men and women they'd failed to reach the standard required to become fast jet pilots, but were good enough to try the rotary stream, I used to try and sweeten the pill by explaining just how exciting flying a helicopter could be.

At the end of the short but memorable flight, we jumped out with our rifles and took cover while the Puma lifted off and sped away at treetop height, presumably to surprise another group with a lift into battle. Such was the exhilaration of our delivery that I can't remember the rest of the exercise at all.

We returned from 6-Day Camp ten days before Black Tuesday, the day most of us would find out whether we'd graduate. But some had their fate decided before this milestone.

As a squadron, it seemed we'd made a complete hash of the exams taken before Camp, a small number performing so badly they were re-coursed several weeks on the spot. Others were allowed to re-take them, but even when they passed, they were on tenterhooks, fearing that the slightest misdemeanour in the run-up to Black Tuesday would spell ruin.

Being an inky swot, I was one of the few that passed first time, and we were allowed to visit the

Royal Tournament, a large military pageant held annually at Earls Court until 1999, when it was discontinued after a defence review. It was a feature of the BBC TV schedule every year, and I was sad to see its demise, partly because I'd always been a fan of the Royal Navy gun crew races that were a central part. I'm glad I managed to see them live at least once.

I was still planning our graduation events, and still wondering whether I'd be among the graduates. Apart from the farting episode, and the recent bollocking for over-exuberance at 6-Day Camp, I'd made no real howlers, but I still wasn't sure whether I'd managed to *make the transition from junior NCO to officer.*

I'll always remember the moment when I first realised I'd passed the course. And I'll always be grateful to the officer who put me out of my misery.

A few days before Black Tuesday, I was having the final fitting of my officers No 1 – Dress - and No 5 – Mess Dress – uniforms at the tailors. To make sure the tailor didn't try to pull a fast one and send us out with ill-fitting uniforms, a flight commander would sit in on the fittings. On this day, it was Flight Lieutenant Mel Kidd, a flight commander on another flight. I'd met him a few times, but only in passing, and he'd never supervised any of the exercises in which I'd been involved.

Throughout the course, in line with military etiquette at the time, our instructors had addressed us exclusively by our surnames. So I expected to be called nothing other than Powell.

When I came out of the tailor's fitting room and rotated in front of the mirror, Flight Lieutenant Kidd smiled, looked me in the eye, and said, 'That looks really smart, Ron.'

To a civilian, this use of my forename must seem a trivial thing, unworthy even of comment. But between Flight Lieutenant Kidd and me, it was a moment of tremendous significance. We both knew he was putting me out of my misery, that beyond the fact that my new Dress uniform was fine, he was telling me I was on track to graduate.

Although we said nothing more at the time, and I never met him after my graduation, I've been eternally grateful to him ever since. He's one of the few people from that period that I took as a role model and have tried to emulate.

Again, it sounds daft, but memory of the event can make me quite emotional. I really had been in an agony of doubt, and he wiped that away with one simple gesture. I think it was another fine example of leadership, similar to that of the Senior Engineering Officer on 35 Squadron at Scampton, who, if you recall, chose not to chastise me for spinning a van in the snow when stopping to offer him a lift.

And just as I've tried to emulate him in not laying into people for every misdemeanour, I've tried to emulate Flight Lieutenant Kidd and throw people lifelines with simple gestures when they've seemed appropriate. I don't suppose I've done it as often as I should, or in the right circumstances, but I've always been grateful to Flight Lieutenant Kidd for showing me how it could be done.

But Flight Lieutenant Kidd and I both knew that being on track to graduate was no guarantee that I would. Even though it was very late in the course, there was still time in the run-up to Black Tuesday and the graduation itself to screw up, and some people did.

My Black Tuesday interview was short and sweet.

If I could avoid making some catastrophic faux pas over the next nine days, I'd be amongst those graduating on the 9th of August. The rest of my flight also survived.

Others were not so lucky. A few were re-coursed to different squadrons. A few who'd already been re-coursed to Blue Squadron from earlier courses were chopped and returned to civilian life. And one or two who'd already been re-coursed, but were still deemed worth the effort, were re-coursed a second time.

And then, someone who'd passed their Black Tuesday interview was re-coursed the following morning. The rumour was that following the party I'd organised – 8pm to 1am, light nibbles and a disco – he'd been caught *in flagrante* with a female member of the Squadron. Why only one of them had been punished remained a mystery, to me at least.

My diary gives few clues about our final days, but from memory they were taken up mainly with drill in preparation for the Graduation Parade, PT and making sure we had all the kit we required for the next stage of training. I had the additional duty of arranging our first Dining-In Night, held two nights before graduation, and the Graduation Lunch and Graduation Ball on the day itself. The sheet of paper on which I planned these events seems to indicate that the seating plans were the biggest headache, with the Graduation Lunch seating over 400, and the Graduation Ball requiring two sittings.

During my end of course interview, I discovered that I'd done very well, showing a steady improvement to the point where I'd been a contender for one of the major prizes, even the Sword of Honour. To say I was surprised would be an understatement.

It seemed I'd been let down by a couple of episodes in major leads where I'd failed to maintain the standard of a prize winner.

One had been the palaver over raising the flagpole for the Ensign ceremony on the first morning of 8-Day Camp – which explained why Flight Lieutenant Kinzett had been so disappointed. Another had been in the office simulator, an exercise in which we'd spent several days pretending to run an RAF station, solving problems devised and acted out by the flight commanders. When acting as Officer Commanding Administration Wing, I'd failed to brief one of my subordinates adequately, and he'd given a poor briefing to a visiting senior officer. I'm sure there'd been other slip-ups, but those were the instances given to explain my lack of a prize.

I suppose I should have been disappointed, but I was so chuffed to be considered anywhere near good enough that the lack of a trophy didn't seem to matter too much. In fact, on our squadron, no-one was deemed good enough to be awarded the Sword of Honour, and the prize for the best overall cadet was awarded to another ex-apprentice.

Unfortunately, the morning of the Graduation Parade dawned cloudy and wet. So, just as at Swinderby six years earlier, it was held in a hangar.

My parents and Brian were driven to Henlow by the warrant officer from my old Air Training Corps squadron, Derek Crowther, the man who'd done so much to put me on the path to joining the RAF. It seemed appropriate that he should be there to see me commissioned. I didn't see him for many years after this, but we met up again recently, and I've promised him a copy of this book when it's published.

Geraldine was also there with her parents, another source of pride on the day.

I'm told the parade went well, but, despite photographic evidence that I was there, I've no recollection of it. After the Lunch I'd organised, during which I found it impossible to relax, all my guests bar Geraldine, who was staying for the Graduation Ball, returned to Shropshire.

Geraldine tells me I spent most of the time at the Ball running around making sure all was going to plan, and sorting out last minute glitches. She was looked after by a couple she'd stayed with when visiting Scampton eight months earlier. The husband, an ex-123 Entry apprentice and fellow corporal on 35 Squadron, had gone to Henlow a few months ahead of me, but been re-coursed, so now we were graduating together. We'd also start flying training together, but we weren't in one another's company long on that occasion, a story for another time.

At some point, I opened a blue envelope I'd been given after the parade. It contained an official letter, printed on high quality blue paper.

Over the years, I came to recognise these distinctive envelopes, and to realise that they tended to bring either very good or very bad news. Receiving one out of the blue, if you'll pardon the pun, could be quite a shock. On this day though, I guessed the envelope held good news. It was my Commissioning Letter. Seven months later, I'd receive a Commissioning Scroll, but for now, the letter was the only written proof that I'd become an officer.

If I was given an end of course report, it no longer exists. This is strange, because my squirreling tendency extends to course and annual reports. I have most, if not all the reports written on me from 1982, when I arrived on my first squadron as a pilot. Perhaps I burned all my earlier reports to cover up the full scale of my inadequacies, but I think it more likely that my officer and flying training pre-dated the era of open reporting.

The letter opens, *I am commanded by the Air Force Board of the Defence Council to inform you that they have approved your appointment to a permanent commission in the Royal Air Force with effect from 9 August 1979, and that you will, at the same time, be discharged from service as an airman. Your appointment, as a pilot in the General Duties Branch, will be in the rank of flying officer with seniority of 22 September 1978.*

I'd known that I'd receive credit for my time as an airman. It was why I'd graduated as a flying officer – one medium stripe – rather than a pilot officer – one very thin stripe. But I was surprised to read that I'd been discharged as an airman, especially as the next sentence seemed to be a thinly veiled threat. *Retention of the commission will be subject to satisfactory completion of the prescribed training,* which I took to mean that if I didn't pass flying training, I'd be busted back to corporal.

In fact, if I failed flying training, I intended to try and become an engineering officer. So a return to airman service was unlikely, although I like to think I'd have reverted to my previous terms of service if the cards had played out that way. I still wanted nothing other than to remain in the RAF and work with aircraft.

The letter also advised that under my new terms of service, my exit date had been extended from 5th November 1982 until 4th April 1993, my 38th birthday.

At the age of 24, this seemed a lifetime away, but I was embarking on something I wanted more than anything else in the world, so it wasn't a matter of concern.

My Commissioning Scroll, when it came through the post in March the next year, was a much more impressive document than the blue letter. I make no apology for repeating the bulk of it here.

Elizabeth II, by the Grace of God OF THE UNITED KINGDOM OF GREAT BRITAIN AND NORTHERN IRELAND AND OF HER OTHER REALMS AND TERRITORIES QUEEN, HEAD OF THE COMMONWEALTH, DEFENDER OF THE FAITH.

To Our Trusty and well beloved Ronald Powell Greeting: We, reposing especial Trust and Confidence in your Loyalty, Courage and good Conduct, do by these Presents Constitute and Appoint you to be an Officer in Our Royal Air Force from the Ninth day of August 1979. You are therefore carefully and diligently to discharge your Duty as such in the rank of Flying Officer or in such other Rank as We may from time to time hereafter be pleased to promote or appoint you to and you are in such manner and on such occasions as may be prescribed by Us to exercise and well discipline in their duties such Officers, Airmen and Airwomen as may be placed under your orders from time to time and use your best endeavours to keep them in good Order and Discipline. And We do hereby Command them to Obey you as their superior Officer and you to Observe and follow such Orders and Directions as from time to time you shall receive from Us, or any superior Officer, according to the Rules and Disciplines of War, in pursuance of the Trust hereby reposed in you.

Given at Our court, at Saint James's the Thirtieth

*day of October 1979 in the Twenty Eighth Year of Our
Reign, By Her Majesty's Command.*

I left Henlow with mixed feelings. I felt great pride at
having gained a commission. But I also harboured
concerns at the example set by some of the flight
commanders, especially during the first part of the
course.

Many of us, and especially the ex-airmen, still felt
that the more extreme hectoring, where necessary at
all, should have been left to the NCOs. We feared that
some of those with less knowledge of the Service
might leave Henlow confused as to how an officer
should behave.

Similarly, we remained concerned at the impression
given that airmen were universally problematic, a
different species to be on your guard against, rather
than, in all but a few cases, colleagues in whom you
could, and would have to, place your trust. Again, we
feared some of our fellow graduates would find it hard
to know how to approach their first dealings with
airmen.

A few instances later in my career seemed to justify
these concerns, but, once again, I've probably over-
stated my case, and it was only in reading my diary
and Henlow notebook that these thoughts came to the
fore. Up until then, it was the pride that I remembered,
and that's as it should be.

The day after graduation, Geraldine and I drove home
to Shropshire and I began three weeks' leave. Mum's
health was okay and all seemed well with the world.
When she wasn't working, I spent most of the time
with Geraldine, and when she was, I played squash and
tennis and ran in the countryside around Ludlow.

The first weekend, we went ten-pin bowling in Wolverhampton and saw the Olympians, Sebastian Coe, Dave Moorcroft and Tessa Sanderson, at an athletics meeting in Telford. The second, we went to Bath.

A week later, on Sunday 2nd September 1979, I set out to try and realise my dream of becoming a pilot in the Royal Air Force.

Epilogue - Onward and Upward

What I didn't realise at the time was that I was commencing a period of 26 years when my life would be completely dominated by my work, almost to the exclusion of anything else. And nowhere was this dominance more apparent than during my flying training.

As an airframe and propulsion fitter, apart from periods of intense study, I'd largely been able to leave work behind when out of uniform. Simplistically, you couldn't take an aircraft home, and neither could you learn all there was to know about how it and its components were put together, taken apart and repaired. And you didn't have to. The skill was in being able to interpret the manuals, and in having the mental and manual dexterity to perform the necessary tasks. By and large, I had these skills, and could only exercise them when I was at work.

This all changed when I left Henlow.

Nowhere is the phrase, 'You never stop learning,' more apt than in the aircrew world. Even as you gain experience, the constant updating of equipment and techniques, changes of aircraft type, and variables such as the weather and differing air traffic control and airfield procedures, mean that you can never learn all there is to learn.

And nowhere is this more apparent than in flying training, where you're trying to assimilate all this knowledge, as well as learn a new motor skill in a fluid, three-dimensional environment. During this period, the effort to master my new profession filled every waking hour. It pushed me to the limit, and I seemed constantly to be on the brink of failure.

Perhaps then, it is no surprise that the next volume of this memoir is dominated by my struggle to succeed in flying training.

Author's Note

Throughout this memoir, where I thought I might cause embarrassment, I've changed people's names. Where I haven't changed the names, and have still caused embarrassment, I apologise.

Special thanks for the cover design go to Martin Butler; and, for their comments on my drafts, to Cardiff Writers' Circle, the Tiny Writers, and Jean Kingdon, freelance writer and former chief reporter of the South Shropshire Journal. Thanks also to David Griffiths and Sandy Sanderson, longstanding RAF mates, and to my Auntie Mary, each of whom corrected some of my mis-rememberings, and prompted a few stories I'd forgotten.

Future volumes of Shropshire Blue will follow me through flying training on the Chipmunk, Jet Provost and Jetstream; flying C130s world-wide, including the South Atlantic; several years as a flying instructor and instructor of instructors; audiences in Buckingham Palace; calling in the flypast for the Queen Mother's 90th Birthday celebration on Horse Guards Parade; responsibility for the careers of all the RAF's junior officer pilots and Ops Support officers; command of a Harrier detachment in southern Italy; two fascinating jobs in the Ministry of Defence; running the Officers and Aircrew Selection Centre, the organisation that twice turned me away when I was a teenager; and my final job running the first stage of flying training for the British Army, Royal Navy and RAF, the dream job which turned sour and led to my early retirement.

You can find out more from my website: http://www.ronpowell.co.uk.